AI
Self-Driving Cars
Convergence

Practical Advances in
Artificial Intelligence and Machine Learning

Dr. Lance B. Eliot, MBA, PhD

Disclaimer: This book is presented solely for educational and entertainment purposes. The author and publisher are not offering it as legal, accounting, or other professional services advice. The author and publisher make no representations or warranties of any kind and assume no liabilities of any kind with respect to the accuracy or completeness of the contents and specifically disclaim any implied warranties of merchantability or fitness of use for a particular purpose. Neither the author nor the publisher shall be held liable or responsible to any person or entity with respect to any loss or incidental or consequential damages caused, or alleged to have been caused, directly or indirectly, by the information or programs contained herein. Every company is different and the advice and strategies contained herein may not be suitable for your situation.

ISBN: 978-1-95-738606-5

DEDICATION

To my incredible daughter, Lauren, and my incredible son, Michael.

Forest fortuna adiuvat (from the Latin; good fortune favors the brave).

CONTENTS

ACKNOWLEDGMENTS

I have been the beneficiary of advice and counsel by many friends, colleagues, family, investors, and many others. I want to thank everyone that has aided me throughout my career. I write from the heart and the head, having experienced first-hand what it means to have others around you that support you during the good times and the tough times.

To Warren Bennis, one of my doctoral advisors and ultimately a colleague, I offer my deepest thanks and appreciation, especially for his calm and insightful wisdom and support.

To Mark Stevens and his generous efforts toward funding and supporting the USC Stevens Center for Innovation.

To Lloyd Greif and the USC Lloyd Greif Center for Entrepreneurial Studies for their ongoing encouragement of founders and entrepreneurs.

To Peter Drucker, William Wang, Aaron Levie, Peter Kim, Jon Kraft, Cindy Crawford, Jenny Ming, Steve Milligan, Chis Underwood, Frank Gehry, Buzz Aldrin, Steve Forbes, Bill Thompson, Dave Dillon, Alan Fuerstman, Larry Ellison, Jim Sinegal, John Sperling, Mark Stevenson, Anand Nallathambi, Thomas Barrack, Jr., and many other innovators and leaders that I have met and gained mightily from doing so.

Thanks to Ed Trainor, Kevin Anderson, James Hickey, Wendell Jones, Ken Harris, DuWayne Peterson, Mike Brown, Jim Thornton, Abhi Beniwal, Al Biland, John Nomura, Eliot Weinman, John Desmond, and many others for their unwavering support during my career.

And most of all thanks as always to Lauren and Michael, for their ongoing support and for having seen me writing and heard much of this material during the many months involved in writing it. To their patience and willingness to listen.

INTRODUCTION

This is a book that provides the newest innovations and the latest Artificial Intelligence (AI) advances about the emerging nature of AI-based autonomous self-driving driverless cars. Via recent advances in Artificial Intelligence (AI) and Machine Learning (ML), we are nearing the day when vehicles can control themselves and will not require and nor rely upon human intervention to perform their driving tasks (or, that allow for human intervention, but only *require* human intervention in very limited ways).

Similar to my other related books, which I describe in a moment and list the chapters in the Appendix A of this book, I am particularly focused on those advances that pertain to self-driving cars. The phrase "autonomous vehicles" is often used to refer to any kind of vehicle, whether it is ground-based or in the air or sea, and whether it is a cargo hauling trailer truck or a conventional passenger car. Though the aspects described in this book are certainly applicable to all kinds of autonomous vehicles, I am focused more so here on cars.

For this book, I am going to borrow my introduction from those companion books, since it does a good job of laying out the landscape of self-driving cars and my overall viewpoints on the topic.

INTRODUCTION TO SELF-DRIVING CARS

This is a book about self-driving cars. Someday in the future, we'll all have self-driving cars and this book will perhaps seem antiquated, but right now, we are at the forefront of the self-driving car wave. Daily news bombards us with flashes of new announcements by one car maker or another and leaves the impression that within the next few weeks or maybe months that the self-driving car will be here. A casual non-technical reader would assume from these news flashes that in we must be on the cusp of a true self-driving car.

We are still quite a distance from having a true self-driving car. A true self-driving car is akin to a moonshot. In the same manner that getting us to the moon was an incredible feat, likewise, is achieving a true self-driving car. Anybody that suggests or even brashly states that the true self-driving car is nearly here should be viewed with great skepticism. Indeed, you'll see that I often tend to use the word "hogwash" or "crock" when I assess much of the decidedly ***fake news*** about self-driving cars.

Indeed, I've been writing a popular blog post about self-driving cars and hitting hard on those that try to wave their hands and pretend that we are on the imminent verge of true self-driving cars. For many years, I've been known as the AI Insider. Besides writing about AI, I also develop AI software. I do what I describe. It also gives me insights into what others that are doing AI are really doing versus what it is said they are doing.

Many faithful readers had asked me to pull together my insightful short essays and put them into another book, which you are now holding.

For those of you that have been reading my essays over the years, this collection not only puts them together into one handy package, I also updated the essays and added new material. For those of you that are new to the topic of self-driving cars and AI, I hope you find these essays approachable and informative. I also tend to have a writing style with a bit of a voice, and so you'll see that I am times have a wry sense of humor and poke at conformity.

As a former professor and founder of an AI research lab, I for many years wrote in the formal language of academic writing. I published in referred journals and served as an editor for several AI journals. This writing here is not of the nature, and I have adopted a different and more informal style for these essays. That being said, I also do mention from time-to-time more rigorous material on AI and encourage you all to dig into those deeper and more formal materials if so interested.

For those of you that are reading this book and have a penchant for writing code, you might consider taking a look at the open-source code available for self-driving cars. This is a handy place to start learning how to develop AI for self-driving cars. There are also many new educational courses spring forth. There is a growing body of those wanting to learn about and develop self-driving cars, and a growing body of colleges, labs, and other avenues by which you can learn about self-driving cars.

This book will provide a foundation of aspects that I think will get you ready for those kinds of more advanced training opportunities. If you've already taken those classes, you'll likely find these essays especially interesting as they offer a perspective that I am betting few other instructors or faculty offered to you. These are challenging essays that ask you to think beyond the conventional about self-driving cars.

THE MOTHER OF ALL AI PROJECTS

In June 2017, Apple CEO Tim Cook came out and finally admitted that Apple has been working on a self-driving car. As you'll see in my essays, Apple was enmeshed in secrecy about their self-driving car efforts. We have only been able to read the tea leaves and guess at what Apple has been up to. The notion of an iCar has been floating for quite a while, and self-driving engineers and researchers have been signing tight-lipped Non-Disclosure Agreements (NDA's) to work on projects at Apple that were as shrouded in mystery as any military invasion plans might be.

Tim Cook said something that many others in the Artificial Intelligence (AI) field have been saying, namely, the creation of a self-driving car has got to be the mother of all AI projects. In other words, it is in fact a tremendous moonshot for AI. If a self-driving car can be crafted and the AI works as we hope, it means that we have made incredible strides with AI and that therefore it opens many other worlds of potential breakthrough accomplishments that AI can solve.

Is this hyperbole? Am I just trying to make AI seem like a miracle worker and so provide self-aggrandizing statements for those of us writing the AI software for self-driving cars? No, it is not hyperbole. Developing a true self-driving car is really, really, really hard to do. Let me take a moment to explain why. As a side note, I realize that the Apple CEO is known for at times uttering hyperbole, and he had previously said for example that the year 2012 was "the mother of all years," and he had said that the release of iOS 10 was "the mother of all releases" – all of which does suggest he likes to use the handy "mother of" expression. But, I assure you, in terms of true self-driving cars, he has hit the nail on the head. For sure.

When you think about a moonshot and how we got to the moon, there are some identifiable characteristics and those same aspects can be applied to creating a true self-driving car. You'll notice that I keep putting the word "true" in front of the self-driving car expression. I do so because as per my essay about the various levels of self-driving cars, there are some self-driving cars that are only somewhat of a self-driving car. The somewhat versions are ones that require a human driver to be ready to intervene. In my view, that's not a true self-driving car. A true self-driving car is one that requires no human driver intervention at all. It is a car that can entirely undertake via automation the driving task without any human driver needed. This is the essence of what is known as a Level 5 self-driving car. We are currently at the Level 2 and Level 3 mark, and not yet at Level 5.

Getting to the moon involved aspects such as having big stretch goals, incremental progress, experimentation, innovation, and so on. Let's review how this applied to the moonshot of the bygone era, and how it applies to the self-driving car moonshot of today.

Big Stretch Goal

Trying to take a human and deliver the human to the moon, and bring them back, safely, was an extremely large stretch goal at the time. No one knew whether it could be done. The technology wasn't available yet. The cost was huge. The determination would need to be fierce. Etc. To reach a Level 5 self-driving car is going to be the same. It is a big stretch goal. We can readily get to the Level 3, and we are able to see the Level 4 just up ahead, but a Level 5 is still an unknown as to if it is doable. It should eventually be doable and in the same way that we thought we'd eventually get to the moon, but when it will occur is a different story.

Incremental Progress

Getting to the moon did not happen overnight in one fell swoop. It took years and years of incremental progress to get there. Likewise, for self-driving cars. Google has famously been striving to get to the Level 5, and pretty much been willing to forgo dealing with the intervening levels, but most of the other self-driving car makers are doing the incremental route. Let's get a good Level 2 and a somewhat Level 3 going. Then, let's improve the Level 3 and get a somewhat Level 4 going. Then, let's improve the Level 4 and finally arrive at a Level 5. This seems to be the prevalent way that we are going to achieve the true self-driving car.

Experimentation

You likely know that there were various experiments involved in perfecting the approach and technology to get to the moon. As per making incremental progress, we first tried to see if we could get a rocket to go into space and safety return, then put a monkey in there, then with a human, then we went all the way to the moon but didn't land, and finally we arrived at the mission that actually landed on the moon.

Self-driving cars are the same way. We are doing simulations of self-driving cars. We do testing of self-driving cars on private land under controlled situations.

We do testing of self-driving cars on public roadways, often having to meet regulatory requirements including for example having an engineer or equivalent in the car to take over the controls if needed. And so on. Experiments big and small are needed to figure out what works and what doesn't.

Innovation

There are already some advances in AI that are allowing us to progress toward self-driving cars. We are going to need even more advances. Innovation in all aspects of technology are going to be required to achieve a true self-driving car. By no means do we already have everything in-hand that we need to get there. Expect new inventions and new approaches, new algorithms, etc.

Setbacks

Most of the pundits are avoiding talking about potential setbacks in the progress toward self-driving cars. Getting to the moon involved many setbacks, some of which you never have heard of and were buried at the time so as to not dampen enthusiasm and funding for getting to the moon. A recurring theme in many of my included essays is that there are going to be setbacks as we try to arrive at a true self-driving car. Take a deep breath and be ready. I just hope the setbacks don't completely stop progress. I am sure that it will cause progress to alter in a manner that we've not yet seen in the self-driving car field. I liken the self-driving car of today to the excitement everyone had for Uber when it first got going. Today, we have a different view of Uber and with each passing day there are more regulations to the ride sharing business and more concerns raised. The darling child only stays a darling until finally that child acts up. It will happen the same with self-driving cars.

SELF-DRIVING CARS CHALLENGES

But what exactly makes things so hard to have a true self-driving car, you might be asking. You have seen cruise control for years and years. You've lately seen cars that can do parallel parking. You've seen YouTube videos of Tesla drivers that put their hands out the window as their car zooms along the highway, and seen to therefore be in a self-driving car. Aren't we just needing to put a few more sensors onto a car and then we'll have in-hand a true self-driving car? Nope.

Consider for a moment the nature of the driving task. We don't just let anyone at any age drive a car. Worldwide, most countries won't license a driver until the age of 18, though many do allow a learner's permit at the age of 15 or 16. Some suggest that a younger age would be physically too small to reach the controls of the car. Though this might be the case, we could easily adjust the controls to allow for younger aged and thus smaller stature. It's not their physical size that matters. It's their cognitive development that matters.

To drive a car, you need to be able to reason about the car, what the car can and cannot do. You need to know how to operate the car. You need to know about how other cars on the road drive. You need to know what is allowed in driving such as speed limits and driving within marked lanes. You need to be able to react to situations and be able to avoid getting into accidents. You need to ascertain when to hit your brakes, when to steer clear of a pedestrian, and how to keep from ramming that motorcyclist that just cut you off.

Many of us had taken courses on driving. We studied about driving and took driver training. We had to take a test and pass it to be able to drive. The point being that though most adults take the driving task for granted, and we often "mindlessly" drive our cars, there is a significant amount of cognitive effort that goes into driving a car. After a while, it becomes second nature. You don't especially think about how you drive, you just do it. But, if you watch a novice driver, say a teenager learning to drive, you suddenly realize that there is a lot more complexity to it than we seem to realize.

Furthermore, driving is a very serious task. I recall when my daughter and son first learned to drive. They are both very conscientious people. They wanted to make sure that whatever they did, they did well, and that they did not harm anyone. Every day, when you get into a car, it is probably around 4,000 pounds of hefty metal and plastics (about two tons), and it is a lethal weapon. Think about it. You drive down the street in an object that weighs two tons and with the engine it can accelerate and ram into anything you want to hit. The damage a car can inflict is very scary. Both my children were surprised that they were being given the right to maneuver this monster of a beast that could cause tremendous harm entirely by merely letting go of the steering wheel for a moment or taking your eyes off the road.

In fact, in the United States alone there are about 40,000 deaths per year by auto accidents, which is more than 100 per day. Given that there are about 263 million cars in the United States, I am actually more amazed that the number of fatalities is not a lot higher.

During my morning commute, I look at all the thousands of cars on the freeway around me, and I think that if all of them decided to go zombie and drive in a crazy maniac way, there would be many people dead. Somehow, incredibly, each day, most people drive relatively safely. To me, that's a miracle right there. Getting millions and millions of people to be safe and sane when behind the wheel of a two-ton mobile object, it's a feat that we as a society should admire with pride.

So, hopefully you are in agreement that the driving task requires a great deal of cognition. You don't' need to be especially smart to drive a car, and we've done quite a bit to make car driving viable for even the average dolt. There isn't an IQ test that you need to take to drive a car. If you can read and write, and pass a test, you pretty much can legally drive a car. There are of course some that drive a car and are not legally permitted to do so, plus there are private areas such as farms where drivers are young, but for public roadways in the United States, you can be generally of average intelligence (or less) and be able to legally drive.

This though makes it seem like the cognitive effort must not be much. If the cognitive effort was truly hard, wouldn't we only have Einstein's that could drive a car? We have made sure to keep the driving task as simple as we can, by making the controls easy and relatively standardized, and by having roads that are relatively standardized, and so on. It is as though Disneyland has put their Autopia into the real-world, by us all as a society agreeing that roads will be a certain way, and we'll all abide by the various rules of driving.

A modest cognitive task by a human is still something that stymies AI. You certainly know that AI has been able to beat chess players and be good at other kinds of games. This type of narrow cognition is not what car driving is about. Car driving is much wider. It requires knowledge about the world, which a chess playing AI system does not need to know. The cognitive aspects of driving are on the one hand seemingly simple, but at the same time require layer upon layer of knowledge about cars, people, roads, rules, and a myriad of other "common sense" aspects. We don't have any AI systems today that have that same kind of breadth and depth of awareness and knowledge.

As revealed in my essays, the self-driving car of today is using trickery to do particular tasks. It is all very narrow in operation. Plus, it currently assumes that a human driver is ready to intervene. It is like a child that we have taught to stack blocks, but we are needed to be right there in case the child stacks them too high and they begin to fall over.

AI of today is brittle, it is narrow, and it does not approach the cognitive abilities of humans. This is why the true self-driving car is somewhere out in the future.

Another aspect to the driving task is that it is not solely a mind exercise. You do need to use your senses to drive. You use your eyes as vision sensors to see the road ahead. You vision capability is like a streaming video, which your brain needs to continually analyze as you drive. Where is the road? Is there a pedestrian in the way? Is there another car ahead of you? Your senses are relying a flood of info to your brain. Self-driving cars are trying to do the same, by using cameras, radar, ultrasound, and lasers. This is an attempt at mimicking how humans have senses and sensory apparatus.

Thus, the driving task is mental and physical. You use your senses, you use your arms and legs to manipulate the controls of the car, and you use your brain to assess the sensory info and direct your limbs to act upon the controls of the car. This all happens instantly. If you've ever perhaps gotten something in your eye and only had one eye available to drive with, you suddenly realize how dependent upon vision you are. If you have a broken foot with a cast, you suddenly realize how hard it is to control the brake pedal and the accelerator. If you've taken medication and your brain is maybe sluggish, you suddenly realize how much mental strain is required to drive a car.

An AI system that plays chess only needs to be focused on playing chess. The physical aspects aren't important because usually a human moves the chess pieces or the chessboard is shown on an electronic display. Using AI for a more life-and-death task such as analyzing MRI images of patients, this again does not require physical capabilities and instead is done by examining images of bits.

Driving a car is a true life-and-death task. It is a use of AI that can easily and at any moment produce death. For those colleagues of mine that are developing this AI, as am I, we need to keep in mind the somber aspects of this. We are producing software that will have in its virtual hands the lives of the occupants of the car, and the lives of those in other nearby cars, and the lives of nearby pedestrians, etc. Chess is not usually a life-or-death matter.

Driving is all around us. Cars are everywhere. Most of today's AI applications involve only a small number of people. Or, they are behind the scenes and we as humans have other recourse if the AI messes up. AI that is driving a car at 80 miles per hour on a highway had better not mess up. The consequences are grave.

Multiply this by the number of cars, if we could put magically self-driving into every car in the USA, we'd have AI running in the 263 million cars. That's a lot of AI spread around. This is AI on a massive scale that we are not doing today and that offers both promise and potential peril.

There are some that want AI for self-driving cars because they envision a world without any car accidents. They envision a world in which there is no car congestion and all cars cooperate with each other. These are wonderful utopian visions.

They are also very misleading. The adoption of self-driving cars is going to be incremental and not overnight. We cannot economically just junk all existing cars. Nor are we going to be able to affordably retrofit existing cars. It is more likely that self-driving cars will be built into new cars and that over many years of gradual replacement of existing cars that we'll see the mix of self-driving cars become substantial in the real-world.

In these essays, I have tried to offer technological insights without being overly technical in my description, and also blended the business, societal, and economic aspects too. Technologists need to consider the non-technological impacts of what they do. Non-technologists should be aware of what is being developed.

We all need to work together to collectively be prepared for the enormous disruption and transformative aspects of true self-driving cars.

WHAT THIS BOOK PROVIDES

What does this book provide to you? It introduces many of the key elements about self-driving cars and does so with an AI based perspective. I weave together technical and non-technical aspects, readily going from being concerned about the cognitive capabilities of the driving task and how the technology is embodying this into self-driving cars, and in the next breath I discuss the societal and economic aspects.

They are all intertwined because that's the way reality is. You cannot separate out the technology per se, and instead must consider it within the milieu of what is being invented and innovated, and do so with a mindset towards the contemporary mores and culture that shape what we are doing and what we hope to do.

WHY THIS BOOK

I wrote this book to try and bring to the public view many aspects about self-driving cars that nobody seems to be discussing.

For business leaders that are either involved in making self-driving cars or that are going to leverage self-driving cars, I hope that this book will enlighten you as to the risks involved and ways in which you should be strategizing about how to deal with those risks.

For entrepreneurs, startups and other businesses that want to enter into the self-driving car market that is emerging, I hope this book sparks your interest in doing so, and provides some sense of what might be prudent to pursue.

For researchers that study self-driving cars, I hope this book spurs your interest in the risks and safety issues of self-driving cars, and also nudges you toward conducting research on those aspects.

For students in computer science or related disciplines, I hope this book will provide you with interesting and new ideas and material, for which you might conduct research or provide some career direction insights for you.

For AI companies and high-tech companies pursuing self-driving cars, this book will hopefully broaden your view beyond just the mere coding and development needed to make self-driving cars.

For all readers, I hope that you will find the material in this book to be stimulating. Some of it will be repetitive of things you already know. But I am pretty sure that you'll also find various eureka moments whereby you'll discover a new technique or approach that you had not earlier thought of. I am also betting that there will be material that forces you to rethink some of your current practices.

I am not saying you will suddenly have an epiphany and change what you are doing. I do think though that you will reconsider or perhaps revisit what you are doing.

For anyone choosing to use this book for teaching purposes, please take a look at my suggestions for doing so, as described in the Appendix. I have found the material handy in courses that I have taught, and likewise other faculty have told me that they have found the material handy, in some cases as extended readings and in other instances as a core part of their course (depending on the nature of the class).

In my writing for this book, I have tried carefully to blend both the practitioner and the academic styles of writing.

It is not as abstract as is typical academic journal writing, but at the same time offers depth by going into the nuances and trade-offs of various practices.

The word "deep" is in vogue today, meaning getting deeply into a subject or topic, and so is the word "unpack" which means to tease out the underlying aspects of a subject or topic. I have sought to offer material that addresses an issue or topic by going relatively deeply into it and make sure that it is well unpacked.

In any book about AI, it is difficult to use our everyday words without having some of them be misinterpreted. Specifically, it is easy to anthropomorphize AI. When I say that an AI system "knows" something, I do not want you to construe that the AI system has sentience and "knows" in the same way that humans do. They aren't that way, as yet. I have tried to use quotes around such words from time-to-time to emphasize that the words I am using should not be misinterpreted to ascribe true human intelligence to the AI systems that we know of today. If I used quotes around all such words, the book would be very difficult to read, and so I am doing so judiciously. Please keep that in mind as you read the material, thanks.

Some of the material is time-based in terms of covering underway activities, and though some of it might decay, nonetheless I believe you'll find the material useful and informative.

COMPANION BOOKS BY DR. ELIOT

1. **"Introduction to Driverless Self-Driving Cars"** by Dr. Lance Eliot
2. **"Innovation and Thought Leadership on Self-Driving Driverless Cars"**
3. **"Advances in AI and Autonomous Vehicles: Cybernetic Self-Driving Cars"**
4. **"Self-Driving Cars: The Mother of All AI Projects"** by Dr. Lance Eliot
5. **"New Advances in AI Autonomous Driverless Self-Driving Cars"**
6. **"AV Driverless Self-Driving Cars & AI"** by Dr. Lance Eliot and Michael B. Eliot
7. **"Transformative Artificial Intelligence Driverless Self-Driving Cars"**
8. **"Disruptive Artificial Intelligence and Driverless Self-Driving Cars"**
9. "**State-of-the-Art AI Driverless Self-Driving Cars**" by Dr. Lance Eliot
10. "**Top Trends in AI Self-Driving Cars**" by Dr. Lance Eliot
11. **"AI Innovations and Self-Driving Cars"** by Dr. Lance Eliot
12. **"Crucial Advances for AI Driverless Cars"** by Dr. Lance Eliot
13. **"Sociotechnical Insights and AI Driverless Cars**" by Dr. Lance Eliot.
14. **"Pioneering Advances for AI Driverless Cars"** by Dr. Lance Eliot
15. **"Leading Edge Trends for AI Driverless Cars"** by Dr. Lance Eliot
16. **"The Cutting Edge of AI Autonomous Cars"** by Dr. Lance Eliot
17. **"The Next Wave of AI Self-Driving Cars"** by Dr. Lance Eliot
18. **"Revolutionary Innovations of AI Driverless Cars"** by Dr. Lance Eliot
19. **"AI Self-Driving Cars Breakthroughs"** by Dr. Lance Eliot
20. **"Trailblazing Trends for AI Self-Driving Cars"** by Dr. Lance Eliot
21. **"Ingenious Strides for AI Driverless Cars"** by Dr. Lance Eliot
22. **"AI Self-Driving Cars Inventiveness"** by Dr. Lance Eliot
23. **"Visionary Secrets of AI Driverless Cars"** by Dr. Lance Eliot
24. **"Spearheading AI Self-Driving Cars"** by Dr. Lance Eliot
25. **"Spurring AI Self-Driving Cars"** by Dr. Lance Eliot
26. **"Avant-Garde AI Driverless Cars"** by Dr. Lance Eliot
27. **"AI Self-Driving Cars Evolvement"** by Dr. Lance Eliot
28. **"AI Driverless Cars Chrysalis"** by Dr. Lance Eliot
29. **"Boosting AI Autonomous Cars"** by Dr. Lance Eliot
30. **"AI Self-Driving Cars Trendsetting"** by Dr. Lance Eliot
31. **"AI Autonomous Cars Forefront"** by Dr. Lance Eliot
32. **"AI Autonomous Cars Emergence"** by Dr. Lance Eliot
33. **"AI Autonomous Cars Progress"** by Dr. Lance Eliot
34. **"AI Self-Driving Cars Prognosis"** by Dr. Lance Eliot
35. **"AI Self-Driving Cars Momentum"** by Dr. Lance Eliot
36. **"AI Self-Driving Cars Headway"** by Dr. Lance Eliot
37. **"AI Self-Driving Cars Vicissitude"** by Dr. Lance Eliot
38. **"AI Self-Driving Cars Autonomy"** by Dr. Lance Eliot
39. **"AI Driverless Cars Transmutation"** by Dr. Lance Eliot
40. **"AI Driverless Cars Potentiality"** by Dr. Lance Eliot
41. **"AI Driverless Cars Realities"** by Dr. Lance Eliot
42. **"AI Self-Driving Cars Materiality"** by Dr. Lance Eliot
43. **"AI Self-Driving Cars Accordance"** by Dr. Lance Eliot
44. **"AI Self-Driving Cars Equanimity"** by Dr. Lance Eliot
45. **"AI Self-Driving Cars Divulgement"** by Dr. Lance Eliot
46. **"AI Self-Driving Cars Consonance"** by Dr. Lance Eliot
47. **"Revelatory AI Self-Driving Cars"** by Dr. Lance Eliot
48. **"Edifying AI Self-Driving Cars"** by Dr. Lance Eliot
49. **"Apprising AI Driverless Cars"** by Dr. Lance Eliot
50. **"Improving AI Self-Driving Cars"** by Dr. Lance Eliot
51. **"Progressing AI Driverless Cars"** by Dr. Lance Eliot
52. **"AI Self-Driving Cars Imminence"** by Dr. Lance Eliot
53. **"AI Self-Driving Cars Convergence"** by Dr. Lance Eliot

These books are available on Amazon and at other major global booksellers.

CHAPTER 1
ELIOT FRAMEWORK FOR AI SELF-DRIVING CARS

This chapter is a core foundational aspect for understanding AI self-driving cars and I have used this same chapter in several of my other books to introduce the reader to essential elements of this field. Once you've read this chapter, you'll be prepared to read the rest of the material since the foundational essence of the components of autonomous AI driverless self-driving cars will have been established for you.

When I give presentations about self-driving cars and teach classes on the topic, I have found it helpful to provide a framework around which the various key elements of self-driving cars can be understood and organized (see diagram at the end of this chapter). The framework needs to be simple enough to convey the overarching elements, but at the same time not so simple that it belies the true complexity of self-driving cars. As such, I am going to describe the framework here and try to offer in a thousand words (or more!) what the framework diagram itself intends to portray.

The core elements on the diagram are numbered for ease of reference. The numbering does not suggest any kind of prioritization of the elements. Each element is crucial. Each element has a purpose, and otherwise would not be included in the framework. For some self-driving cars, a particular element might be more important or somehow distinguished in comparison to other self-driving cars.

You could even use the framework to rate a particular self-driving car, doing so by gauging how well it performs in each of the elements of the framework. I will describe each of the elements, one at a time. After doing so, I'll discuss aspects that illustrate how the elements interact and perform during the overall effort of a self-driving car.

At the AI Self-Driving Car Institute, we use the framework to keep track of what we are working on, and how we are developing software that fills in what is needed to achieve Level 5 self-driving cars.

D-01: Sensor Capture

Let's start with the one element that often gets the most attention in the press about self-driving cars, namely, the sensory devices for a self-driving car.

On the framework, the box labeled as D-01 indicates "Sensor Capture" and refers to the processes of the self-driving car that involve collecting data from the myriad of sensors that are used for a self-driving car. The types of devices typically involved are listed, such as the use of mono cameras, stereo cameras, LIDAR devices, radar systems, ultrasonic devices, GPS, IMU, and so on.

These devices are tasked with obtaining data about the status of the self-driving car and the world around it. Some of the devices are continually providing updates, while others of the devices await an indication by the self-driving car that the device is supposed to collect data. The data might be first transformed in some fashion by the device itself, or it might instead be fed directly into the sensor capture as raw data. At that point, it might be up to the sensor capture processes to do transformations on the data. This all varies depending upon the nature of the devices being used and how the devices were designed and developed.

D-02: Sensor Fusion

Imagine that your eyeballs receive visual images, your nose receives odors, your ears receive sounds, and in essence each of your distinct sensory devices is getting some form of input. The input befits the nature of the device. Likewise, for a self-driving car, the cameras provide visual images, the radar returns radar reflections, and so on. Each device provides the data as befits what the device does.

At some point, using the analogy to humans, you need to merge together what your eyes see, what your nose smells, what your ears hear, and piece it all together into a larger sense of what the world is all about and what is happening around you. Sensor fusion is the action of taking the singular aspects from each of the devices and putting them together into a larger puzzle.

Sensor fusion is a tough task. There are some devices that might not be working at the time of the sensor capture. Or, there might some devices that are unable to report well what they have detected. Again, using a human analogy, suppose you are in a dark room and so your eyes cannot see much. At that point, you might need to rely more so on your ears and what you hear. The same is true for a self-driving car. If the cameras are obscured due to snow and sleet, it might be that the radar can provide a greater indication of what the external conditions consist of.

In the case of a self-driving car, there can be a plethora of such sensory devices. Each is reporting what it can. Each might have its difficulties. Each might have its limitations, such as how far ahead it can detect an object. All of these limitations need to be considered during the sensor fusion task.

D-03: Virtual World Model

For humans, we presumably keep in our minds a model of the world around us when we are driving a car. In your mind, you know that the car is going at say 60 miles per hour and that you are on a freeway.

You have a model in your mind that your car is surrounded by other cars, and that there are lanes to the freeway. Your model is not only based on what you can see, hear, etc., but also what you know about the nature of the world. You know that at any moment that car ahead of you can smash on its brakes, or the car behind you can ram into your car, or that the truck in the next lane might swerve into your lane.

The AI of the self-driving car needs to have a virtual world model, which it then keeps updated with whatever it is receiving from the sensor fusion, which received its input from the sensor capture.

D-04: System Action Plan

By having a virtual world model, the AI of the self-driving car is able to keep track of where the car is and what is happening around the car. In addition, the AI needs to determine what to do next. Should the self-driving car hit its brakes? Should the self-driving car stay in its lane or swerve into the lane to the left? Should the self-driving car accelerate or slow down?

A system action plan needs to be prepared by the AI of the self-driving car. The action plan specifies what actions should be taken. The actions need to pertain to the status of the virtual world model. Plus, the actions need to be realizable.

This realizability means that the AI cannot just assert that the self-driving car should suddenly sprout wings and fly. Instead, the AI must be bound by whatever the self-driving car can actually do, such as coming to a halt in a distance of X feet at a speed of Y miles per hour, rather than perhaps asserting that the self-driving car come to a halt in 0 feet as though it could instantaneously come to a stop while it is in motion.

D-05: Controls Activation

The system action plan is implemented by activating the controls of the car to act according to what the plan stipulates.

This might mean that the accelerator control is commanded to increase the speed of the car. Or, the steering control is commanded to turn the steering wheel 30 degrees to the left or right.

One question arises as to whether or not the controls respond as they are commanded to do. In other words, suppose the AI has commanded the accelerator to increase, but for some reason it does not do so. Or, maybe it tries to do so, but the speed of the car does not increase.

The controls activation feeds back into the virtual world model, and simultaneously the virtual world model is getting updated from the sensors, the sensor capture, and the sensor fusion. This allows the AI to ascertain what has taken place as a result of the controls being commanded to take some kind of action.

By the way, please keep in mind that though the diagram seems to have a linear progression to it, the reality is that these are all aspects of the self-driving car that are happening in parallel and simultaneously. The sensors are capturing data, meanwhile the sensor fusion is taking place, meanwhile the virtual model is being updated, meanwhile the system action plan is being formulated and reformulated, meanwhile the controls are being activated.

This is the same as a human being that is driving a car. They are eyeballing the road, meanwhile they are fusing in their mind the sights, sounds, etc., meanwhile their mind is updating their model of the world around them, meanwhile they are formulating an action plan of what to do, and meanwhile they are pushing their foot onto the pedals and steering the car. In the normal course of driving a car, you are doing all of these at once. I mention this so that when you look at the diagram, you will think of the boxes as processes that are all happening at the same time, and not as though only one happens and then the next.

They are shown diagrammatically in a simplistic manner to help comprehend what is taking place. You though should also realize that they are working in parallel and simultaneous with each other. This is a tough aspect in that the inter-element communications involve latency and other aspects that must be taken into account. There can be delays in one element updating and then sharing its latest status with other elements.

D-06: Automobile & CAN

Contemporary cars use various automotive electronics and a Controller Area Network (CAN) to serve as the components that underlie the driving aspects of a car.

There are Electronic Control Units (ECU's) which control subsystems of the car, such as the engine, the brakes, the doors, the windows, and so on.

The elements D-01, D-02, D-03, D-04, D-05 are layered on top of the D-06, and must be aware of the nature of what the D-06 is able to do and not do.

D-07: In-Car Commands

Humans are going to be occupants in self-driving cars. In a Level 5 self-driving car, there must be some form of communication that takes place between the humans and the self-driving car. For example, I go into a self-driving car and tell it that I want to be driven over to Disneyland, and along the way I want to stop at In-and-Out Burger. The self-driving car now parses what I've said and tries to then establish a means to carry out my wishes.

In-car commands can happen at any time during a driving journey. Though my example was about an in-car command when I first got into my self-driving car, it could be that while the self-driving car is carrying out the journey that I change my mind. Perhaps after getting stuck in traffic, I tell the self-driving car to forget about getting the burgers and just head straight over to the theme park. The self-driving car needs to be alert to in-car commands throughout the journey.

D-08: V2X Communications

We will ultimately have self-driving cars communicating with each other, doing so via V2V (Vehicle-to-Vehicle) communications. We will also have self-driving cars that communicate with the roadways and other aspects of the transportation infrastructure, doing so via V2I (Vehicle-to-Infrastructure).

The variety of ways in which a self-driving car will be communicating with other cars and infrastructure is being called V2X, whereby the letter X means whatever else we identify as something that a car should or would want to communicate with.

The V2X communications will be taking place simultaneous with everything else on the diagram, and those other elements will need to incorporate whatever it gleans from those V2X communications.

D-09: Deep Learning

The use of Deep Learning permeates all other aspects of the self-driving car. The AI of the self-driving car will be using deep learning to do a better job at the systems action plan, and at the control's activation, and at the sensor fusion, and so on.

Currently, the use of artificial neural networks is the most prevalent form of deep learning. Based on large swaths of data, the neural networks attempt to "learn" from the data and therefore direct the efforts of the self-driving car accordingly.

D-10: Tactical AI

Tactical AI is the element of dealing with the moment-to-moment driving of the self-driving car. Is the self-driving car staying in its lane of the freeway? Is the car responding appropriately to the controls commands? Are the sensory devices working?

For human drivers, the tactical equivalent can be seen when you watch a novice driver such as a teenager that is first driving. They are focused on the mechanics of the driving task, keeping their eye on the road while also trying to properly control the car.

D-11: Strategic AI

The Strategic AI aspects of a self-driving car are dealing with the larger picture of what the self-driving car is trying to do. If I had asked that the self-driving car take me to Disneyland, there is an overall journey map that needs to be kept and maintained.

There is an interaction between the Strategic AI and the Tactical AI. The Strategic AI is wanting to keep on the mission of the driving, while the Tactical AI is focused on the particulars underway in the driving effort.

If the Tactical AI seems to wander away from the overarching mission, the Strategic AI wants to see why and get things back on track. If the Tactical AI realizes that there is something amiss on the self-driving car, it needs to alert the Strategic AI accordingly and have an adjustment to the overarching mission that is underway.

D-12: Self-Aware AI

Very few of the self-driving cars being developed are including a Self-Aware AI element, which we at the Cybernetic Self-Driving Car Institute believe is crucial to Level 5 self-driving cars.

The Self-Aware AI element is intended to watch over itself, in the sense that the AI is making sure that the AI is working as intended. Suppose you had a human driving a car, and they were starting to drive erratically. Hopefully, their own self-awareness would make them realize they themselves are driving poorly, such as perhaps starting to fall asleep after having been driving for hours on end. If you had a passenger in the car, they might be able to alert the driver if the driver is starting to do something amiss.

This is exactly what the Self-Aware AI element tries to do, it becomes the overseer of the AI, and tries to detect when the AI has become faulty or confused, and then find ways to overcome the issue.

D-13: Economic

The economic aspects of a self-driving car are not per se a technology aspect of a self-driving car, but the economics do indeed impact the nature of a self-driving car. For example, the cost of outfitting a self-driving car with every kind of possible sensory device is prohibitive, and so choices need to be made about which devices are used. And, for those sensory devices chosen, whether they would have a full set of features or a more limited set of features.

We are going to have self-driving cars that are at the low-end of a consumer cost point, and others at the high-end of a consumer cost point. You cannot expect that the self-driving car at the low-end is going to be as robust as the one at the high-end.

I realize that many of the self-driving car pundits are acting as though all self-driving cars will be the same, but they won't be. Just like anything else, we are going to have self-driving cars that have a range of capabilities. Some will be better than others. Some will be safer than others. This is the way of the real-world, and so we need to be thinking about the economics aspects when considering the nature of self-driving cars.

D-14: Societal

This component encompasses the societal aspects of AI which also impacts the technology of self-driving cars. For example, the famous Trolley Problem involves what choices should a self-driving car make when faced with life-and-death matters. If the self-driving car is about to either hit a child standing in the roadway, or instead ram into a tree at the side of the road and possibly kill the humans in the self-driving car, which choice should be made?

We need to keep in mind the societal aspects will underlie the AI of the self-driving car. Whether we are aware of it explicitly or not, the AI will have embedded into it various societal assumptions.

D-15: Innovation

I included the notion of innovation into the framework because we can anticipate that whatever a self-driving car consists of, it will continue to be innovated over time. The self-driving cars coming out in the next several years will undoubtedly be different and less innovative than the versions that come out in ten years hence, etc.

Framework Overall

For those of you that want to learn about self-driving cars, you can potentially pick a particular element and become specialized in that aspect. Some engineers are focusing on the sensory devices. Some engineers focus on the controls activation. And so on. There are specialties in each of the elements.

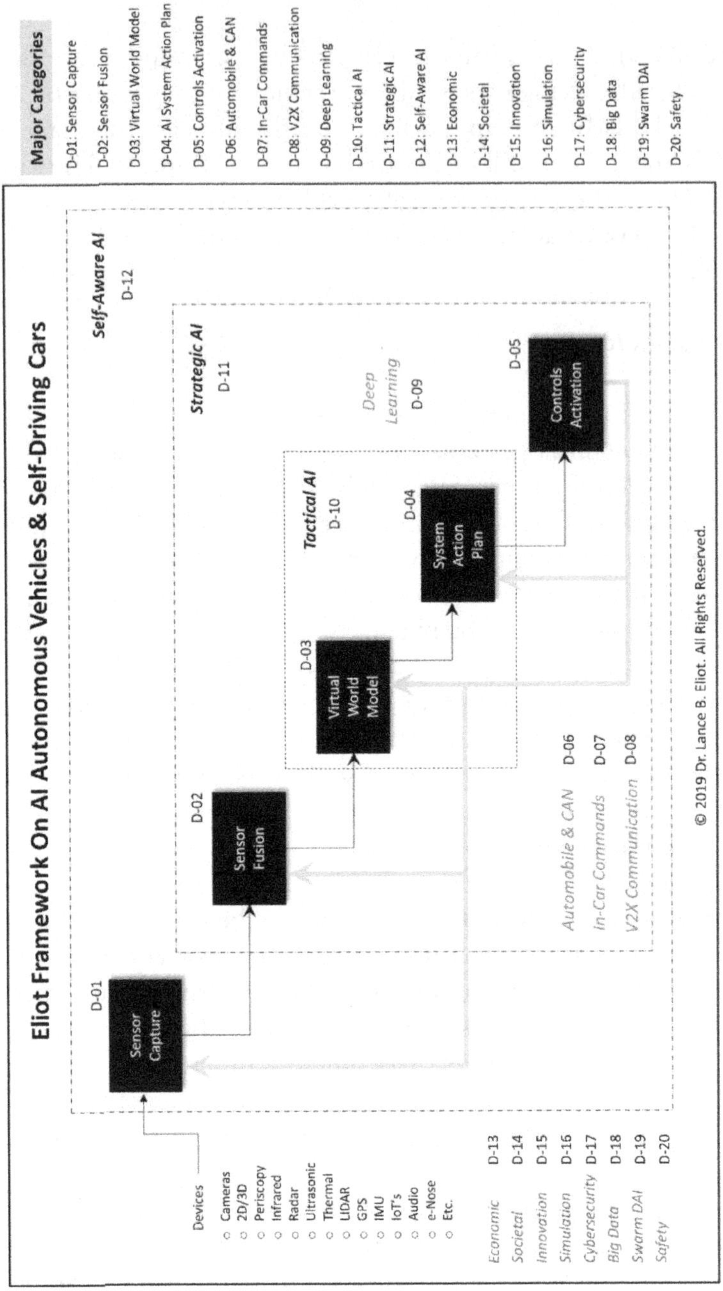
Eliot Framework On AI Autonomous Vehicles & Self-Driving Cars
Self-Aware AI
D-12
Strategic AI
D-11
Tactical AI
D-10
Deep Learning
D-09
D-01
Sensor Capture
D-02
Sensor Fusion
D-03
Virtual World Model
D-04
System Action Plan
D-05
Controls Activation
Automobile & CAN D-06
In-Car Commands D-07
V2X Communication D-08
Devices
Cameras
2D/3D
Periscopy
Infrared
Radar
Ultrasonic
Thermal
LIDAR
GPS
IMU
IoT's
Audio
e-Nose
Etc.
Economic D-13
Societal D-14
Innovation D-15
Simulation D-16
Cybersecurity D-17
Big Data D-18
Swarm DAI D-19
Safety D-20
© 2019 Dr. Lance B. Eliot. All Rights Reserved.
Major Categories
D-01: Sensor Capture
D-02: Sensor Fusion
D-03: Virtual World Model
D-04: AI System Action Plan
D-05: Controls Activation
D-06: Automobile & CAN
D-07: In-Car Commands
D-08: V2X Communication
D-09: Deep Learning
D-10: Tactical AI
D-11: Strategic AI
D-12: Self-Aware AI
D-13: Economic
D-14: Societal
D-15: Innovation
D-16: Simulation
D-17: Cybersecurity
D-18: Big Data
D-19: Swarm DAI
D-20: Safety

CHAPTER 2

VARIABLE SPEED LIMITS AND SELF-DRIVING CARS

When you get into your car today and go driving, I'd bet that you pretty much know the speed limits of wherever you are headed.

Assuming that you are driving in a locale that you know well, the odds are that you already have learned over time what the speed limits are. Perhaps you pull out of your driveway and drive initially past a school ground. Next, you get onto a major street that takes you to the freeway. Upon entering the freeway, you proceed for a while and eventually take an exit into a downtown area.

For each of the portions encompassing that daily trip, there are speed limits that you are to comply with.

Generally, the speed limits are lower in a neighborhood setting and then heightened on the open highways and freeways. This makes indubitable sense. On those smaller and local streets, there is a chance of encountering pedestrians, coming upon loose dogs, etc. Once you get onto a freeway, the roadway is purposely set aside and somewhat guarded by railings to prevent anything other than fellow vehicular traffic.

In a locale that you know by heart, you've memorized the speed limits or perhaps developed "muscle memory" that intuitively informs you about the speed limits. You don't need to look for any posted speed signs, since you already know well what the accepted speed is. When first driving in that area, you probably looked high and low to spot the various speed limit signs during your driving journeys. As a result of your avid familiarity with those roads, you barely notice the posted speed limit signs anymore.

Those signs are still there, but your mind blots them out as though they are invisible.

It's a natural thing to do.

For teenagers just learning to drive, the newbies usually notice the speed limit signs. They are taught in driver-training classes to explicitly look for the speed limit and then make sure to obey whatever the posting says. You can see the anxious young drivers swiveling their heads and using their panicky eyes while immensely struggling and searching to find those crucial speed limit postings.

This can be difficult to do.

Speed limit signs are supposed to be posted in rather obvious spots. Unfortunately, they are at times ostensibly hidden from view, often placed nearby other objects that attract your attention. Or, put near to trees or businesses that you notice more so than the speed limit sign. Looking for speed limit signs can be akin to doing the Where's Waldo kind of puzzles.

People have a love-hate relationship with speed limits.

Upon reflective thought, you have to admit that speed limits are exceedingly appropriate in many circumstances.

On your neighborhood block, suppose that the speed limit was set at 65 miles per hour. I dare say that you would likely find it quite daunting to go outside. Cars would be zipping past your house. If your children perchance wandered into the street, dire consequences could sadly arise. There is also the ample chance that a car might veer off the street and plow into your beloved domicile, which at a speed over sixty is going to cause a massive amount of damage and destruction.

In that sense, I would respectfully suggest that we love speed limits in situations such as establishing a suitable speed limit in an everyday neighborhood. The same goes for speed limits around school grounds. And so on.

The hate part of the speed limits usually arises when you are late to work or otherwise in a hurry. At that point, you might carp that the speed limit is too low, even in a peaceful community setting. For sure you are going to be upset about the speed limit on a freeway or open highway. That seems downright stupid as a place to put constraining bounds on the allowed speeds, or at least we ought to make the speed limit high enough that people can travel at "expedient" rates.

Part of the basis for speed limits is that it presumably saves lives. Besides the obvious aspects of lives saved nearby school grounds, there are lives to be saved on freeways too. Studies tend to show that car crashes at higher speeds are more likely to produce fatalities. By keeping the speed limit at a more "reasonable" level, the argument goes that any car crashes will be less injurious and less death-producing.

Not everyone buys into that logic.

Some assert that the freeways especially ought to be more open-ended as to the speed limits imposed. Furthermore, in some places, there are lots of wide-open cross-country roads and many miles to be covered if you want to get from one part of a state to another. Those vast and nearly empty passages are going to be driven at heightened speeds anyway, some point out, and thus having set narrow speed limits is impractical and a bit of a joke.

One concern too is that if people don't believe that a speed limit is sensible, it makes them question our driving laws overall. By the act of speeding, doing so when people think it is reasonable to flaunt the legally stated speed limit, perhaps this is sending a kind of signal that the law is capricious and not to be observed. A slippery slope is said to extend from there.

There is an interesting dynamic involving human behavior and speed limits.

When people see a posted speed, they are supposed to construe the stated speed as a maximum allowed. In addition, this maximum is based on presumed relatively ideal conditions. If the roadway is slick due to rain, the posted speed limit is not the speed you likely should be going. The notion is that the speed is indicative of what you can do if the road is pristine, and all is good to proceed.

It seems that many people perceive the speed limit in an entirely different way. They consider the speed limit to be the target speed, though you can certainly go higher than the number indicated. Driving faster than the posted speed is fine, in their minds. You might ultimately average out to that stated speed, based on at times going a lot faster and at other times having to go slower due to traffic impedance.

There is also the belief that you won't get a ticket unless you are going at least 5 to maybe 10 miles per hour faster than the posted speed limit. Thus, the sign that says 35 mph is really telling you that you can go 40 to 45 mph, fully legally so. Sorry to burst your bubble but that's not how speed limits work. You can readily get a ticket for going even a rudimentary one mph over the speed limit.

And you can also get a speeding ticket for doing the speed limit. Yes, that's the case, if the conditions of the roadway are not suitable for attaining and maintaining the posted speed limit, you can get a ticket. It will be a bona fide ticket and unlikely to be overturned, assuming that in fact, the driving you were doing was unsuitable according to the conditions at the time.

Most of the time, the speed limit is the speed limit.

That seems a rather oddball way to express things. Allow me to explain.

You see a posted speed and it says 45 miles per hour. Later that day, you drive on that same stretch of road. The odds are pretty high that the sign still says 45 mph. No matter what time of day, and no matter which day of the week, the posted speed limit is set in stone.

We know this isn't entirely the case. For example, school zones have one stated speed when children are present, and a different allowed speed when children are not there. Nonetheless, they are fixed speed limits, though there are two fixed values involved.

Another example of speeds that are somewhat changing includes construction zones. You drive toward a roadway construction crew and they might be holding up signs that adjust the normal speed limit in that vicinity. There are also often electronic speed limit signboards that are hauled around by construction teams and put in place to blink repeatedly about the temporary speed limit wherever they are placed.

In short, we do accept the general idea that speed limits are not always static and fixed in place. There are many occasions wherein a speed limit is stated as being able to vary, depending upon the circumstances. I would respectively submit that we are accustomed to this notion in a somewhat narrow and preordained way, for which we can be taken aback if the roadway does not abide by that convention (as will be discussed in a moment). In essence, the examples I've given are the types of situations that we today accept and realize that the speed limit might vary.

Here's a different angle on the speed limit variability.

Suppose that there were speed limit signs that displayed one speed at one time of the day, and then displayed a different speed limit at a different time of the day. Let's add to this variability by also having the speed limits be one set of speeds on weekdays versus the weekends.

We can also mix things up a bit further by allowing that the variable speed does not need to be consistent per se. In other words, you are not guaranteed that on every Monday morning the variable speed limit will be a certain preset number. Instead, the traffic conditions, weather conditions, and other factors might contribute toward a final determination of what the speed limit will be on any given day and at any given time.

In that sense, you have no means beforehand of knowing exactly what the speed limit will be. You might say this is a variable speed limit (VSL) and that it also varies over time. It is a *varying* variable speed limit, as it were (in contrast to a predictable, predetermined scheduled change of speed limits that are of a fixed nature for when they occur and how long they last).

Why would VSL be used?

The theory underlying variable speed limits is that it potentially can smooth out traffic, reduce risks, decrease car crashes, and minimize injuries and fatalities. Meanwhile, this accommodates the needs of the driving public. Rather than always having to go at a slower speed on a given roadway, there might be times that it is okay to go faster.

A static speed limit would not normally allow for that kind of flexibility, while a variable speed limit would.

Here's how this works.

You are driving along and the posted speed limit is shown on an electronic display. Let's assume it is morning and the roadway is jampacked with cars. Perhaps the display is showing a speed of 35 mph as the speed limit. During your lunch break, you get back onto the roadway and you then observe that the speed limit sign now says 50 mph. Upon the end of your workday, you once again are driving your car on that same road and notice that the speed limit is now set at 30 mph.

Reportedly, at least a dozen states or more have tried using VSL.

Indeed, a recent news story indicated that there will be seventy-two of the variable speed limit signs set up on a 14-mile stretch of road on Interstate 76 in Pennsylvania (between the locales of King of Prussia and Philadelphia). That comes to about five of those VSL signs per mile on average. The speeds to be displayed will range from a low of 35 mph to a high of 55 mph.

There is a bit of a rub.

That same stretch has customarily been around 50 to 55 mph. As such, from the perspective of the everyday driver, they are not gaining any speed and only (presumably) losing speed. On the other hand, one argument is that by regulating the speed at lower rates of speed, there is a solid chance of smoothing out the flow and averting long delays due to traffic accidents. In that manner of thinking, you might be able to proceed at a faster pace than you did when the legally posted speed limit was ostensibly higher (which, as a reminder, was only the maximum allowed anyway and not the stated expected speed). And, crucially, the hope is that the number of car crashes (and fatalities) will be reduced.

One of the overarching issues about using VSL is that drivers might get confused by the changing speed limits. What the heck, some drivers might say, yesterday it was 55 mph, today it is 35 mph, and tomorrow it is anyone's guess as to what it might be.

The retort is that the speed limit is the speed limit. You are supposed to be paying attention and obeying the speed limit. Rather than relying on your gut or a hunch, the VSL makes things rather apparent as to what the speed limit is. Just obey it and stop carping.

Where the mix-up can be injurious or at times fatal entails a driver that thought the speed limit was faster than it currently is, and meanwhile another driver is let's assume abiding by the now-lowered speed limit. The driver that thinks the speed limit is 55 mph might readily ram into the slower moving car that is going at the legally stated VSL-posted speed of 35 mph.

It is easy to point fingers at the faster-moving driver. The dolt should have been looking for the variable speed limit and adjusted accordingly. You are hard-pressed to point a finger at the slower moving driver since they were obeying the posted VSL, though you can likely anticipate that the faster moving driver would try to contend that the slower moving driver was the problem (this is seemingly not going to pass muster with a judge).

One can also readily make the counter case too, namely in the use case of the VSL stating 55 mph, and meanwhile, other cars are being driven at 35 mph due to those drivers thinking that the speed limit is still 35 mph. All told, there is a heightened chance of confusion about what the speed limit is since the number keeps varying and there is no particular set pattern involved.

Some would point the finger at the VSL itself, in the sense that it is a system devised by mankind that is rife with problems. Human drivers have enough to deal with when behind the wheel, besides also throwing at them a continually shifting target of what the speed limit might be. The cognitive overload on the driver is already much too high in today's chaotic driving world.

Adding a changing speed limit is the proverbial last straw on the camel's back, some would assert.

Another consideration is whether the VSL can be legally enforced. A driver might justifiably claim they were confused by the signage. Judges might or might not allow such rationalization for getting out of a speeding ticket.

Yet another concern is the visibility of the VSL. Depending upon how the electronic display works, it could be that the sunshine can make seeing the speed an altogether tough proposition. Or, maybe when it is cloudy and raining the VSL sign is hard to see. The point is that by visually displaying the speed and doing so on a variable basis, if you don't perchance see the sign, you are up a creek without a paddle.

An especially disturbing complaint is that the VSL can be used as a speed trap.

That's right, catch those unaware drivers by shifting around the speed limit and ostensibly entrapping them into a speeding charge. This could be a lucrative money maker for a municipality or roadway authority. Though people that live in the area might get used to the changing speed limits, visitors from out-of-town might have no idea what the signs mean, nor whether they are valid.

You can hear the surprised and dismayed speeding ticket holders insisting that they had never seen such signage before. They assumed that the signage was a practical joke or possibly intended for some purpose other than regulating the speed.

The bottom line is this: Can human drivers manage to deal with variable speed limits?

The research on this topic is still being conducted and the results of using VSL are typically mushy. VSL admittedly might be overly challenging for humans. Then again, perhaps if it was more prevalent as a technique, human drivers would get accustomed to the approach. You could persuasively argue that the biggest hurdle to be overcome is the inherent newness or uniqueness of the technique, rather than the abstract conceptual underpinnings per se.

Now that we've covered many of the aspects underlying what human drivers do when confronted with variable speed limits, let's shift our attention. The future of cars consists of self-driving cars. Self-driving cars are going to be using AI-based driving systems and there won't be a human driver at the wheel.

Here is an intriguing question: *How will AI-based true self-driving cars contend with variable speed limits, and will they be challenged by or find it easy to abide by VSL?*

Let's unpack the matter and see.

Understanding The Levels Of Self-Driving Cars

As a clarification, true self-driving cars are ones that the AI drives the car entirely on its own and there isn't any human assistance during the driving task.

These driverless vehicles are considered Level 4 and Level 5 while a car that requires a human driver to co-share the driving effort is usually considered at Level 2 or Level 3. The cars that co-share the driving task are described as being semi-autonomous, and typically contain a variety of automated add-on's that are referred to as ADAS (Advanced Driver-Assistance Systems).

There is not yet a true self-driving car at Level 5, which we don't yet even know if this will be possible to achieve, and nor how long it will take to get there.

Meanwhile, the Level 4 efforts are gradually trying to get some traction by undergoing very narrow and selective public roadway trials, though there is controversy over whether this testing should be allowed per se (we are all life-or-death guinea pigs in an experiment taking place on our highways and byways, some contend).

Since semi-autonomous cars require a human driver, the adoption of those types of cars won't be markedly different than driving conventional vehicles, so there's not much new per se to cover about them on this topic (though, as you'll see in a moment, the points next made are generally applicable).

For semi-autonomous cars, it is important that the public needs to be forewarned about a disturbing aspect that's been arising lately, namely that despite those human drivers that keep posting videos of themselves falling asleep at the wheel of a Level 2 or Level 3 car, we all need to avoid being misled into believing that the driver can take away their attention from the driving task while driving a semi-autonomous car.

You are the responsible party for the driving actions of the vehicle, regardless of how much automation might be tossed into a Level 2 or Level 3.

Self-Driving Cars And Variable Speed Limits

For Level 4 and Level 5 true self-driving vehicles, there won't be a human driver involved in the driving task.

All occupants will be passengers.

The AI is doing the driving.

One aspect to immediately discuss entails the fact that the AI involved in today's AI driving systems is not sentient. In other words, the AI is altogether a collective of computer-based programming and algorithms, and most assuredly not able to reason in the same manner that humans can.

Why this added emphasis about the AI not being sentient?

Because I want to underscore that when discussing the role of the AI driving system, I am not ascribing human qualities to the AI. Please be aware that there is an ongoing and dangerous tendency these days to anthropomorphize AI. In essence, people are assigning human-like sentience to today's AI, despite the undeniable and inarguable fact that no such AI exists as yet.

With that clarification, you can envision that the AI driving system doesn't natively somehow "know" about variable speed limits. This is an aspect that needs to be programmed as part of the hardware and software of the self-driving car.

Let's dive into the myriad of aspects that come to play on this topic.

First, the AI driving system has to become aware of the speed limit in whichever locale it is driving. This is usually done by pre-mapping the area that will be traveled by the self-driving car. Data is collected about the roadway particulars, including the speed limits. This is then fed into the AI driving system and used as part of the overall template about the roadway infrastructure and its contours.

Does a self-driving try to detect actual speed limit signs?

On the one hand, you might argue that it doesn't need to do so if the speed limits are already pre-mapped and available on-board the self-driving car. That being said, it is certainly possible that a speed limit has changed, and the posted speed sign was updated after the pre-mapping was performed. As such, the AI driving system should rightfully be expected to scan in real-time for existing speed limit signs.

In addition, as already discussed, there are commonplace instances wherein the speed limit is adjusted on the fly by roadway construction and for other reasons. In that sense, a pre-mapping is only handy as an overall guide and not a definitive indication of what will be encountered during an actual driving journey.

The self-driving car can use its cameras to try and detect and interpret speed limit signs. This is somewhat harder than you think it might be. If a speed limit sign is well-hidden or marred, it can be difficult to discern via the computational image processing taking place. In any case, the detection of speed limit signs would be argued as essential and can be utilized in conjunction with the pre-mapping.

As an aside, a fleet of self-driving cars also has an advantage in that if one of the self-driving cars comes upon a speed limit sign that heretofore was differently stated via pre-mapping, this updated info can be pushed up into the cloud of the fleet operator via OTA (Over-The-Air) electronic communications. In turn, this could be downloaded and shared with the other self-driving cars in that fleet.

What about detecting those variable speed limits or VSL signs?

Yes, those too must be scanned for.

The good news is that they are usually easier to spot. This is partly because they are usually placed in very conspicuous placements and made as abundantly apparent as feasible, primarily for aiding human drivers to see them. They are usually well-maintained too, keeping in mind that much of the time they are currently used on an experimental or pilot basis.

The other handy aspect about modern VSL is that the signboards can be equipped to electronically transmit the speed too. Self-driving cars are going to leverage V2I, vehicle-to-infrastructure, which consists of roadway devices that are electronically beaming out signals. The beauty is that even if the visual sign is hard to visually detect (maybe the onboard cameras are having trouble spotting a VSL sign), electronic messaging can be utilized.

This electronic messaging does not have to pertain only to self-driving cars. The odds are that conventional human-driven cars will be equipped with V2I and allow human drivers to receive machine-generated verbal or visual messages inside their vehicle about the speed that a nearby VSL is emitting.

Conclusion

You could assert that AI driving systems are going to have an easy time dealing with VSL. Assuming that the VSL transmission or display can be readily detected, the AI driving system will smoothly adjust to the speed limit changes as needed.

Easy-peasy.

Unlike human drivers, the AI doesn't have any feelings about whether the speed is too slow or too fast. The speed limit is the speed limit. That's all there is to it.

I'm sure the passengers inside the self-driving car might see the world a different way. In particular, if the self-driving car is going 35 miles per hour in an area that the riders have driven before at higher speeds, they might question why the AI driving system is proceeding so slowly. Those devising self-driving cars are likely to incorporate an explanatory component that would inform the passengers that the variable speed in that locale is now at say 35 mph.

Presumably, this will be sufficient to placate the passengers.

On the other hand, don't be surprised if passengers inside self-driving cars try to stoke the AI driving system to go faster than the allowed speed limit. It isn't clear-cut as to what those passengers might use to induce this unlawful behavior, though perhaps a quick deposit of some cryptocurrency into the Swiss bank account of the AI system might do the trick.

.

.

.

CHAPTER 3
ARTIFICIAL LIGHT POLLUTION AND SELF-DRIVING CARS

Let there be darkness.

That is the potential catchphrase for those that are concerned about nighttime light pollution.

More formerly known as Artificial Light At Night (ALAN), there is an ongoing bruhaha that our modern way of living is generating way too much light during the evening darkness. It is an ongoing issue and the amount of such pollution is likely to keep on increasing due to further industrialization and expansion of societies into additional geographical areas.

In short, you can expect more light to be emitted in existing populated areas, along with nighttime light being unleashed in regions that had so far not been especially well lit due to insufficient means or lack of a light-producing populace. When you start adding more office buildings, more homes, more cars, more lampposts, and the like, this all translates into a tsunami of unbridled light at night.

You might be puzzled as to why the mere shepherding of artificial light is considered a pollution monstrosity.

One obvious facet is that you cannot see the stars at nighttime, or they are otherwise generally blotted out of view by the abundance of overwhelming artificial light.

How does this happen?

Well, there is the artificial light that comes from say a skyscraper, considered to be a point source of such light, and there is the skyglow type of light, proffering a combined effect that muddles together the thousands upon thousands of point source lights. I'm sure you have noticed this effect whenever taking a flight over a sizable part of the country and observed the glowing lights from any big city. Particularly striking is the evening glow around Las Vegas which is a look-here lights-on-steroids city plopped down into the middle of an otherwise utterly darkened desert.

Some researchers estimate that about 80% of the global populace lives in light-polluted areas. This is somewhat concentrated geographically because there are vast parts of the world that are relatively uninhabited or sparsely so. Research suggests that perhaps one-fourth of the world has those polluted nighttime skies.

Besides undercutting the ability to readily see the stars, there are other quite notable qualms about ALAN.

For example, some assert that artificial lighting is impacting the everyday life cycle of nature. Animals that are cued naturally to act at nighttime are at times taken aback by the appearance of artificial light, and likewise, animals that focus on daytime lighting are seemingly triggered to act in the evening when they normally would not do so. It is believed that humans can also be impacted by all of the artificial light at night, perhaps being linked in some ways to poorer sleep quality amid disturbances to circadian rhythms, might spur or promote impaired memory capacity, can possibly foster obesity, and so on.

Various recommendations have been made about corralling this out-of-control artificial light abundance. Experts ask that artificial lighting only be used when fully justified. Artificial lighting should not occur simply by default and indeed there ought to be adequate attention allotted toward the polluting properties that can arise. When feasible, artificial lighting should be kept to the lowest usable intensity, it should be shielded and guided toward whatever the intended lighting purpose requires, etc.

You might not realize that you are probably a nighttime artificial light polluter.

How so?

When you go for a drive at nighttime, your headlights become a source of artificial light pollution. That being said, do not foolishly think that you should not be using your headlights. The use of your headlights is a vital safety measure and wholeheartedly needs to be used. You have to see the roadway to properly drive a car. Without headlights, you'd be driving in the dark, dangerously so, and undoubtedly the outcome would be disastrous.

You might have noticed from time-to-time cars driving along in traffic that do not have their headlights on, even though it is completely nighttime and all the other nearby vehicles have their headlights on. We usually assume that the driver might be intoxicated and not aware that they are driving without their headlights employed. Oftentimes, police will pull over a vehicle that doesn't have its headlights on and do so to find out why the driver is driving without this needed safety capability engaged.

During times of dusk and sunrise, you'll often see that some cars have their headlights on and some do not. The somewhat gray aspect of whether to turn on your headlights when there is a modicum of natural light still available or emerging is one that drivers make a judgment call about. Of course, most modern cars have an automated feature that senses the available lighting (or lack thereof) and will turn on the headlights for the driver, thus the driver doesn't have to take into account per se the headlight engaging chore.

Why all this talk about artificial light pollution?

A reader of my column recently sent me an intriguing question about the future of cars and the matter of artificial light pollution. As you likely know, cars will gradually become self-driving cars. Those are cars in which an AI-based driving system acts as the driver and there isn't a human driver at the wheel.

The question was this: *Will the advent of AI-based true self-driving cars potentially allow for the turning off of headlights at nighttime due to the self-driving cars orchestrating automatically their movement and traffic flow?*

This posits the conjecture that perhaps self-driving cars will electronically communicate their positions and align to avoid each other and proceed seamlessly as though like the flowing of water in a stream. The hook regarding headlights is that presumably there won't be a need to use headlights when those self-driving cars are all dancing together with aplomb. Just imagine, if it was possible to turn off the headlights and yet still had utter safety of traffic (in this imagined self-driving vehicular vision), there would be a substantive reduction in the artificial light pollution (at least due to headlights).

Let's consider whether that makes sense.

Before we jump into the fray, it will be helpful to clarify what is meant by the notion of AI-based true self-driving cars.

Understanding The Levels Of Self-Driving Cars

As a clarification, true self-driving cars are ones that the AI drives the car entirely on its own and there isn't any human assistance during the driving task.

These driverless vehicles are considered Level 4 and Level 5 while a car that requires a human driver to co-share the driving effort is usually considered at Level 2 or Level 3. The cars that co-share the driving task are described as being semi-autonomous, and typically contain a variety of automated add-on's that are referred to as ADAS (Advanced Driver-Assistance Systems).

There is not yet a true self-driving car at Level 5, which we don't yet even know if this will be possible to achieve, and nor how long it will take to get there.

Meanwhile, the Level 4 efforts are gradually trying to get some traction by undergoing very narrow and selective public roadway trials, though there is controversy over whether this testing should be allowed per se (we are all life-or-death guinea pigs in an experiment taking place on our highways and byways, some contend).

Since semi-autonomous cars require a human driver, the adoption of those types of cars won't be markedly different than driving conventional vehicles, so there's not much new per se to cover about them on this topic (though, as you'll see in a moment, the points next made are generally applicable).

For semi-autonomous cars, it is important that the public needs to be forewarned about a disturbing aspect that's been arising lately, namely that despite those human drivers that keep posting videos of themselves falling asleep at the wheel of a Level 2 or Level 3 car, we all need to avoid being misled into believing that the driver can take away their attention from the driving task while driving a semi-autonomous car.

You are the responsible party for the driving actions of the vehicle, regardless of how much automation might be tossed into a Level 2 or Level 3.

Self-Driving Cars And Artificial Light

For Level 4 and Level 5 true self-driving vehicles, there won't be a human driver involved in the driving task.

All occupants will be passengers.

The AI is doing the driving.

One aspect to immediately discuss entails the fact that the AI involved in today's AI driving systems is not sentient. In other words, the AI is altogether a collective of computer-based programming and algorithms, and most assuredly not able to reason in the same manner that humans can.

Why this added emphasis about the AI not being sentient?

Because I want to underscore that when discussing the role of the AI driving system, I am not ascribing human qualities to the AI. Please be aware that there is an ongoing and dangerous tendency these days to anthropomorphize AI. In essence, people are assigning human-like sentience to today's AI, despite the undeniable and inarguable fact that no such AI exists as yet.

With that clarification, you can envision that the AI driving system won't natively somehow "know" about the facets of driving. Driving and all that it entails will need to be programmed as part of the hardware and software of the self-driving car.

Let's dive into the myriad of aspects that come to play on this topic.

The first aspect to consider is whether self-driving cars will possibly be orchestrated by a centralized means that will coordinate their actions. This is a commonly expressed notion by some pundits. A centralized controller would attempt to maximize the flow of traffic and seek to reduce or entirely eliminate any semblance of congestion or traffic snarls.

Generally, though that might work in a simulation, you would be hard-pressed to make this contrivance viable in the real world.

Part of the reason that some believe this could work is that the AI driving systems will presumably take any strict orders about where to drive, what speed to drive at, and so on. Unlike human drivers that would likely balk at a centralized command that tells them what to do, the AI driving systems would simply carry out whatever instructions were provided (well, that's assuming that the AI was programmed to do so).

Unfortunately, there are a lot of gotchas and traps involved in trying to bring to fruition that kind of centralized control. In brief, this would require an ostensibly flawless electronic communications network that would transmit the car-going instructions and ensure that each self-driving car got a timely indication of what needed to be done. Even a split-second delay or if there was noise on the transmission could lead to a calamity in this rather farfetched scenario.

Another false assumption underlying the Utopian-like setting is that the roadway could have all sorts of imperfections and considerations that this centralized command might be unaware of. Suppose a piece of debris suddenly slips onto the roadway. Meanwhile, the centralized command is telling the self-driving cars to proceed ahead. Wham, a self-driving car hits the debris and then a cascading series of car crashes occur.

Yet another issue that sometimes is forgotten entails the aspect that we aren't likely to have only self-driving cars on our roadways, namely there will also be human-driven vehicles too. The emergence of self-driving cars will be gradual and take many years to become prevalent. During that time, likely many decades, there will be a mixture of self-driving cars and human-driven cars in traffic. In fact, some human drivers insist that they will never give up driving, until the day that you pry their cold dead hands from the steering wheel.

The point is that you might be able to get the self-driving cars to abide by the centralized commands approach, but one wonders whether human drivers will be willing to do so. Also, if a human driver decided to divert from the centralized command, doing this while in the middle of a sea of self-driving cars, it could once again cause quite a shebang akin to the example earlier about the appearance of debris. The human-driven car would be where it is not expected to be, and the nearby self-driving cars might ram into the human-driven car or take evasive action, upon which the centralized command might be delayed in being informed.

Let's then reasonably agree to set aside, for now, the centralized command notion as a means of trying to turn off those self-driving car headlights.

We might also amicably agree that headlights are a necessary enabler for vision-based driving.

Humans primarily use their vision as the key or core sensory apparatus needed to drive a car. When there is sufficient natural lighting, our eyeballs or ordinary vision can see the road. When there is a lack of sufficient natural lighting, our eyeballs cannot fully see the road. We, therefore, use artificial lighting to support our vision-based driving.

Lampposts near a roadway are handy to artificially light the roadway and aid our eyeballs as we drive. In theory, we could dispense with headlights if there was sufficient lamppost lighting on every nook and cranny of wherever you might want to drive. The beauty of headlights is that you bring them with you wherever your car goes. You don't need to depend upon any external source of lighting such as lampposts, and instead, you are carrying with you the ability to project artificial lighting when needed, where needed, as needed.

This brings up some interesting considerations worth pondering.

One aspect entails whether self-driving cars need to use vision or perhaps could be devised to use other sensory types.

As you might know, self-driving cars are usually loaded with video cameras and those cameras are collecting data about the driving scene. The AI driving system interprets the images coming from the cameras. Using Machine Learning (ML) and Deep Learning (DL), which are computational pattern matching techniques, the AI driving system tries to ascertain where other cars are, where pedestrians are, and other objects within the range of the self-driving vehicle.

In addition to video cameras, many of the self-driving cars are equipped with radar, LIDAR, thermal imaging, ultrasonic units, and other kinds of sensors. If we wanted to do away with the headlights, we might do so if we could rely entirely on the other types of sensory devices during the driving task. Thus, by somehow excising the vision elements of driving, a self-driving car would no longer need to light the way via headlights.

Sorry to say, this seems untenable in today's world. Not using vision is just not in the cards for now. The opposite is actually being generally pursued, wherein some automakers and self-driving tech firms are pushing further ahead on vision, aiming to make vision even more crucial, and downplay the role of the other sensory types.

Scratch for now the idea that you could eliminate the need for vision in self-driving cars as a scheme to get rid of the headlights and reduce the artificial light pollution at nighttime.

Let's try a different angle.

Have you ever noticed that when you are driving adjacent to other cars that have their headlights on that you can oftentimes see the road due to their headlights as an afterglow or spillover effect? I'm sure you've noticed this. I doubt that you considered turning off your headlights since you did not know how long those other nearby cars would be near you. No sense in taking a chance of having no lighting when those other vehicles change lanes, slow down, or otherwise change their traffic positions.

But with self-driving cars, there is a chance of knowing where and when the other nearby self-driving cars will change their positions. Using V2V which is vehicle-to-vehicle electronic communications, self-driving cars will be sending messages to each other. This might include for example the possibility of one self-driving car detecting debris on the roadway and then alerting electronically other self-driving cars to watch out for the obstruction.

Okay, we might then do this.

Whenever self-driving cars are near to each other, while at nighttime, they would electronically communicate about the use of their headlights. The headlights from one self-driving car could be illuminating the roadway sufficiently for another self-driving car nearby, such that the self-driving car getting the spillover could turn off its headlights momentarily. This might last for a few seconds or maybe minutes, depending upon where the self-driving cars are going and the nature of the roadway being used.

Upon an electronic communication from the self-driving car with its headlights on that, it is intending to shortly move away from the other headlight "borrowing" self-driving car, the self-driving car without its headlights on would need to turn on its headlights. All of this could happen very quickly. Electronic messages would be zipping around and you would see a seemingly oddball-looking scene as the self-driving cars all were turning off and on their headlights. Envision a potential twinkling effect similar to those sparkling lights on a Christmas tree.

In theory, maybe this would balance out that perhaps on the average you would have one out of every two self-driving cars using its headlights entirely on a driving journey, or maybe just one out of every ten, or every hundred, etc. It would depend greatly on where these self-driving cars are, how close they get to each other, and a myriad of other factors.

Would the logistics of this be worthwhile in terms of the reduction of ALAN?

A back of the napkin analysis suggests this would be quite a reach of achieving any significant dent in the artificial light pollution matter. We also need to once again consider how this might impact nearby human drivers. And so on.

Do we give up on this?

No!

Consider another possibility that involves throttling the amount of light being emitted from your headlights.

Imagine that headlights were able to showcase a beam of light that could be ratcheted between a numeric range of perhaps one to ten (a zero would mean the headlights are not on). The headlights at a setting of one were barely on. Headlights at a level of ten are super high beams.

For a human driver to try and continually throttle or adjust their headlights would seem onerous and a severe distractor from the driving task. On the other hand, this would be a relatively easy task for the AI driving system to computationally perform and assuredly not distract from the driving activity. The video cameras or other akin sensors would detect the needed level of lighting and the headlights would be electronically commanded to adjust accordingly. This could happen in split seconds and be a routine function of the vehicle.

Here's how this might help to reduce artificial light pollution.

Suppose that most of the cars on the roadways are eventually self-driving cars. Those self-driving cars can quickly and efficiently adjust the amount of light needed from their headlights. If they are all doing this, it could add up to a lot less light being emitted, in total and on average. Assuming that safety is not compromised, this could be a means of reducing the ALAN aspects as spurred by car headlights.

Would the reduction in ALAN be worth the tradeoffs of employing such a feature?

That's an open question.

Conclusion

There are additional twists and turns on this topic.

Some assert that we might use cars at nighttime more so than we do today as a result of the advent of self-driving cars.

This seems like a sensible piece of guesswork. Self-driving cars will be running 24x7 and there won't be a need for a driver to take breaks, rest, or grow weary of driving. People that want to go from point A to point B might be more willing to do so at nighttime than they are today, especially since the self-driving cars might be less costly for riders than when using human drivers (we don't know this to be the case, but it is highly speculated to occur).

The bad news then is that we might produce more artificial light pollution due to the use of self-driving cars. Not because the self-driving cars are producing more light, but because they will be used at nighttime in larger volumes than potentially human-driven cars of today are used. Yikes, it seems like self-driving cars are going to contribute to ALAN and not reduce ALAN if you buy into the foregoing logic.

Wait for a second, there could be a countervailing aspect.

Some claim that we will have fewer cars on the roadways as a result of self-driving cars becoming available. People will no longer own cars and will instead use ridesharing self-driving cars. You could therefore contend that though there might be more nighttime trips, perhaps it might occur via a lesser number of vehicles, and ergo the amount of light pollution is the same or reduced in comparison to human-driven and personally owned vehicles.

Whew, that seems a potential relief.

The thing is, we are all pretty much in the darkness right now about how self-driving cars are going to turn out. There is no magic light that shows what way self-driving cars are going to go (a bit of an extended pun, thanks for noticing).

Aristotle famously said that the light of day is followed by night, as a shadow follows a body. We are unlikely to be able to do anything directly about nighttime, but we can do something about the artificial light that we use when it is dark out. The headlights topic is pretty low on the priority list right now for attaining self-driving cars. Upon eventually giving due consideration to the headlights topic, it would tend to imply that we've already solved the zillions of other unsolved more pressing problems facing the advent of self-driving cars.

That will then be the (shining) light of day for self-driving cars, one might say.

CHAPTER 4
AMBIENT INTELLIGENCE AND SELF-DRIVING CARS

You invite someone over to your home.

If you are the type of host that cares about providing a cozy experience, you will attempt to fine-tune your household environment toward the specific interests and preferences of your guest. Turns out that the guest is known to be somewhat sensitive to bright light and loud noises. So, you draw closed many of the curtains, keep the interior lights dimmed, and politely ask other occupants to refrain from earsplitting vocal outbursts.

This is part of an effort to accommodate the needs of your guest.

Of course, you don't necessarily have to take those actions. It could be that you merely let your guest contend with whatever the normal conditions within your home are. Tough luck to them about any of their ambient desires as a visitor. Your place is your place, and the onus is upon any guest to self-adjust to the surroundings within your domicile.

I would optimistically suggest that few hosts tend to take that ostensibly harsh uncaring perspective and will instead do what they reasonably can to adjust the ambiance as best feasible. Might as well seek to make the environs palatable to a guest, thus likely increasing their satisfaction and comfort, along with indubitably making things better for yourself too (a happy guest would presumably spur being a happy host).

Another place where tuning the ambiance comes to play is inside a car.

You are giving a lift to a friend.

The ride will take about two hours. This is a long enough time period that it would seem worthwhile to try and do something for the comfort of your pal. Maybe you like rap music and your friend prefers classical music. As such, you prepare a slate of enthralling songs that includes both styles. Your friend relishes those indoor air fresheners and especially the sweet smell of forest pines. Though you normally don't use air fresheners in your vehicle, you nonetheless purchase one that has a wooded scent and install it into your car.

Pat yourself on the back for being a conscientious host.

All of this talk about setting the ambiance or surroundings is due to the rising aspects of something referred to as Ambient Intelligence (AmI).

The gist is that rather than you having to adjust the environment to the needs of a fellow human, there is state-of-the-art technology that will automatically do so. When someone walks into a house, the high-tech systems inside the structure will quietly and unobtrusively adjust the interior environment for the preferences of that person. This could make use of technology such as Internet of Things (IoT) devices, and likely leverage the latest in Artificial Intelligence (AI).

The IoT devices serve as sensors that can detect the conditions within the structure. That data can be fed into an AI-based controller that is able to electronically set and reset the devices of the home that pertain to the ambiance. For example, the Air Conditioning (A/C) might be electronically interconnected, and the AI will turn on or off the A/C as needed, per the temperate readings flowing in from the numerous IoT sensors throughout the house.

Ambient Intelligence is also coming to our cars.

Right now, you usually switch on the A/C when you need a flow of fresh cool air in your vehicle. Many cars also have a temperature gauge that can detect when the interior gets overly hot and will directly engage the A/C to cool down the compartment. Few cars though have a more sophisticated range of detection and action-taking tech.

The kind of space-age arrangement being envisioned would include the aspect that the tech would attempt to ascertain how warm the passengers are becoming and to what degree the A/C should be engaged. Have you ever had today's A/C suddenly bring forth a jet force blast of cold air? That is a crude way to try and cool off the interior and at times startles and rankles the riders.

If the Ambient Intelligence system had thermal detectors, it could read the temperatures of the people inside the car. When someone in the backseat seems to be getting especially overheated, the A/C would utilize just the jets in the backset and orient those directly toward that specific person. Rather than bluntly trying to get the entire car cooler, the idea is that the A/C usage is being tailored or customized to individual needs.

You might say that Ambience Intelligence entails using high-tech to be a good host.

This can be trickier than it might seem at first glance.

Just because that person in the backseat is showing a slightly heightened temperature does not necessarily mean that they welcome getting a jet of cool air upon them. Perhaps the person prefers being a bit warm. Or the person would instead like to open their window and not make use of the A/C at all.

The AI aspects of Ambient Intelligence are intended to make the ambient capabilities "smart" in that the use of ambient-related technology befits the person and the circumstances. In this scenario of the person in the backseat, the tech could open a car window for them, but this might not make sense if the outside temperature is a roasting hot wind. The AI would be attempting to ascertain for the given situation what options exist and which ones to prudently employ.

Another tricky element involves trying to set the ambiance when you have two or more people that are being accommodated.

In the backseat, assume that we have two passengers.

The one seated on the right likes the interior to be warm. The person seated on the left has a preference for cooler temps. Yikes, this is a bit of a dilemma. I'm sure you've had similar conundrums as a driver and having to cope with the disparate preferences of your fellow riders. Do you turn on the A/C or not? If one person complains that the A/C should not be operating, any action you take to rectify the ambiance could end up stoking the temperature to a degree that the other one starts to complain.

Trying to satisfy all passengers, all of the time can be quite a daunting dilemma. This takes a bit of finesse. A crucial element is ascertaining the preferences of each passenger. We'll come back to that topic in a moment.

Speaking of cars, the future of cars consists of self-driving cars. Self-driving cars are driven by an AI driving system. There is no need for and indeed no provision for a human to drive the vehicle.

People inside a self-driving car will entirely be passengers and there won't be a human driver at the wheel. In a conventional car, we expect the human driver to try and adjust and establish the interior ambiance for the benefit of their riders. Well, there won't be that human driver anymore, and as such, the matter of setting the ambiance becomes open-ended.

A passenger can set the ambiance for themselves. A passenger can set the ambiance for the vehicle and try to accommodate the needs and preferences of their fellow passengers. In short, a human can still control the internal environment and make whatever settings might seem preferable.

It sure would be nice though if the AI system could do this chore since it is now considered the driver of the vehicle. In addition to performing the driving task, it might as well also take on the job of trying to create an interior ambiance that is suitable for those inside the self-driving car.

This brings up an important question: *Will AI-based true self-driving cars leverage the use of Ambient Intelligence capabilities to try and instill an interior environment for the comfort of the passengers?*

Before jumping into the details, I'd like to clarify what is meant when referring to true self-driving cars.

Understanding The Levels Of Self-Driving Cars

As a clarification, true self-driving cars are ones that the AI drives the car entirely on its own and there isn't any human assistance during the driving task.

These driverless vehicles are considered Level 4 and Level 5 while a car that requires a human driver to co-share the driving effort is usually considered at Level 2 or Level 3. The cars that co-share the driving task are described as being semi-autonomous, and typically contain a variety of automated add-on's that are referred to as ADAS (Advanced Driver-Assistance Systems).

There is not yet a true self-driving car at Level 5, which we don't yet even know if this will be possible to achieve, and nor how long it will take to get there.

Meanwhile, the Level 4 efforts are gradually trying to get some traction by undergoing very narrow and selective public roadway trials, though there is controversy over whether this testing should be allowed per se (we are all life-or-death guinea pigs in an experiment taking place on our highways and byways, some contend).

Since semi-autonomous cars require a human driver, the adoption of those types of cars won't be markedly different than driving conventional vehicles, so there's not much new per se to cover about them on this topic (though, as you'll see in a moment, the points next made are generally applicable).

For semi-autonomous cars, it is important that the public needs to be forewarned about a disturbing aspect that's been arising lately, namely that despite those human drivers that keep posting videos of themselves falling asleep at the wheel of a Level 2 or Level 3 car, we all need to avoid being misled into believing that the driver can take away their attention from the driving task while driving a semi-autonomous car.

You are the responsible party for the driving actions of the vehicle, regardless of how much automation might be tossed into a Level 2 or Level 3.

Self-Driving Cars And Ambient Intelligence

For Level 4 and Level 5 true self-driving vehicles, there won't be a human driver involved in the driving task.

All occupants will be passengers.

The AI is doing the driving.

One aspect to immediately discuss entails the fact that the AI involved in today's AI driving systems is not sentient. In other words, the AI is altogether a collective of computer-based programming and algorithms, and most assuredly not able to reason in the same manner that humans can.

Why this added emphasis about the AI not being sentient?

Because I want to underscore that when discussing the role of the AI driving system, I am not ascribing human qualities to the AI. Please be aware that there is an ongoing and dangerous tendency these days to anthropomorphize AI. In essence, people are assigning human-like sentience to today's AI, despite the undeniable and inarguable fact that no such AI exists as yet.

With that clarification, you can envision that the AI driving system won't natively somehow "know" about the facets of driving. Driving and all that it entails will need to be programmed as part of the hardware and software of the self-driving car.

Let's dive into the myriad of aspects that come to play on this topic.

First, automakers and self-driving tech makers are not especially focused on the interior ambiance at this time. The difficulties of getting self-driving cars to proceed safely from point A to point B are a higher priority, deservedly so. The preponderance of development efforts is devoted to the AI driving system as a driver, and not toward the AI driving system as an ambiance infusing supervisor.

Second, a question arises whether the AI driving system ought to be undertaking the ambiance chore. Some would stridently assert that the AI driving system should be exclusively dealing with the driving task. No need to divert attention toward the ambiance factors. Any such distraction might be argued as unnecessarily using computer processing cycles that ultimately could be used in the desire for maximum roadway safety considerations.

This brings up an allied point that the Ambient Intelligence system could readily be a separate component from the AI driving system. They do not need to be melded together. That being said, it would be useful for the two to electronically communicate with each other.

Why so?

Consider that one aspect of riding inside a car and the ambiance thereof can include the driving aspects of the vehicle. You might have had passengers in your car that said they get overly nervous when a car takes fast or tight turns. These same passengers might also detest those rapid-fire starts of going from zero to sixty miles per hour that cause them to lose their stomachs or get dizzy.

The Ambient Intelligence system could collaborate with the AI driving system to achieve a totality of ambiance that covers the interior environment and also the nature of how the car is being driven.

You can add to this the path of the self-driving car too. For example, maybe the self-driving car could avoid roads that have potholes and are rocky, which a passenger might wish to avoid due to getting jostled while riding in the vehicle. Thus, when the AI driving system is making use of the GPS and the various maps for navigation, this qualm or desire by the rider ought to be taken into account.

There is a slew of ambiance factors that can be adjusted by a car-based Ambient Intelligence system.

We've already covered some of the temperature aspects. There is the use of an air conditioning system. There is the use of an in-car heater. The seats themselves might also be wired for heating. The windows might be opened to either cool off the interior or perhaps heat the interior. And so on.

Knowing what temperature to establish can be difficult to discern.

As earlier mentioned, thermal sensors might be used to detect the temperatures of the passengers. Another means of trying to figure out the temperatures of the riders could be via using facial recognition. There will be inward-facing cameras in self-driving cars, and those cameras could be used to try and detect if someone is sweating, or otherwise showcasing mannerisms and effects of either being too hot or being too cold.

Lighting inside a self-driving car will be adjustable. There are interior lights that can be switched on or off, along with being dimmed or brightened on a spectrum of illumination. Some expect that self-driving cars will have some form of window shades that can be automatically rolled up or down, allowing for privacy and darkness within the vehicle.

The rationale for those curtaining elements would be that people might opt to take naps or sleep while inside a self-driving car. You no longer need to worry about driving. While commuting to work in the morning, you might want a few additional winks of sleep before arriving at the office. On the way home at night, the self-driving car will deal with the arduous traffic and you meanwhile might be getting a quick nap before arriving at your busy household.

Seats inside a self-driving car are anticipated to be highly adjustable. Currently, there must be a driver's seat at a fixed position in a car. There will no longer be a driver's seat, nor the conventional driving controls. This handily opens up space within a self-driving car and allows for rather interesting new ways of seating passengers.

One commonly designed approach entails the use of swivel seats. The passengers will be able to swivel in whichever direction they prefer. At times, you might be facing forward and opt to watch the road ahead. If there are other passengers on board, you might want to face them and have an engaging dialogue, or maybe play cards or chess together.

The Ambient Intelligence component might glean over time your preferences for which way the swivel seats should be oriented. Those swivel seats are likely to also be reclinable, allowing you to take a snooze. This again could be automatically adjusted for you, rather than you having to do so.

Remember that earlier there was the scenario of a passenger that preferred certain kinds of odors or scents? The Ambient Intelligence system might be armed with a wide array of scents that can be activated. Those would be used in accordance with the preferences of the riders.

This brings us to the vexing topic of how to contend with multiple passengers.

Let's back up for a moment and start with how to cope with just one passenger, and then we'll widen the view toward handling multiple riders.

When you are driving a car, how do you know what your passenger prefers?

The most obvious answer is that you ask the person. For AI systems, there are ongoing advances in Natural Language Processing (NLP), such as the likes of Alexa and Siri. By using that kind of NLP capability, the self-driving car can ask the rider what their preferences are. This certainly simplifies matters greatly.

Ask, and you shall receive, as they say.

The AI system could store the results of a person's preferences and then use those preferences whenever the person gets into the self-driving car. Furthermore, via the use of OTA (Over-The-Air) electronic communications, the AI could store the preferences into the cloud of the fleet operator. The beauty of this is that any other self-driving cars connected to that cloud could potentially look for that person's preferences and then immediately be able to use those preferences.

To clarify, right now if you use a conventional car and set the car settings to your preferences, it is only that particular car that has your settings. When getting into someone else's car, this other car has no ready means of being aware of what your prior settings in that other car. In the case of self-driving cars, they will be routinely using an OTA capability to get updates for the AI onboard software, along with using the OTA to upload data collected by the vehicle.

This means that when you "teach" or tell one self-driving car what your preferences consist of, this can be shared across an entire fleet of self-driving cars. Those other self-driving cars can instantly recognize what your preferences are, doing so without asking you again about them. Do not though falsely assume you will be stuck with whatever preferences you might have originally stated. The capability ought to be written astutely that whenever your preferences change, those would be likewise further uploaded via the OTA.

This takes us to the multiple passengers and the ambiance quandary.

What to do about conflicting ambiance preferences by passengers within the same self-driving car on a collective driving journey?

Using the NLP, the AI system could ask them to resolve their differences amongst themselves, and then instruct the Ambient Intelligence on what they'd like to have done. Imagine those arm-wrestling matches while the riders are seated in their swivel seats.

There could be algorithms that try to figure out mathematically what might be best for all passengers and seemingly calculate a presumed compromise across the disparate preferences. The tough thing here is that you can end up with no one particularly satisfied and everyone altogether dissatisfied.

Well, that kind of is the human condition, at times, one might say.

This is an open problem and one that will increasingly be encountered when Ambient Intelligence systems are used in rather tightly enclosed spaces such as inside a self-driving car.

Conclusion

A critic or skeptic might exhort that this is a bunch of phooey and that they do not want any darned AI system or whatever kind of system deciding their ambiance preferences while inside a self-driving car. These smacks of over-engineering and a veritable much ado about nothing, they would exclaim.

Maybe yes, maybe no.

Once self-driving cars become prevalent, how will you as a prospective passenger decide which self-driving cars to utilize?

Assume that by-and-large self-driving cars will be available via ridesharing or ride-hailing network. In addition, assume that the pricing among the different fleets will be about the same. In that case, passengers will have no particular preference of selecting one fleet over another when they request a lift.

That's not good news for those fleet operators. They want you to pick their specific fleet. This is all going to be a money-making enterprise, and each fleet operator will be trying to lure passengers to use their fleet more so than someone else's fleet.

One answer to this standout desire would be to have a fleet of self-driving cars that are really good at this ambiance matter. When advertising a fleet, the operator could tout that they have the best available Ambient Intelligence systems. Your every whim of interior ambiance will be accommodated by their facility. That might be quite an attractor for some.

Meanwhile, those passengers that don't like the AI doing these interior ambiance adjustments will presumably be able to merely switch off the feature. If you don't like the AI trying to play a game of figuring out your preferences, you don't need to play the game. Indeed, some will likely find it eerie to consider that your in-car ambiance preferences are being stored in a cloud someplace and readily retrievable.

That brings us to a thorny question: *Is this attempt at tailoring ambiance a privacy intrusion?*

That is an unresolved issue that is bound to arise once the Ambient Intelligence systems are incorporated into self-driving cars. For now, no one is thinking about that tough question.

The odds are that you'll need to do things for yourself for the time being, such as setting the A/C, opening the windows, etc. In the future, some will prefer being treated like royalty and have the AI take care of those tasks, thus riding along without a care in the world and amidst an idyllic environment that turns the riding journey into a dreamy experience.

Those are dreams that could someday come true

CHAPTER 5

FLAGGING AND SELF-DRIVING CARS

Not so long ago, it seemed that the hailing of a cab required long arms and a capacity to wave frantically to catch the eye of the taxi driver.

You would be standing at a curb and keep your cool while taxi after taxi seemed to entirely ignore your frantic motions. It was hard to discern why the cabs weren't pulling over to pick you up. They were showing as empty and therefore ought to be avidly seeking a potential fare. Sometimes you would consider that perhaps they didn't like the particular manner in how you waved your arms.

Maybe they thought you were overly excited and this was a worrisome sign by the taxi driver. Or they didn't like the look of your seemingly crudely summoning tactic for getting a pickup. You see, there were lots of other potential cab seekers that had a more subtle approach. Some all-knowing people would nonchalantly do a once wave and that was all it took to get a cab to pull over. Others would merely nod their head or make a quick tip of their hat, as though these were secret signals in a private baseball game between a catcher and a pitcher.

Things could get really competitive at certain times of the day.

If it was rush hour, then all bets were off. There were tons of people fervently attempting to get cabs, all of them at the same time and all across the whole city. You pretty much had to hope for the randomness of the world to come to your aid. When a taxi perchance dropped off a rider at the very spot that you were standing, this gave you the top rights to commandeer the taxi and proclaim that it was yours for the taking.

Many movies and TV shows used to provide a gag whereby a taxi comes up to pick someone up, and then someone else darts into the cab instead. This was more than just a spate of humor. It happened. Quite often. Unless you took to mind the ever-present notion that possession is nine-tenths of the law, a nanosecond of a delay getting into a taxi could mean that an interloper would grab it and you would be left standing high and dry.

I remember getting into a cab at the airport and when I gave the hotel address for my stay, the cabbie gave me the most utterly disgusting of glances. He then explained that the hotel was less than a two-minute drive from the airport. His fare would be peanuts. Meanwhile, he had waited in an enormously long cab line while at the airport, and after dropping me at the hotel he would once again have to sit idly in that same darned line. In short, he emphatically told me that I just cost him nearly two hours of his available cab time, for pretty much nothing at all as a fare.

He pleaded with me to get out. The rules for the cabbies at the airport did not allow them to kick out a rider. It had to be the rider themselves that would decide to back out of a ride. He told me that he had a family and needed to support them. Get another cab, he exhorted. Just don't force him to give me the dinky ride, for which he also suggested I could just walk from the airport and enjoy the fresh air, averting the need for a taxi altogether.

Anyway, the point is that even if you believe you had managed to snag a taxi, there was still a chance that it might get loose from your grip. Either the cab driver would not want you, or someone else might try to intervene and take your cab, sometimes offering a whale of a story.

I recall one time that I had just gotten into a hailed cab and a bystander tapped on the window. The person explained that they had been waiting for twenty minutes to get a cab. They had noticed me standing there too, though I apparently had only been waiting about ten minutes. The explanation turned into a morality play that I ought to voluntarily give up the cab since this other person had waited longer than me. It made no difference that the cabbie stopped in front of me.

It made no difference that we were both humans. The key was that I had gone outside of my fair turn and had cheated this other waiting rider.

How about that?

On another occasion, I luckily hailed a cab and a person came running up to the vehicle. They offered me ten bucks if I would hand the taxi over to them. They were in a hurry and didn't want to wait for a taxi. The logic was that time is money, as we all know, and so this potential rider was willing to pay me for giving up my cab and presumably giving up my waiting time. An interesting proposition. The taxi driver entered into the dialogue and pointed out that the ten dollars ought to go to the driver, or at least a cut of it ought to.

Hailing a cab while in the rain or snow was the worst.

There you are, standing out in the raw elements. The wind nearly blowing you over. Rain pouring sheets of water onto your head, or perhaps onto your umbrella or raincoat. If it was snow, you stood in the icy cold and kept moving your feet to keep the circulation going. An additional problem was that there seemed to be fewer cabs cruising around and thus the wait time was totally elongated.

In today's world, there is a lot less handwaving hailing going on.

In lieu of wantonly hailing a ride, you usually pull up an app on your smartphone and use a ridesharing network or even a cab-hailing network to get yourself a ride. No need to stand around and try to spy on an available roaming vehicle. The computer systems do all that work for you. This is known as e-hailing.

On a digital map displayed on your smartphone screen, you'll see various dots or tiny emoji cars that are moving around in your area. One of them will be usually chosen for you by the computer system, based on factors such as how close the roaming vehicle is, where you want to go, the type of vehicle preference you have, and so on. All you then need to do is wait for the arrival of the assigned vehicle.

No need to wave at anyone or anything.

That being said, upon the arrival of your assigned vehicle, sometimes you do need to wave or make a motion to ensure that the driver sees you. The map is oftentimes not precisely able to indicate where the passenger is standing. Plus, there might be a multitude of people waiting for lifts, perhaps having all gotten out of a theatre at the same time and now seeking rides home.

There is no doubt that merely requesting online to get a ride is a lot smoother than having to play the roulette wheel game of hailing on-the-street a prospective ride.

Besides the ease of no longer needing to make those waving motions, you also now have a somewhat ironclad guarantee that you will get a ride. In the case of standing around and hailing, you never really knew how long it might take and whether you would ever land a ride. That was the terrible uncertainty of it all. This could be especially on your mind if perchance caught in a bad part of town or rotten weather. Your mind was frantically praying for an available ride to come along.

Another nifty aspect about using an app to hail a ride is that you know beforehand the nature of the vehicle and the driver. You are usually presented with some info about the car that is coming to pick you up. There is also the name of the driver and their rating. This helps you to know whether the rider is presumably any good at providing rides.

When you hailed a cab at random, it was a wildcard as to what type of driver you might get. Some drivers were cautious and went relatively slowly, taking turns with great aplomb. Other drivers were like racecar drivers, zipping along. They wanted to get you to your destination as fast as possible, meaning that they then could seek to find their next paying fare that much sooner. More fares in a day were the mantra for making any money at this game.

Those that have never hailed a ride via the standing outside and waving method are at times aghast when they discover that this approach still exists. Many believe it was only something that happened during the times of the dinosaurs, and they assumed that since dinosaurs are extinct that presumably, the traditional method of hailing of a ride was certainly extinct too.

Well, sit down and prepare yourself for a bit of a shock, conventional hailing still happens.

There are though additional twists and turns.

In many locales, there are byzantine rules about which cabs or taxis can provide those impromptu derived rides. Depending upon various conditions, it could be that only e-hailing is legally allowed, per time of day or where you are in a city or town. Anyone trying to do the street hailing has to be brazen to think that it will work since there are fewer and fewer chances of this being feasible.

Some sneaky riders will try to maximize their chances of getting a ride quickly by doing both the e-hailing and the stand-around techniques in unison.

They pull up the app for an e-hail and see what the wait time is like. They simultaneously stand out in the street and start waving at any seeming potential rides. If the wait time seems long on the e-hail, they will temporarily book it and then wait until the last allowed moment to drop it (before incurring any fees for doing so). During that interval, they will be stridently attempting to catch a ride via the waving method. Whichever approach strikes gold first is the winner in that momentary contest.

As they say, all's fair in love and war.

Since we have been discussing cars and taxis, it makes indubitable sense to consider that the future of such vehicles will consist of self-driving cars. Be aware that there isn't a human driver involved in a true self-driving car. True self-driving cars are driven via an AI driving system. There isn't a need for a human driver at the wheel, and nor is there a provision for a human to drive the vehicle.

Here's an intriguing question that is worth pondering: *Once self-driving cars are acting as robo-taxis and cruising around on our streets to do so, will you be able to hail one by hand or only via e-hailing?*

Before jumping into the details, I'd like to further clarify what is meant when referring to true self-driving cars.

Understanding The Levels Of Self-Driving Cars

As a clarification, true self-driving cars are ones that the AI drives the car entirely on its own and there isn't any human assistance during the driving task.

These driverless vehicles are considered Level 4 and Level 5 while a car that requires a human driver to co-share the driving effort is usually considered at Level 2 or Level 3. The cars that co-share the driving task are described as being semi-autonomous, and typically contain a variety of automated add-on's that are referred to as ADAS (Advanced Driver-Assistance Systems).

There is not yet a true self-driving car at Level 5, which we don't yet even know if this will be possible to achieve, and nor how long it will take to get there.

Meanwhile, the Level 4 efforts are gradually trying to get some traction by undergoing very narrow and selective public roadway trials, though there is controversy over whether this testing should be allowed per se (we are all life-or-death guinea pigs in an experiment taking place on our highways and byways, some contend).

Since semi-autonomous cars require a human driver, the adoption of those types of cars won't be markedly different than driving conventional vehicles, so there's not much new per se to cover about them on this topic (though, as you'll see in a moment, the points next made are generally applicable).

For semi-autonomous cars, it is important that the public needs to be forewarned about a disturbing aspect that's been arising lately, namely that despite those human drivers that keep posting videos of themselves falling asleep at the wheel of a Level 2 or Level 3 car, we all need to avoid being misled into believing that the driver can take away their attention from the driving task while driving a semi-autonomous car.

You are the responsible party for the driving actions of the vehicle, regardless of how much automation might be tossed into a Level 2 or Level 3.

Self-Driving Cars And Hailing A Robo-Taxi

For Level 4 and Level 5 true self-driving vehicles, there won't be a human driver involved in the driving task.

All occupants will be passengers.

The AI is doing the driving.

One aspect to immediately discuss entails the fact that the AI involved in today's AI driving systems is not sentient. In other words, the AI is altogether a collective of computer-based programming and algorithms, and most assuredly not able to reason in the same manner that humans can.

Why this added emphasis about the AI not being sentient?

Because I want to underscore that when discussing the role of the AI driving system, I am not ascribing human qualities to the AI. Please be aware that there is an ongoing and dangerous tendency these days to anthropomorphize AI. In essence, people are assigning human-like sentience to today's AI, despite the undeniable and inarguable fact that no such AI exists as yet.

With that clarification, you can envision that the AI driving system won't natively somehow "know" about the facets of driving. Driving and all that it entails will need to be programmed as part of the hardware and software of the self-driving car.

Let's dive into the myriad of aspects that come to play on this topic.

Assume for sake of discussion that self-driving cars are inevitably sufficiently able to drive around and at least achieve Level 4 capabilities (this means that there is a defined ODD or Operational Design Domain for which the autonomous vehicle is capable of driving within).

There is a hefty debate about whether individuals will be able to own and operate self-driving cars or whether only large companies will be able to do so. Part of the logic is that a self-driving car will need to be kept in tiptop shape else the AI driving system will not be able to safely provide rides. The assumption is that a company responsible for operating a fleet of self-driving cars is more likely to maintain and upkeep the autonomous vehicles than might individual owners do so.

I generally disagree with that contention and argue that we will indeed have individual ownership of self-driving cars.

Putting that whole brouhaha to the side, I think we can generally all agree that there will be self-driving cars offered on ridesharing or ride-hailing basis, regardless of whom the owner is. When you go to use an app to request a ridesharing lift, the odds are that the app will present you with one of two options, you can select a human-driven car or you can select a self-driving car. Some people will relish using a self-driving car, while others will eschew it and prefer instead to use a human-driven ridesharing car.

Each to their own preference.

Most pundits agree that self-driving cars will be on the go for much of their available traversal time. The nice thing about a self-driving car is that the AI driving system doesn't need any rest, nor lunch breaks, or even bathroom breaks. The expectation is that self-driving cars will be able to be driving around 24x7, except for times when they need to refuel or need some maintenance or fixing up.

For an entity that owns a self-driving car, there is the opportunity to potentially make big bucks by this always on the move capability (and, without the labor costs of needing a human driver). For example,

I assert that a person could own a self-driving car, have it take them to the office for a normal workday, and while at work the self-driving car is made available on a ridesharing basis. The person then has the self-driving car take them home after work, and for the rest of the night, the self-driving car continues making money by providing more lifts. In short, their self-driving car makes money for them when they otherwise don't need it.

Without getting mired into any messy arguments, the emphasis is that a self-driving car can be a ridesharing or ride-hailing vehicle and provide rides to those making such a request. That seems abundantly clear-cut and inarguable.

The question we are considering herein is the matter of how to request a self-driving car for those that are seeking a lift.

We can already assume that the most likely approach consists of app-based e-hailing.

Either the company operating the self-driving car will provide a dedicated app for this purpose, or might list the self-driving car on some existing ridesharing network. If they list via a network, the odds are that a cut of the fare is bound to be required (i.e., a split between the operator of the self-driving car and the network operator). Ergo, the chances are that the operator of the self-driving car would prefer that people use the specialized app and not have to split any fees.

It is a tradeoff of course, as to whether the dedicated app will ensure enough use of the self-driving car versus being listed on a ridesharing network.

Will a self-driving car be occupied at all times while on a ridesharing basis with a passenger inside the vehicle?

Nope.

There will be times during which the self-driving car will be absent of a passenger. It could be that the self-driving car is doing delivery of a package, thus, there isn't a person inside the autonomous vehicle.

Other times the self-driving car might be making its way to a requested lift and is empty until it reaches the person seeking a ride.

One other possibility is that there aren't any ride requests at the moment and so the conundrum of what to do with the self-driving car then logistically arises. Do you opt to park the self-driving car at some locale, and have it wait for a requested ride? That might not be as advantageous as having the self-driving car roaming around, for which it might be in a better place when a request occurs.

The operator of a self-driving car will need to make this balancing act decision. In some instances, it might be better to park the self-driving car, while in other instances it is more prudent to keep it underway. A variety of factors come to play.

All told, we can seemingly agree that there will be times at which self-driving cars will be roaming empty of any passengers and awaiting a request for a ride.

We are now at the moment of truth.

Should a self-driving car that is acting in this robo-taxi manner be able to pick up passengers that might undertake a traditional hailing gesture, or will self-driving cars only be summoned via e-hailing?

My claim is that we potentially *could* have self-driving cars programmed to handle the streetwise hailing approach.

This probably though will not occur at first. The mainstay will be the e-hailing avenue. Once that has become firmly established, I believe we will see some self-driving cars that are adjusted to be responsive to street-level hailing. This will primarily be due to competitive forces that require self-driving car operators to increasingly find ways to outshine their competition.

Now, it could be that the human drivers take the same stance too.

In other words, if self-driving cars start to become commonplace on ridesharing networks, the question naturally comes up about how human drivers will remain competitive. Assuming that a self-driving car is less expensive to use and that it won't have the human foibles of driving, the logical progression is that riders will aim to select a self-driving car over a human-driven car (all else being equal, as it were). A means for a human driver to remain competitive would be to offer something that the self-driving cars aren't offering, namely the traditional street hailing approach.

Let's dig briefly into the complications of having a self-driving car attempt to perform the conventional hailing method.

As mentioned earlier, a person seeking a ride is customarily expected to make a motion that will serve to relatively definitively indicate that they are seeking a ride. This usually consists of waving an arm, along with perhaps looking directly at the targeted cab or taxi, and possibly pointing at the cab too. All of this is intended to catch the attention of the human driver.

Self-driving cars will be outfitted with a variety of sensors, including video cameras, radar, LIDAR, ultrasonic units, thermal imaging, and so on. Via the use of techniques such as Machine Learning (DL) and Deep Learning (DL), the data from those sensors is computationally analyzed and various patterns are being scanned for.

In theory, the image processing of the video camera's live stream could be used to try and detect a person that seems to be hailing the self-driving car. It would be easiest if the person had some special token or signal that was known for this purpose, such as a special flag or even just a specific gesture. But this might be a bit much for people to keep with them or have to know, so we'll assume that the traditional waving motion is the preferred method per se.

Admittedly, a person could be simply waving at a friend across the street, or perhaps swatting at a buzzing bee. It will be hard to discern with absolute certainty that the person is hailing the self-driving car. You could make the same case for human taxi drivers too, namely that they do not know for sure that a person is doing a hailing action. The context of the moment and the movements of the potential rider have to be carefully combined to reach such a conclusion.

Okay, so trying to spot a person seeking a ride that is doing a streetwise hailing will be somewhat computationally tough to do, but not insurmountable. There will be instances of an AI driving system skipping past the person due to the lack of detecting that a hailing activity was underway. There will also be instances of mistakenly coming to the person to provide a ride when they were not genuinely in the act of hailing a ride.

We can also assume some dolts will just for kicks decide to falsely attempt a hailing to see what the self-driving car will do.

In the case of a human taxi driver, the driver would likely be irked at the jokester and provide a rather stern talking to (or worse). One supposes that the AI driving system could send the video to a remote agent for review, and if the trickster is seen to have been playing false games, perhaps there would be some means of legitimately issuing a ticket or something along those lines (unfortunately, that could be a slippery slope too).

Conclusion

Flagging down a self-driving car that is being operated as a robo-taxi is not likely in the cards for the near term, but certainly can be envisioned for the future.

This is going to be tricky to program.

Nonetheless, it is possible.

We will likely initially have disgruntled indications of situations that the AI driving system that went right past someone and ignored them. Similar to how there have been concerns about human taxi drivers that cherry-pick whom they will pick up, we would need to test and validate that the AI driving systems do not have any built-in patterns of biases (see my column for coverage on this and other AI Ethics issues).

There won't be much cause to out-the-gate have self-driving cars operate in this manner. The easiest approach entails doing e-hailing.

Given that the AI developers already have their hands full as they aim to just get self-driving cars to safely go from point A to point B, the notion of including a conventional ride-hailing capability is ostensibly considered an edge or corner case. Those edge or corner cases are ranked as low priority and construed as outside the core of what needs to be developed.

Besides hand waving, perhaps we can program the AI driving system to detect a ride-hailing gesture such as a quick wink of the eye. Imagine though how confusing that might be when the self-driving car is going down a crowded street of pedestrians.

I know, maybe we can use mind-reading instead. If a person merely thinks about needing a lift, the AI driving system can make use of that type of hailing. As you likely know, the desire for mind-reading computers is right up there with the aspiration for autonomous vehicles (see my coverage).

Just don't read whatever else is in our minds, and stick with the earnest and singular desire of hailing a ride.

CHAPTER 6
TALL TRUCKS AND SELF-DRIVING CARS

Let's go on a safari!

As you head out onto the savanna, you keenly observe that the area is rife with wildlife. Whoa, right over there is a zebra. Say, look, some warthogs are meandering near those trees. Majestic gazelles are grazing nearby. You even spy an ostrich or two. A truly marvelous safari experience.

Amongst a clump of trees, you notice a giraffe that is pulling at and chewing on leaves and twigs, high up on a tall tree. That's how giraffes tend to eat. With their long necks and long legs, they usually dine on the upper parts of trees. Few other animals are able to reach those topmost locales and thus there is almost always a guaranteed meal by naturally being in that heightened position.

Wait for a second, the giraffe is furtively looking around.

What's is happening?

Off in the distance, a lion is being sneaky and gradually approaching this spot where a slew of animals are innocently enjoying their day. The animals that are low to the ground have no inkling that the lion is making its way in this direction. Those animals cannot see far enough away due to being so close to the ground. Meanwhile, relying on merely the odor of a lion to detect its presence is a dicey proposition since the lion is cleverly upwind and won't be sniffed until the last moment.

By the last moment, this means that the lion will already be within striking distance and these regal animals will be in dire straits, unlikely able to escape a fierce attack.

The giraffe though can plainly see what the lion is trying to do. Even though giraffes oftentimes fight off a lion, the effort expends a tremendous amount of energy and the outcome is not always going to be in the favor of the giraffe. Giraffes usually prefer the option of fleeing in a choice between the proverbial and existential fight-or-flight conundrum, all else being equal.

So, the giraffe makes a bit of noise and starts quickly to move to another further away spot.

The animals nearby had been watching the giraffe intently, noticing observantly that the giraffe was clearly on edge about something. When the giraffe subsequently decided to abruptly take leave of this particular locale, the other animals quickly scattered too. They didn't necessarily know why the giraffe got spooked, but the very fact that the giraffe was alarmed provided sufficient indication that they too needed to be apprehensive.

You could assert that those animals were wise to use the giraffe as an early warning signal. By doing so, the animals were able to leverage the survival advantages of a giraffe to their own benefit, namely, its tall stature. While those animals were grazing or lolling around, they had an eye on the giraffe. If the giraffe showed signs of unease, those attentive animals would get an early heads-up to be on their toes.

After the giraffe opted to skedaddle, the now alerted animals figured they ought to do so too.

Furthermore, the direction that the giraffe is headed is yet another helpful clue.

Presumably, the giraffe would seek to proceed in a direction that would have the least amount of impending danger. You see, perhaps lions are coming from multiple directions, and as such, the other animals would be going directly into a deathly trap if they perchance tried to escape in the wrong direction.

The giraffe provides a potential signpost of where safety might be.

For those of you that have been on a safari, you've assuredly seen this type of behavior. For those of you that are aiming to go on safari now that the world is opening up again, please keep your eyes peeled for these kinds of animalistic machinations. Nature is wonderful to observe in action.

The good news is that you can observe the same behavior right here, during your daily commute. You don't need to fly to a faraway savanna.

How so?

Simply stated, savvy drivers, keep their eye on tall trucks when in the throes of navigating those thorny traffic snarls and roadway trips across town. Tall trucks are akin to the giraffes of a safari journey, except they just so happen to be on our existent freeways, highways, and local byways.

Here's the deal.

You are in traffic on the freeway and the traffic is, fortunately, moving relatively steadily. This has been going on for a while and you have gotten accustomed to the free-flowing effect. Your thoughts drift to that baseball game that you have tickets to attend later that night. Perhaps you are also daydreaming about a vacation planned to the African savanna (well, la-di-dah, that's quite a coincidence since that's what I've just been discussing herein!).

While your mind drifts, unbeknownst to you a ladder has fallen onto the freeway, occurring about a half-mile up ahead. There is no immediate way that you would know this has happened.

Vehicles that are directly behind the fallen ladder are beginning to jockey wildly. Some drivers are choosing to straddle the ladder. Other drivers are ramming the ladder and forcing it to skirt around in the lanes of traffic. This is a really bad situation. The odds are that someone is going to veer and smash into other vehicles, doing so to avoid the now fractured ladder that is menacing the traffic.

As you know, there is a kind of cascading course of events that usually takes place in these circumstances. The vehicles closest to the obstructing ladder will do a dance of avoidance. Other vehicles just behind those dancing vehicles will begin to shortly also get engaged in the dance. A rippling effect will have other vehicles further behind that start to do a dance, either using their brakes, changing lanes, or at times making crazy maneuvers.

The ripple can take many precious moments to arrive at your further back position. By the time that the cascading reaches you, it could be that you'll need to radically jam on the brakes. Had you been able to somehow spy beforehand that the traffic was reacting in this untoward manner, you could have been prepared for what was going to occur.

Wouldn't it be nice if a giraffe was grazing up ahead and could showcase that danger lurked on the roadway?

No need for a giraffe to be on our roadways when we have tall trucks.

The chances are reasonably good that a truck driver might see the transpiring and evolving events in an early bird manner. Being seated up high in a tall truck does have its intrinsic advantages. You can frequently see further ahead and therefore anticipate what is going to happen on the roadway.

Sure enough, a trucker is moving over into the slow lane and the brake lights suggest the truck is decreasing speed. Several trucks are doing this. All at once. Unless you are truly asleep at the wheel (I hope not), you are bound to see that the trucks are in unison taking evasive action.

You might not have any clue that a ladder is causing troubles up ahead. All that you know is that those trucks sure seem concerned. And if the trucks are concerned, you ought to be too. You are thankfully prodded out of your daydream stupor and now are on full alert. At the same time, you decide to get into the slow lane.

A smart move. The ladder continues to foul traffic in the faster lanes. Those vehicles stuck in the faster lanes are all having a devil of a time. You're having gotten into the slow lane was timely and saved you from the trauma of coping directly with the fallen ladder.

Who do you owe gratitude to?

Tall trucks and truck drivers are paying attention to the roads.

I suppose you can thank giraffes too, though that's not pertinent per se to having averted disaster with that ladder. Giraffes are worth thanking, just for the sake of things.

Not all car drivers opt to use tall trucks as an early warning.

Some car drivers are oblivious to the very notion that tall trucks can serve as an early bird. This has never occurred to those car drivers as a type of driving technique. They blissfully drive along and take no notice of trucks, other than when they perchance find themselves immediately behind a giant truck. In that case, their view is entirely obscured and they are hopping mad about it.

Other drivers do take notice of tall trucks.

Within that camp, there are the car drivers that always watch for tall trucks. They watch them intently. It is both a fun game to play and derives that early warning opportunity. Then there are the car drivers that sometimes notice tall trucks. This is pretty much one of those veritable "out of sight, out of mind" considerations until a tall truck suddenly does something unusual.

If a tall truck starts to do something out of the usual pattern, such as trying quickly to change lanes, rather than doing so slowly and gradually, this becomes a noticeable behavior change. Of course, you don't know that this portends for anything untoward up ahead. There could be lots of reasons for the tall truck to make such moves.

Your mind is usually exploring patterns in the behavior of traffic.

All the tall trucks are consistently aligned and moving along at a steady pace. That's one pattern. They each turn on their blinkers and appear to be each scrambling to make a lane change. Aha, this is a pattern that suggests something is amiss. They might know something that you don't yet know.

In short, you cannot blankly assume that the behavior of tall trucks is going to for sure be an indicator of what might lay ahead. On the other hand, you would be remiss in not giving this early indicator its proper due. Like the animals that are low to the ground on the savanna rightly know, you ignore the giraffe at your own peril.

Speaking of cars, the future of cars consists of AI-based true self-driving cars.

Allow me a moment to elaborate.

There isn't a human driver involved in a true self-driving car. Keep in mind that true self-driving cars are driven via an AI driving system. There isn't a need for a human driver at the wheel, and nor is there a provision for a human to drive the vehicle.

Here's an intriguing question that is worth pondering: *Will AI-based true self-driving cars leverage the early bird indications of tall trucks, and if so what might this portend?*

Before jumping into the details, I'd like to further clarify what is meant when I refer to true self-driving cars.

Understanding The Levels Of Self-Driving Cars

As a clarification, true self-driving cars are ones that the AI drives the car entirely on its own and there isn't any human assistance during the driving task.

These driverless vehicles are considered Level 4 and Level 5 while a car that requires a human driver to co-share the driving effort is usually considered at Level 2 or Level 3. The cars that co-share the driving task are described as being semi-autonomous, and typically contain a variety of automated add-on's that are referred to as ADAS (Advanced Driver-Assistance Systems).

There is not yet a true self-driving car at Level 5, which we don't yet even know if this will be possible to achieve, and nor how long it will take to get there.

Meanwhile, the Level 4 efforts are gradually trying to get some traction by undergoing very narrow and selective public roadway trials, though there is controversy over whether this testing should be allowed per se (we are all life-or-death guinea pigs in an experiment taking place on our highways and byways, some contend).

Since semi-autonomous cars require a human driver, the adoption of those types of cars won't be markedly different than driving conventional vehicles, so there's not much new per se to cover about them on this topic (though, as you'll see in a moment, the points next made are generally applicable).

For semi-autonomous cars, it is important that the public needs to be forewarned about a disturbing aspect that's been arising lately, namely that despite those human drivers that keep posting videos of themselves falling asleep at the wheel of a Level 2 or Level 3 car, we all need to avoid being misled into believing that the driver can take away their attention from the driving task while driving a semi-autonomous car.

You are the responsible party for the driving actions of the vehicle, regardless of how much automation might be tossed into a Level 2 or Level 3.

Self-Driving Cars And Tall Trucks As Tipsters

For Level 4 and Level 5 true self-driving vehicles, there won't be a human driver involved in the driving task.

All occupants will be passengers.

The AI is doing the driving.

One aspect to immediately discuss entails the fact that the AI involved in today's AI driving systems is not sentient. In other words, the AI is altogether a collective of computer-based programming and algorithms, and most assuredly not able to reason in the same manner that humans can.

Why this added emphasis about the AI not being sentient?

Because I want to underscore that when discussing the role of the AI driving system, I am not ascribing human qualities to the AI. Please be aware that there is an ongoing and dangerous tendency these days to anthropomorphize AI. In essence, people are assigning human-like sentience to today's AI, despite the undeniable and inarguable fact that no such AI exists as yet.

With that clarification, you can envision that the AI driving system won't natively somehow "know" about the facets of driving. Driving and all that it entails will need to be programmed as part of the hardware and software of the self-driving car.

Let's dive into the myriad of aspects that come to play on this topic.

The initial reaction that many non-insiders have about this matter of today's self-driving cars giving due attention to the movement of tall trucks is usually quite consistent and pronounced. There is one line that I often hear over and over.

Here it is.

Don't self-driving cars already do this?

The answer is generally nope, few of the self-driving car efforts underway are giving much attention to observing the far ahead movement of tall trucks. Not at least with respect to serving as an early bird indicator.

To clarify, by and large, any well-devised self-driving cars and their accompanying AI driving system are ostensibly detecting any tall trucks that are *immediately* nearby such as in front of or adjacent to the self-driving car.

That's kind of a given.

This though is pretty much a classic monkey-see-monkey-do type of detection.

Via the sensors on the self-driving car, the AI driving system is computationally analyzing the nearby driving scene. The sensor suite can contain a variety of sensing devices, including video cameras, radar, LIDAR, ultrasonic units, thermal imagining, and so on. The devices are collecting raw data about the surroundings. By using various image processing and other sensory analysis techniques, including Machine Learning (ML) and Deep Learning (DL), the objects and their positions are being internally noted and plotted.

The mainstay of this computational analysis is aimed at closer objects. A tall truck that is in the adjacent lane and paralleling the self-driving car is given top priority for detection. This makes indubitable sense since that truck could suddenly swerve into the lane of the self-driving car. Similarly, a tall truck that is directly in front of the self-driving car deserves some rapt computational focus.

Scanning the horizon up ahead and examining the driving scene for tall trucks that are quite further ahead in traffic is something that few AI driving systems are yet programmed to do. That's considered an advanced feature or piece of functionality. Indeed, it is something that many would claim is an edge or corner case, meaning that it is low in priority, does not merit being rated or ranked as in the core realm of driving, and can be dealt with someday in the future.

An AI driving system can be bereft of this capability and still drive a car, they would contend.

You could say the same about human drivers.

On the other hand, any added means to try and improve safety while driving is certainly worthy of getting some serious attention. We might be willing to accept the idea that not all humans are going to be considering the tall truck early bird indications, but we are bound to be less lenient regarding AI driving systems that are not exploiting this advantage.

You might expect that lawsuits will later on land on this same type of consideration.

In other words, a self-driving car gets caught up in a traffic accident on the freeway. Assume that the AI driving system itself is not at direct fault. Meanwhile, assume that there were passengers inside the self-driving car and they got injured. In essence, the self-driving car got carried into a cascading series of human-driven car crashes for which the human passengers that were within the self-driving car were harmed accordingly.

This is a very realistic scenario.

Suppose that the AI driving system lacked any semblance of using tall trucks as an early predictor of traffic. And, let's envision that a post-crash expert-performed forensic analysis demonstrates that had the AI driving system been scanning for the behaviors of tall trucks, the odds are that the self-driving car could have averted getting carried into the melee.

Could the automaker and self-driving tech firm be sued on the basis that they failed to provide a necessary and crucial element for their AI driving system?

We'll see how that plays out.

Insiders right now would exhort that the tall truck early bird detection is no more than a flighty distractor from the real issues that need to be addressed for making the AI driving system readied to drive on our public roadways. To them, the idea is certainly an intriguing notion and one that perhaps deserves attention someday, it is just not worthy at this time. Getting self-driving cars to drive safely from point

A to point B is the urgent call to order. Messing around with detecting tall trucks that are out of immediate reach and seemingly beyond the "danger zone" is a lofty ideal and more theory than something required in practical terms.

You can say that if you wish, but if it made the difference between harm or even life-or-death for passengers inside a self-driving car, those will be words of hollow value to loved ones and the harmed riders.

Insiders would likely take another stance on this matter too.

They would assert that V2V will otherwise solve this open-ended concern.

V2V refers to vehicle-to-vehicle electronic communications.

Self-driving cars are expected to be outfitted with V2V so that AI driving systems can readily communicate with each other. A self-driving car that is up ahead in traffic could presumably send an electronic signal that there is a ladder in the roadway. All other self-driving cars coming up upon the situation will receive the V2V message. Hopefully, the AI driving systems of those self-driving cars will then use that as a heads-up.

Problem solved.

No need to visually try to figure out what is going on with those tall trucks. Just rely upon V2V and you'll be fine.

Well, that's not quite the case.

First, suppose there aren't any V2V equipped vehicles up ahead. That's a high likelihood right now and certainly for the foreseeable future. It is going to take years upon years, probably decades before V2V gets widely adopted.

During that long period of time, you are merely hanging your hat on something that might eventually become widespread. You are rolling the dice for those passengers inside the self-driving car. If they are lucky, perchance a self-driving car or self-driving truck up ahead has V2V. I'm not sure that luck ought to be a vital component of safe driving.

Let's pretend that by your lucky stars that indeed there is a V2V equipped vehicle up ahead.

Think about what has to take place to effectively utilize that capability.

A V2V equipped vehicle first confronting the ladder has to detect whatever problem is underway. That's obviously the cornerstone needed step. Whether it does this or not, there is a high chance it will do so, but still, some chance that it might not.

The AI driving system presumably should be primarily focusing on the safety efforts immediately needed for that self-driving car, and secondarily be considering the need to send out V2V messages about the debris or roadway obstruction. This seems prudent and logical.

Once the V2V is transmitted, other self-driving cars have to be within range to pick up the V2V. It could be that the transmission is not able to be received. Include this consideration in your odds making.

Assuming that a further back self-driving car does receive the V2V, and does so on a timely basis, the receiving AI driving system has to computationally take into account this added piece of driving-related data.

But how much weight should the V2V message be given?

In some theoretical nirvana, the V2V message is completely apt, timely, and utterly trustworthy. The AI driving system can heed whatever the V2V message has provided. No questions asked. Take cover or otherwise evasive actions simply based on the V2V indication.

This seems like a doubtful proposition, or downright scary.

I believe most passengers would hope that the AI driving system does at least a "trust, but verify" of whatever the V2V has indicated. I know that I would want that to happen.

And, this leads us to the following somewhat ironic point, the AI driving system should probably be then analyzing the traffic up ahead to see that it comports with whatever the V2V has alerted. This has a semblance of irony because the very thing that we are saying the AI driving system ought to be doing anyway, namely looking ahead at those tall trucks, now becomes a vital element of the AI driving system, to begin with.

Conclusion

Before anyone has a bellyache or conniption, let's also agree that just because the early bird detection of tall trucks might be included in the AI driving system, this does not make self-driving cars somehow impervious to traffic problems.

Heck no.

Just as stated earlier when considering how human drivers make use of the tall truck scenario, there are plenty of ways that the tall truck movement can be interpreted. It is easy to get a false impression based on the behaviors of those tall trucks. They do not provide certainty. They only provide an added basis for judiciously making driving decisions.

One final set of thoughts.

A smarmy person might point out that via the use of drones, none of this tall truck stuff is needed. To some extent, this is a valid point and I have discussed at length the coming use of drones as paired with the advent of self-driving cars. As a polite retort to the drones prognosticator, we do not know when drones will be actively adopted for these purposes. In addition, we don't know whether drones will be available in all places and at all times (such as being grounded during foul weather conditions).

In short, those tall trucks can still matter.

Notice that I've not said anything about whether those tall trucks are driven by a human truck driver or by an AI driving system. All told, it really doesn't make that much of a difference in terms of utilizing the tall trucks in their giraffe capacity.

A giraffe is a giraffe, and we can be darned happy that they stand tall.

Go, giraffes, go.

CHAPTER 7
MONOPOLISTIC PRICES AND SELF-DRIVING CARS

I had both Park Place and Boardwalk in my gleeful hands.

Yes, in the venerated game of Monopoly, you can be darned happy when you manage to acquire various keystone properties on the gameboard. By establishing a monopoly in Monopoly, you can take decisive actions that will allow you to charge immense rents. When other players land on your monopoly, or perhaps monopolies if you've finagled a bunch of them, you know that those unlucky players will pay through the nose for the privilege of being on your monopolistic property.

That's just how the game is played.

In the real world, there is also a chance that a marketplace can be dominated in a monopolistic manner.

If that happens, there is a distinct possibility that the monopoly owner or producer will be able to charge sky-high prices for their goods or services. A lack of competition provides an opportunity to attain what is referred to as monopoly rent. Consumers of the desired goods or services will be paying more so than they would otherwise if the monopoly was not a monopoly, thus sometimes our laws seek to break up monopolies and flatten out prices.

It could be that competitors have been unable to readily enter into the particular marketplace and are being shut out in some strident fashion. The monopoly wielder might be able to create barriers that keep competitors at bay. Or perhaps competitors are able to land in the marketplace but the monopolistic player is able to knock them out.

And so on it goes.

A monopoly that comes into existence can likely glean so-called excess profits. This implies that the pricing of their goods or services is not only high, but it is also presumably sky-high. We would usually expect that purveyors of goods or services ought to be able to achieve a profit of some kind. That's common sense and the notion behind for-profit entities. The rub comes when it seems like the profits are woefully out of proportion and appear to be gouging those that are buying the goods or services being proffered.

These issues arise especially in the instances of new innovations.

Suppose a pharmaceutical company comes up with a new miracle drug that can cure some terrible ailment. If they are the only provider of this innovative new drug, they can possibly charge sky-high prices for it. Upon any backlash, the reply could be that they invested a tremendous amount into creating the new drug and are simply trying to achieve a profit that will cover those earlier costs. In addition, they would likely argue that without charging those high prices they would not be able to fund their other ongoing development efforts, for which similar miracle drugs might someday be invented.

The same kind of logic applies to technological innovations.

Sometimes a company will invent a new technological piece of wizardry and seek to charge an arm and a leg to those that wish to use or license the shiny item. How much profit should they be able to garner? For some people, the sky is the limit in the sense that to the victor go the spoils. Others though are likely to begrudge the use of outlandish pricing and point out that some could demonstratively benefit from the invention and yet are priced out of the chance of doing so.

Back and forth the pendulum swings. Trying to ferret out what constitutes a monopoly rent can be hard to do. Experts can readily get into heated debates, whereby one expert swears that a monopoly is underway and the prices are outrageously high, while another expert mildly admits that some taint of a monopoly might exist but the pricing is commensurate with the investment and subsistence of the entity involved.

Not going to solve that conundrum here.

The preceding discussion does though bring up the notion that we ought to be keeping our eyes wide open and always on the alert for potential monopolistic practices and situations. One belief is that the sooner such a circumstance is detected, the better off we all are. Perhaps by knowing beforehand that a monopoly is possibly being formulated, it can be headed off at the pass. There might be ways to aid or guide the shaping of the monopoly so that it does not seem quite so onerous, or presumably, stop it before things get out of hand (others would recoil at that idea and would instead fervently clamor that whatever will happen should be allowed to happen).

Where else might a monopoly be just modestly now forming and that we can take a keen look at it in the early stages of growth?

Answer: *Self-driving cars.*

There is quite a bit of handwringing going on that AI-based true self-driving cars are going to be a monopoly. This is based on the assumption that only a few purveyors will be able to attain true self-driving cars. A tiny set of automakers or self-driving tech firms will hold all the cards when it comes to self-driving cars.

We are not there yet, since the invention of self-driving cars is still being figured out.

But, if you are thinking ahead, those purveyors might be the only entities able to field self-driving cars and therefore be able to charge monopoly rent, as it were. This could include charging sky-high prices for the use of self-driving cars.

Why care about that, you might be wondering?

Some pundits have been advocating that those vaunted self-driving cars will finally allow society to enter into a mobility-for-all era.

Members of society that have been mobility disadvantaged will finally have ready access to the use of cars, namely via self-driving cars. This will happen due to the logic that self-driving cars are going to be a lot less costly to deploy and maintain in comparison to conventional human-driven cars. In short, there is no human driver needed and ergo you've excised that cost entirely out of the equation related to the costs for making use of a car.

The thing is, the pricing might <u>not</u> be less than a human-driven car. Even if the costs do drop tremendously, it could be that the small set of purveyors opts to charge sky-high prices for the use of their divined self-driving cars. They could perceive that they are rightfully able to do so. Again, using the earlier indicated argument, the rationale would be that they invested the big dough to get to the point of being able to place self-driving cars into real-world use. They, therefore, need to recoup those sky-high costs, they would vehemently insist.

This brings up another factor about the hopes associated with self-driving cars.

Currently, in the United States, there are about 6.7 million car crashes annually. This produces about 2.5 million injuries and around 40,000 fatalities each year, see my analysis of such stats. Many of those car crashes are due to human driver foibles, including drunk driving, drowsy driving, distracted driving, and the like. Self-driving cars won't presumably have those same predilections since there isn't a human driver at the wheel anymore.

The point being that those revered self-driving cars will essentially make our public roads safer by hopefully reducing the number of car crashes, along with correspondingly reducing the number of said injuries and fatalities thereof. If that is going to be the case, we would all want self-driving cars to as soon as possible be widespread. It stands to reason since our highways and byways will be safer for us all.

In that case, a purveyor of self-driving cars might eloquently argue that even if sky-high prices are being charged, this is pricing that takes into account the societal benefits that accrue from the safer driving aspects. We ought to ergo accept the heightened pricing as part of the strident deal toward saving lives, foregoing injuries, and dramatically lessen the number of car crashes.

That does seem compelling.

A retort to that argument is that the sky-high pricing means that very few will be able to afford the use of self-driving cars. This in turn implies that the number of miles driven via self-driving cars will be minuscule in comparison to the total number of miles of driving (i.e., which includes human-driven cars). Therefore, you won't get much bang for your buck in the sense that so few miles are being undertaken via self-driving cars that it won't materially reduce the volume of car crashes.

Self-driving cars would be nothing more than a tiny drop in the tsunami of human driving. You would not reasonably expect that this minuscule usage would move the needle on lowering the number of car crashes. As such, the sky-high pricing is not justifiable as based on the said-to-be hollow argument that lives are going to be saved.

Dizzying!

No matter how you view these matters, it would seem nearly inarguable that the future of cars consists of AI-based true self-driving cars.

To clarify, there isn't a human driver involved in a true self-driving car. Keep in mind that true self-driving cars are driven via an AI driving system. There isn't a need for a human driver at the wheel, and nor is there a provision for a human to drive the vehicle.

Here's an intriguing question that is worth pondering: *Are we headed toward a potential of monopoly rents as associated with the advent of AI-based true self-driving cars?*

Before jumping into the details, I'd like to further clarify what is meant when I refer to true self-driving cars.

Understanding The Levels Of Self-Driving Cars

As a clarification, true self-driving cars are ones that the AI drives the car entirely on its own and there isn't any human assistance during the driving task.

These driverless vehicles are considered Level 4 and Level 5 while a car that requires a human driver to co-share the driving effort is usually considered at Level 2 or Level 3. The cars that co-share the driving task are described as being semi-autonomous, and typically contain a variety of automated add-on's that are referred to as ADAS (Advanced Driver-Assistance Systems).

There is not yet a true self-driving car at Level 5, which we don't yet even know if this will be possible to achieve, and nor how long it will take to get there.

Meanwhile, the Level 4 efforts are gradually trying to get some traction by undergoing very narrow and selective public roadway trials, though there is controversy over whether this testing should be allowed per se (we are all life-or-death guinea pigs in an experiment taking place on our highways and byways, some contend).

Since semi-autonomous cars require a human driver, the adoption of those types of cars won't be markedly different than driving conventional vehicles, so there's not much new per se to cover about them on this topic (though, as you'll see in a moment, the points next made are generally applicable).

For semi-autonomous cars, it is important that the public needs to be forewarned about a disturbing aspect that's been arising lately, namely that despite those human drivers that keep posting videos of themselves falling asleep at the wheel of a Level 2 or Level 3 car, we all need to avoid being misled into believing that the driver can take away their attention from the driving task while driving a semi-autonomous car. You are the responsible party for the driving actions of the vehicle, regardless of how much automation might be tossed into a Level 2 or Level 3.

Self-Driving Cars And Monopoly

For Level 4 and Level 5 true self-driving vehicles, there won't be a human driver involved in the driving task.

All occupants will be passengers.

The AI is doing the driving.

One aspect to immediately discuss entails the fact that the AI involved in today's AI driving systems is not sentient. In other words, the AI is altogether a collective of computer-based programming and algorithms, and most assuredly not able to reason in the same manner that humans can.

Why this added emphasis about the AI not being sentient?

Because I want to underscore that when discussing the role of the AI driving system, I am not ascribing human qualities to the AI. Please be aware that there is an ongoing and dangerous tendency these days to anthropomorphize AI. In essence, people are assigning human-like sentience to today's AI, despite the undeniable and inarguable fact that no such AI exists as yet.

With that clarification, you can envision that the AI driving system won't natively somehow "know" about the facets of driving. Driving and all that it entails will need to be programmed as part of the hardware and software of the self-driving car.

Let's dive into the myriad of aspects that come to play on this topic.

One of the most forgotten factors when it comes to thinking about the advent of self-driving cars is something known as human-driven cars. I say that somewhat facetiously, but with a notable point in hand.

Much of the painted picture of the future envisions self-driving cars roaming across our many streets, freeways, and public roadways.

Indeed, the only thing that you seem to see in these visionary portrayals is self-driving cars.

Where did the human-driven cars go?

I ask this question because the answer is relatively straightforward. Human-driven cars are not going anywhere, at least not in any near-term or medium-term timeframe.

You cannot just wish away human-driven cars. In the United States, there are approximately 250 million conventional human-driven cars. Even if self-driving cars become feasible and practical tomorrow, it would take many years, likely decades, before there would be a substantive proportion of self-driving cars in comparison to human-driven cars. Nobody realistically is going to junk human-driven cars due to the emergence of self-driving cars.

Some believe we might have to legislate the demise of human-driven cars. It could be that laws are enacted that put an expiration date on all human-driven cars. Perhaps that might come to pass, but I seriously doubt it, and certainly not in any near-term perspective. Many people insist that you will take away their driving only when you've pried their dead cold hands from their steering wheel.

A kind of utopia that has exclusively self-driving cars is not at all realistic in today's world. A long, long time from now, perhaps that will emerge as a societal norm. Not now. Not soon. Sure, there might be narrow settings that this happens, such as a city that puts its foot down and declares that only self-driving cars can enter into the downtown areas. That might happen. This though has little to do with the notion that the proportion of self-driving cars will magically outnumber the volume of human-driven cars all told.

I trust that you are perhaps persuaded that we will have both self-driving cars and human-driven cars, co-existing on our public roadways for quite a while into the future.

Why have I dragged you through that seemingly now obvious point?

Because of the matter entailing competition.

Those that are decrying the possibility of purveyors of self-driving cars being monopolistic are forgetting or overlooking the dominance of human-driven cars.

Look at it this way.

You are trying to decide whether to use a self-driving car to get to your local grocery for a shopping trip or whether you might use a human-driven car.

Assume that both are readily available.

Go along with the overall notion that self-driving cars are known for being somewhat safer as a driver than the average human-driven car. But this is a relatively short driving journey and you perceive that the risk-safety factor involved is a negligible difference in this brief trip.

Both options will take you door-to-door. This means that the self-driving car will pick you up at your house and take you directly to the grocery store. Likewise, a human-driven car would do the same. We will assume that this is all taking place on ridesharing or ride-hailing basis.

There is a kind of novelty associated with taking the self-driving car. On the other hand, you've used a self-driving car for some previous rides and you now realize that there is nothing special about doing so.

The thrill has worn off. At this juncture, you assess the self-driving car option as simply an alternative form of transit, nothing especially remarkable otherwise.

Okay, now we make use of the monopoly rents scenario.

Turns out that the price to use a human-driven car is vastly less than using a self-driving car. This is because the self-driving car purveyors are charging sky-high prices.

Which do you choose, the lower costing human-driven car or the sky-high-priced self-driving car?

Assuming that you are no longer enamored with the aura of using a self-driving car, and all else being rather equal, it would seem that you are bound to choose the human-driven car.

In that manner, there is competition facing those self-driving cars.

Whether the purveyors of those self-driving cars will be able to keep those sky-high prices in place is an open question. If they are getting only minimal use out of their self-driving cars, it would seem that they would need to take some kind of action to overcome the marketplace reticence. There are several ploys they could try. One would be to bring their prices down.

Conclusion

It seems that the odds of having a sustainable monopolistic rent in the case of self-driving cars will be a bit unlikely due to the competition fostered by human-driven cars. Human-driven cars are available aplenty. They aren't going to be whisked away overnight.

This doesn't though mean that the purveyors of self-driving cars will have to set their prices on a less than sky-high basis. Not at all.

They could go ahead and use sky-high prices. The implication is that consumers would on the balance be more likely to choose a human-driven car versus using those self-driving cars. Nonetheless, there would be some that would opt to use self-driving cars and pay the premium price to do so.

This then brings us into some dicey territory for those purveyors of self-driving cars that set their prices sky-high. I've previously pointed out that there are some worries that self-driving cars will only be ridden by the wealthy and the famous, for which a societal backlash could develop.

You can easily imagine the kind of stink that this would create for those purveyors that are charging sky-high prices for the use of their self-driving cars. Lawmakers and others that are hoping for the mobility-for-all era to emerge would be shocked and dismayed at the pricing tomfoolery (so it would seem).

Fortuitously, there would appear to be many crucial factors that would tend to inhibit the sky-high pricing, or at least create pressures to get the pricing to come down.

Here's an added twist for you.

You might be surprised to know that many of the self-driving car makers are in fact worried about the general acceptance regarding the use of self-driving cars. If self-driving cars out-the-gate get a bad rap, perhaps due to being exorbitantly priced, this could squelch the whole deal. All that investment in the creation of a self-driving car could become a heavy anchor that cannot be recouped.

Going with a sky-high price might seem like an initial wise choice, and the novelty factor will potentially sustain that pricing for a while, but the long run of things will undoubtedly cast doubt on such a pricing strategy.

Oddly enough, things might go in the opposite direction. It could be that self-driving cars are priced at extraordinarily low rates, much lower than the comparable pricing for a human-driven car. In that case, there is a likely attack that this is some form of predatory pricing, trying to put human drivers out of existence.

Well, by gosh, that is pretty much kind of the general idea overall.

We are bound to see quite a hefty discussion about that concern, perhaps more so than the qualms about monopolistic rents. Getting humans out from behind the steering wheel does have merits, as mentioned previously about the challenges associated with human-led car crashes.

How will society adjust when all of those human drivers that rely upon driving as a source of income and for making a living are dealt a blow by the advent of self-driving cars?

The good news, if that's what we can call it, will be that this is going to happen gradually and over a lengthy period of time. Rather than waking up one morning and all that you see are a plethora of self-driving cars driving on your streets, you will instead see a mixture of self-driving cars and human-driven cars for a long time to come.

At first, it will be very few self-driving cars and a lot of everyday human-driven cars. When that proportion inevitably shifts, taking place seemingly at a glacial pace, we will have step by step morphed into a world of self-driving cars. Keep your eyes open and make sure to pay attention during this coming rugged road toward the advent of self-driving cars.

And keep looking out your window to see how things are looking, and always remember, do not pass go (or, maybe that should be to *always* pass go).

CHAPTER 8
ANIMAL COGNITION AND SELF-DRIVING CARS

Let's talk about common sense.

We all have it, presumably.

Some more so than others.

When we hear about someone performing a seemingly nonsensical act, there is a strong impulse to immediately decry that the person lacked common sense. You either have it or you don't.

Well, more likely, you sometimes have it and sometimes you do not. There are occasions where we either skirt our reservoir of common sense or it might be altogether blank in a particular setting or context.

A popular way of characterizing common sense is to suggest that there are two primary components involved.

First, there is the knowledge itself that underlies the basis for common sense. Those are the bits and pieces of information stored in your memory banks and utilized for tapping into a kind of mental database about the nuances and substance of common sense.

Second, there is the use of common-sense reasoning that comes to play. This entails the enactment of the common sense that is retrievable from within your mind. You reason about a particular matter and are doing so by applying the common-sense cornerstone that you've prior established.

We'll get to this in a moment with some handy examples to illuminate the matter.

A person can have a large store of common sense and yet fail to reason with it. This can happen if you are suddenly startled and do not have the presence of mind to mentally process what is happening. The reasoning process does not get engaged or is tardy to the party and ergo unable to timely leverage the available common-sense mental embodiments.

On the other side of that coin, a person might have a notable semblance of common-sense reasoning but lack a sufficient common-sense foundation to do much with it. Suppose that you are a city slicker and not familiar with being out in the woods. Though you might be generally adroit at common-sense reasoning, upon wandering into a wooded forest you realize that you know so little about nature and forests that your reasoning prowess is going to come up short. Until you've gleaned more about what kinds of facts and considerations underlie a forested realm, your reasoning ability can only provide a limited advantage.

How do we come upon our building up of common sense?

Children are considered to have only a modicum of common sense and the assumption is that by the time they reach adult age, they will have a more seasoned repertoire of common sense under their belt. In that sense of things, the acquisition of common sense is usually characterized as amorphously acquired over time. You cannot particularly take a class on common sense and somehow gleefully graduate with a heady adoption of common sense now firmly implanted in your noggin.

Trying to pin down the exact facets of common sense is squishy and challenging to finitely define. Some would say that it is akin to the famous line about art, namely that you know it when you see it. The thing is, those without ardent common sense are likely to find themselves in a world of hurt, potentially taking actions that are seriously injurious or harmful, unknowingly so.

Besides common sense occurring in humans and the human mind, the field of AI is eager to crack the code on what common sense consists of.

Those in the AI field are well-aware of the slipperiness of getting a handle on how to codify common sense. Many have tried and are continuing doggedly to find ways to embody this elusive form of cognition into computer-based systems. By and large, the attempts to codify common sense and plop it into AI capabilities have been fraught with great difficulty and exasperating disappointment.

Some initially believed that a gigantic facts database might be sufficient for giving rise to AI-based common-sense implementation. The sky is blue. Clouds can float across the sky. Objects seen in the side mirror are closer than they appear. On and on, the hope was to try and articulate every kind of fact or piece of knowledge that mankind has accumulated.

That's a tall order.

Plus, even if you could manage to populate a system with tons and tons of those minuscule and seemingly randomly arrayed facts, the question arises as to how they would be made into the goldenrod of common sense (note that some efforts have opted to categorize and try to structure the factual database). This then led to efforts of proposing a myriad of ways to have machine-based common-sense reasoning algorithms that could exploit the (presumed) common-sense embodied knowledge bases.

I dare say, AI is still not even in the ballpark of approaching the human capacity of common-sense and common-sense reasoning. Not anywhere seemingly close to it.

The road ahead is long and bumpy.

Speaking of roads, we can use the everyday act of driving a car as a helpful means of exploring the realm of common sense and common-sense reasoning.

Do you use common sense when you are driving a car?

Absolutely.

You might not be directly aware that you are leveraging your common sense aptitudes, but you are abundantly doing so. I mention this key aspect because some would say that driving is a specific skill that needs to be acquired and in a sense denotes a kind of expertise. To drive a car, you need to learn about how to use the steering wheel, how to use the brake pedal, how to use the accelerator, etc. You need to learn the driving laws that stipulate how you are allowed to drive.

Yes, there is no question that driving does involve quite an amount of specifics in terms of particular knowledge and reasoning needed for the chore of driving. No doubt about that. Indeed, there are driving schools and we test people before they are granted a license to drive.

Meanwhile, silently and generally unnoticed, your common sense is residing resolutely at the core of your driving efforts. You could argue that this is partially why you cannot get a driver's license until around the age of 16. The logic is that you need the cognitive maturity for driving, and we also are in an unstated way implying that you would have hopefully gained sufficient common sense by that age to warrant the privilege of driving.

Keep in mind that driving is a life-or-death act.

I don't want to seem sour or downbeat, but the reality is that each time you get behind the steering wheel, you are ascertaining the life or death possibilities for yourself, for your passengers, for other nearby drivers, and their passengers, for pedestrians, and the like. We seem to take for granted the driving of a car and do not explicitly realize the somber and quite risky aspects that we incur daily. Just to mention, there are sadly about 6.7 million car crashes in the US each year, producing approximately 2.5 million injuries and over 40,000 fatalities (see my analysis and coverage about such stats).

A driver needs to have the proper skills associated with driving to appropriately drive a car. In addition, a driver needs to have sufficient common sense to be able to adequately drive a car. I think you would be hard-pressed to argue otherwise.

Consider the following scenario.

You slide into the driver's seat of your car and decide to go for a cheery Sunday drive.

Using your honed driving skills, you start the engine, you back out of your garage, you continue in reverse and drive down your driveway, finally edging slightly into the street. Looking both ways, you decide it is safe to fully enter the street. After backing a little way further and slowly turning the wheels of the car, you are ready to put the car into forward drive. You then nonchalantly drive down the block and begin your joyous driving trek.

Was there any use of common sense in that seemingly perfunctory effort of getting underway on a driving road trip?

Zillions upon zillions of common-sense instances arose, though few would realize the importance and infused nature of common sense in this situation.

Let's unpack it.

You knew what a car is and what a car can do, which otherwise you wouldn't have gotten into the car, to begin with. You knew that you would have to go in reverse and back out of the garage since going forward would be disastrous and you would summarily ram into the wall of the garage. You knew that there could be obstructions or possibly kids or dogs nearby to your driveway and thus you scanned around to make sure that you weren't going to hit something or someone. Likewise, when you reached the street, you looked for cars or bikes or anything that might strike your vehicle.

You know that objects such as bikes can be in motion. You know that things in motion can come toward you. You know that when one object encounters another object, this gives rise to a collision. You know that collisions can cause damage. You know that the type of damage can include the injury. You know that injuries can potentially lead to deaths.

I trust that it is readily apparent that you are using a lot of common sense about the world and how things operate and interact in the real world, doing so during the routine effort of getting underway on your driving journey. Multiply this by all the other common-sense aspects that will come to play as you drive down the street, and as you drive on open highways, and so on.

Another means of revealing the cognitive subtleties of common sense can be shown via our use of language.

Here is a sentence that I'd like you to carefully read: *The moving car hit the Stop sign because it was in the way.*

What did you glean from that sentence?

I'm assuming that you figured out that a car was in motion and it came upon a Stop sign, perhaps sitting in the street and somewhat in the path of oncoming cars. The car struck the Stop sign. We don't know how hard the blow was. We seem to be told that the driver was not necessarily at fault. The Stop sign was seemingly not where it should have been in terms of normally being outside the realm of where cars might be going.

Here is the same sentence with one notable change: *The moving car hit the Stop sign because it was speeding.*

Is the meaning different?

Yes, gobs yes. We are logically going to infer that the car was speeding and this presumably reckless act led to the driver ramming the Stop sign.

I want you to reinspect those two sentences and keep your eye on the word "it" within the sentences.

In the first sentence, we have "because it was in the way" and you are left to your own devices to semantically grasp what the "it" is. Does the "it" refer to the car or the Stop sign? We don't know for sure, but you do know by common sense that the Stop sign is more likely to be the object that was in the way, rather than the car.

In the second sentence, we have "because it was speeding" and you are left to your own devices to semantically grasp what the "it" is. Once again, I ask you, does the "it" refer to the car or the Stop sign? In this case, our common sense suggests that since the "it" is speeding, the car is most likely the object being referred to rather than the Stop sign.

That exercise of cognitive analysis is insightful.

We have discussed the role of common sense in an everyday real-world setting of backing up a car and going for a drive. This involves numerous dimensions of common sense. A vital dimension or frame of reference entails the physics of the world. Objects and their manifestations underlie our common sense regarding physical interactions.

The language exercise proffered another variant of how we use common sense. I gave you some sentences and you mulled them over in your mind. There wasn't something physically that happened akin to the aforementioned effort of driving a car out of a garage and into the street. This was the use of common sense in a pure thought experiment fashion.

You are perhaps convinced by now that common sense is a core component of human reasoning. And, you are hopefully also persuaded that common sense is hard to delineate in any codified way. It is somewhat nebulous and everywhere, largely hazy and mushy to get your arms around.

We have also used driving as an exemplar of the importance of having common sense. Furthermore, the field of AI is seeking to decode common sense and include this sorely needed capacity into AI systems.

Whoa, this brings us to a monumental juncture or conjunction.

The future of cars consists of AI-based true self-driving cars.

There isn't a human driver involved in a true self-driving car. Keep in mind that true self-driving cars are driven via an AI driving system. There isn't a need for a human driver at the wheel, and nor is there a provision for a human to drive the vehicle.

Here's an intriguing question that is worth pondering: *Do we need common sense reasoning to achieve AI-based true self-driving cars, and if so how will we get there?*

I'd like to first further clarify what is meant when I refer to true self-driving cars.

Understanding The Levels Of Self-Driving Cars

As a clarification, true self-driving cars are ones that the AI drives the car entirely on its own and there isn't any human assistance during the driving task.

These driverless vehicles are considered Level 4 and Level 5 while a car that requires a human driver to co-share the driving effort is usually considered at Level 2 or Level 3. The cars that co-share the driving task are described as being semi-autonomous, and typically contain a variety of automated add-on's that are referred to as ADAS (Advanced Driver-Assistance Systems).

There is not yet a true self-driving car at Level 5, which we don't yet even know if this will be possible to achieve, and nor how long it will take to get there.

Meanwhile, the Level 4 efforts are gradually trying to get some traction by undergoing very narrow and selective public roadway trials, though there is controversy over whether this testing should be allowed per se (we are all life-or-death guinea pigs in an experiment taking place on our highways and byways, some contend).

Since semi-autonomous cars require a human driver, the adoption of those types of cars won't be markedly different than driving conventional vehicles, so there's not much new per se to cover about them on this topic (though, as you'll see in a moment, the points next made are generally applicable).

For semi-autonomous cars, it is important that the public needs to be forewarned about a disturbing aspect that's been arising lately, namely that despite those human drivers that keep posting videos of themselves falling asleep at the wheel of a Level 2 or Level 3 car, we all need to avoid being misled into believing that the driver can take away their attention from the driving task while driving a semi-autonomous car.

You are the responsible party for the driving actions of the vehicle, regardless of how much automation might be tossed into a Level 2 or Level 3.

Self-Driving Cars And The Need For Common Sense

For Level 4 and Level 5 true self-driving vehicles, there won't be a human driver involved in the driving task.

All occupants will be passengers.

The AI is doing the driving.

One aspect to immediately discuss entails the fact that the AI involved in today's AI driving systems is not sentient. In other words, the AI is altogether a collective of computer-based programming and algorithms, and most assuredly not able to reason in the same manner that humans can.

Why is this added emphasis about the AI not being sentient?

Because I want to underscore that when discussing the role of the AI driving system, I am not ascribing human qualities to the AI. Please be aware that there is an ongoing and dangerous tendency these days to anthropomorphize AI. In essence, people are assigning human-like sentience to today's AI, despite the undeniable and inarguable fact that no such AI exists as yet.

With that clarification, you can envision that the AI driving system won't natively somehow "know" about the facets of driving. Driving and all that it entails will need to be programmed as part of the hardware and software of the self-driving car.

Let's dive into the myriad of aspects that come to play on this topic.

Some assert that the AI of today will not become bona fide AI until we can ascertain how humans embody common sense. There is even a naming that some use, referring to today's AI as so-called narrow AI. This is meant to convey the notion that AI is narrowly focused and not able to work in any broadly based manner.

One strong case being made is that without AI systems having a common-sense component, they will forever be limited in what they can do. They will be narrow. They will be fragile and brittle. They won't at all approach the vaunted goal of attaining *artificial intelligence* in the full sense of what we aspire to achieve.

Let's consider the advent of AI-based true self-driving cars in that bailiwick.

Level 4 self-driving cars are considered to be bounded by a pre-defined ODD (Operational Design Domain). This consists of an automaker or self-driving tech firm specifying the context in which their AI driving system can properly operate. For example, an AI driving system might be established to work in a particular geographical area such as a designated part of a city, and do so only when the weather is moderate (won't operate in rain or snow).

Some believe that we might be able to muddle along and get self-driving cars to generally operate in various strictly prescribed ODDs. One implied basis for keeping the ODD's strictly bounded has to do with the lack of common-sense reasoning capabilities of AI.

In short, we aren't likely going to attain Level 5, which essentially ditches the ODDs concept and be able to have AI that can drive in a wide variety of open-ended settings (within limits) unless we conquer the embodiment of common sense and common sense reasoning into AI systems.

But as earlier stated, progress has been stunted and many are wondering what other outside-of-the-box ways could we pursue to overcome the existing hurdles. That being said, if trying to ferret out the deep secrets of human common sense is arduous and having troubles progressing, there is another avenue that might be considered.

Sit down and prepare yourself for a bit of a surprise.

Animal common sense.

Say what?

The argument is that animals also have common sense.

Of course, you can quibble with this and contend that the common sense exhibited by animals is not nearly as sophisticated and advanced as that of humans. Maybe so, but the notion is that we might start there and see if that gives us a leg-up toward figuring out the fuller blown human-based common sense.

A clever research article entitled "Artificial Intelligence and the Common Sense of Animals" published in *Trends In Cognitive Sciences* makes an intriguing case for making such a pursuit.

Authored by researchers at DeepMind, and the Imperial College of London, plus the University of Cambridge (Murray Shanahan, Matthew Crosby, Benjamin Beyret, and Lucy Cheke), they provide this salient point: "Here, we argue that common sense in humans is founded on a set of basic capacities that are possessed by many other animals, capacities pertaining to the understanding of objects, space, and causality. The field of animal cognition has developed numerous experimental protocols for studying these capacities and, thanks to progress in deep reinforcement learning (RL), it is now possible to apply these methods directly to evaluate RL agents in 3D environments."

Is this farfetched?

Not at all.

It makes solid sense. I've covered previously that there have been efforts to see if dogs could drive a car. There are studies of mice brains that are hoping to reveal how the thinking process works, possibly revealing insights that will aid in explorations of the human brain. Etc.

You can readily make the case that animals do have a semblance of common sense. Perhaps by figuring out their form of common sense, we can generalize and make added progress on human-based common sense.

It is the proverbial *take a step back and rethink our approach* solution, namely that we can start small or smaller and ultimately make our way to the bigger machination.

Conclusion

There is a famous old fable about a donkey that might be relevant to consider.

It seems that a donkey had fallen into a well. The farmer hears the crying sounds of the trapped donkey. Upon looking closely at the situation, the farmer decides that there is nothing much that can be done since the donkey is too heavy to be lifted out of the well. With great sadness in his heart, he decides that he will at least cover the donkey with dirt and provide a suitable burial.

As each scoop of dirt is summarily dumped into the well, the donkey at first is surprised but then starts shaking off the dirt. This continues repeatedly. Eventually, to the surprise of the farmer, the donkey is near to the top of the well and easily leaps out, continuing on its merry way.

Turns out that the donkey had iteratively shaken the dirt to the floor of the well, pounded on the dirt to compact it, and gradually the floor level rose and rose, reaching a point that the donkey could readily jump out.

The moral of the story that we'll consider here is the donkey employed better common sense than did the farmer. This illustrates that not all common sense is necessarily bright or inspiring. As they say, sometimes common sense isn't as common as you might think it is.

Plus, this is a handy parable since it highlights what we hope to glean from studying animal cognition and the role of common sense.

For those in AI development or AI research that find themselves stuck down inside a well and seemingly at wit's end about how to figure out common sense, the lowly and stubborn donkey might provide insightful clues about discovering the heart and soul of common sense and inexorably lead to instilling that into more advanced AI.

Per the classic proverb, the patience of donkeys is a laudable virtue.

CHAPTER 9
HEDGEHOG PARABLE AND SELF-DRIVING CARS

There is a famous line by an Ancient Greek poet named Archilochus that goes something like this: *Multa novit vulpes, verum echinus unum magnum.*

Roughly translated, this is interpreted as ascertaining the revered and yet some say perhaps wholly misunderstood contention that a fox knows many things, but a hedgehog knows one big thing. If you prefer, you are seemingly able to put that in the other order, namely that a hedgehog knows one big thing while a fox knows many things.

You are further welcome to kind of make-up whatever you wish about the meaning of this sage wisdom.

There is no abundantly agreed and nor absolute rock-solid indication of precisely what the declaration portends. That being said, the general consensus is that this might be a parable telling us that there are two major ways to view the world.

Let's start with the hedgehog.

We are informed that the hedgehog knows one big thing. This potentially means that you can seemingly gauge the world around you by cultivating and adopting a singular comprehensive perspective. You are seeking to adopt a presumably cohesive and all-telling vision of what the world is and how it operates. Thereafter, everything you do or say is guided by that grand vision.

That sure sounds nifty and worthy of aspiring toward.

Maybe not all of the time, depending upon how you take up the hedgehog mantle, as it were.

I had a friend in college that seemed to act in this hedgehog-affected manner, sort of. His philosophy about life was that everyone is in it for themselves. The moment that he met someone or heard someone speak, an immediate reaction was to scour the person for their presumed self-greediness. Especially alarming to him were people that alluded to doing things for the good of mankind or that said they were acting altruistically. That was utterly contrary to his one-view of existence.

Now, I don't want to leave the improper impression that the hedgehog is somehow necessarily in the wrong. The contrary sentiment is actually the normative stance.

Suppose for example that my friend instead held a one-view that everyone in the world ought to be given their due chance and were to be granted the cornerstone assumption of being intrinsically good and altogether kind. We would probably give this type of one-view a lot of street cred and bonus points for showcasing the smiley face side of existence.

You can philosophically argue in favor of the hedgehog as being the "best" approach, while others might exhort there are potential downsides to having a one-view. You can readily dance back and forth on this. For example, any one-view that you postulate, I can undercut it by finding some untoward weakness or qualm about it. At the same time, the one-view can be pretty darned useful and apt, depending upon what scope or targeted arena the viewpoint is aimed at.

To ratchet this up further, another interpretation is that the hedgehog is not just any of the myriad of one big thing that we could come up with, but instead represents the grandest and holistic of all big things. In essence, the hedgehog holds the keys to the entirety of all meaning and all existence, bound up into one singular viewpoint that can explain everything about everything.

That's one mighty hedgehog.

Very few utilize that interpretation.

All this talk about the hedgehog has almost led us to forget about the other counterpart in the parable, the wily fox. We ought to give some due attention to the fox since so far we've only shined the light on the hedgehog in this discussion.

We are steadfastly informed by this famed poetic utterance that the fox knows many things.

Yeh, well, I dare say that we can make the same assertion about nearly all animals and humans on this planet. It seems like everyone knows a bunch of things. We'll upgrade that notion of a bunch to the unlimited aspect of knowing many things. How many are many? Does the fox know five things, five hundred things, five thousand things, or maybe zillions and zillions of things?

Anyway, setting aside that perhaps microscopic teardown, we need to remember that this is about the fox versus the hedgehog in terms of providing a yin and yang of comparison. We are told that the fox knows many things, but a hedgehog knows one big thing. This implies that the fox knows many *small* things. We might also reasonably take this to suggest that the fox does assuredly not know the one big thing.

We can continue this form of logic-based unpacking and deduce that the hedgehog does not know those small things and in lieu of this is only knowledgeable about the one big thing.

Wait for a second. That puts us though on somewhat shaky ground. We aren't sure whether the one big thing might encapsulate some or all of the small things that the fox knows. Maybe so, maybe not. For the moment, assume that the one big thing and the many small things are completely separate and a part of each other (otherwise, it would seem like a hands-down knockout punch that the hedgehog has got to be better off than the fox, in this context).

In any case, based on the fox knowing many small things and the hedgehog knows one big thing, we might try to interpret this as being more favorable toward the hedgehog strategy than the fox strategy. We are perhaps being told that you are better off by knowing a big thing than you are by knowing a slew of smaller things.

One supposes this is akin to saying that the hedgehog can see the forest for the trees. Meanwhile, the fox is ostensibly lost among the trees and does not grasp the totality of the forest around it. The proverbial seeing of the big picture versus getting caught in the weeds.

You see, we can use lots of other witticisms to try and decipher the fox and the hedgehog allegory.

A provocative essay in the 1950s by philosopher Isaiah Berlin brought the fox and hedgehog into a modern-day focus. His interpretation of the ancient piece of poetry brought new life into its usage. Indeed, his work has spawned a cavalcade of splintering analyses and uses that has nearly become a cottage industry. Just about anybody nowadays is more than happy to jump on the fox and hedgehog bandwagon.

In short, the most popular leveraging consists of asserting that people fall into either the fox category or the hedgehog category.

For example, some have claimed that business leaders and top executives can be characterized in this fashion. You've got the bold and visionary CEO that has a singular vision for their firm and this serves as a lighthouse kind of guiding light for the entity. That is the CEO as a hedgehog.

On the other hand, you have CEOs that are like the fox, seemingly lacking a grand vision and instead are hopelessly focused on the day-to-day business battles and become swayed by the changing winds around them. There isn't a designated north star for this type of CEO. As a result, the employees and other stakeholders have no definitive clue about where the firm is heading. This in turn makes things hard to align in a particular direction and is contrary to ensuring that everyone is rowing together in unison.

Under this kind of portrayal, I'd bet that any CEO worth their salt would seek vigorously to become the hedgehog and avoid getting branded as a fox. Being labeled as a fox seems unsuitable to being a leader and you don't want to get your reputation and career smeared by being so stamped.

Whoa, which do you think of generally as more favorable in terms of the animal kingdom, the fox or the hedgehog?

We consider the fox to be a cunning character. A fox has a multitude of tricks up its sleeve. If you've ever seen a fox trying to evade predators, you can readily witness the many tools it has in its evasive machination toolbox. Likewise, a fox is a clever hunter too and can be a daring and crafty predator.

When you think about it, our everyday language positively incorporates the fox. We say that a person has outfoxed someone else, doing so in a complementary fashion. The fox is cool. Getting the tagline of being a foxy person is usually a quite flattering label. Etc.

I don't believe that the hedgehog has the same cachet.

Few would go around touting the fact that they are emulating a hedgehog. You would get some rather disconcerting stares. Furthermore, most people tend to think of a hedgehog as that animal that rolls itself into a ball when confronted with danger. This becomes a stationary tactic of hoping that whatever is attacking the hedgehog will be dissuaded by this seemingly imposing ball of spikes.

A leader that gets associated with being a hedgehog might discover to their dismay that this can be turned around on them. Maybe this is the type of person that when the business gets into trouble they merely roll into a tight ball and hide. Oopsie, not a good look for any CEO.

All of this suggests that the ancient choice of using a fox and a hedgehog is somewhat at odds with today's regard for what a fox is and what a hedgehog is. There is a decidedly uphill battle to try and place a hedgehog onto the pinnacle of whatever you want people of today to be or aspire to become. It is a public relations nightmare and you'd be better off elevating the fox to the top position of the metaphor and putting the hedgehog as the undercard.

Sure enough, some have done just that.

They make somewhat disparaging remarks about the hedgehog and proffer circumstances whereby the singular view was brittle and fell apart when business conditions changed. The fox is shown as being adaptable and resilient. When business circumstances evolved, the fox adroitly was able to pivot and reposition accordingly.

There are even those that ditch the hedgehog entirely. They turn the parable into the fox and the dog, or the fox and the cat, or the fox and the whale, and so on. The fox usually gets to remain in the story. This is logically required, pretty much. If you made your parable about say a bear and a horse, nobody would have any immediate means of tying this to the fox and the hedgehog. By keeping the fox in the mix, you can always quickly connect your metaphor to the more famous one of the Ancient Greeks.

One final twist, for now, is that perhaps this is not about the fox *versus* the hedgehog in any bitter head-to-head skirmish about which is better and which is worse. Some have argued that the fox and the hedgehog are not mutually exclusive in a parable visionary sense. Perhaps we are wise to consider that sometimes we need to be the fox and sometimes we need to be the hedgehog. Our best bet is to try and simultaneously embody *both* strategies, employing whichever one is most suitable to the situation at hand.

Now that we've covered this veritable Swiss army knife of allegories (you can seemingly deploy it as you wish, applying it as desired), let's shamelessly see what we can use it for herein.

Are you ready?

My assertion is that the field of Artificial Intelligence (AI) can be likened to the fox and the hedgehog.

Yes, you read that correctly, namely that the latest in advanced technology incorporating AI and machine learning can be characterized by this altogether delightful and insightful one-liner fable. We can mindfully take the wisdom of the ancients and apply it to how AI is being developed today.

On top of that assertion, I'll add to the matter by providing a decided bonus.

We can use the fox and hedgehog parable to glean something quite telling about the advent of AI-based true self-driving cars. I make this connection so that the discussion will not seem entirely abstract and somehow lacking in firm grounding.

Self-driving cars are essentially an outcome of advances in AI. As such, we can see how the fox and hedgehog apply to AI overall, and we can then also bring the discussion further down to earth by examining how the matter applies to those burgeoning self-driving cars.

This necessitates providing a bit of helpful background for you about self-driving or driverless cars. In brief, the future of cars consists of AI-based true self-driving cars. There isn't a human driver involved in a true self-driving car.

Keep in mind that true self-driving cars are driven via an AI driving system. There isn't a need for a human driver at the wheel, and nor is there a provision for a human to drive the vehicle.

Here's an intriguing question that is worth pondering: *How does the parable about the fox and the hedgehog apply to AI all told, and also apply in particular to the emergence of AI-based true self-driving cars?*

I'd like to first further clarify what is meant when I refer to true self-driving cars.

Understanding The Levels Of Self-Driving Cars

As a clarification, true self-driving cars are ones that the AI drives the car entirely on its own and there isn't any human assistance during the driving task.

These driverless vehicles are considered Level 4 and Level 5 while a car that requires a human driver to co-share the driving effort is usually considered at Level 2 or Level 3. The cars that co-share the driving task are described as being semi-autonomous, and typically contain a variety of automated add-on's that are referred to as ADAS (Advanced Driver-Assistance Systems).

There is not yet a true self-driving car at Level 5, which we don't yet even know if this will be possible to achieve, and nor how long it will take to get there.

Meanwhile, the Level 4 efforts are gradually trying to get some traction by undergoing very narrow and selective public roadway trials, though there is controversy over whether this testing should be allowed per se (we are all life-or-death guinea pigs in an experiment taking place on our highways and byways, some contend).

Since semi-autonomous cars require a human driver, the adoption of those types of cars won't be markedly different than driving conventional vehicles, so there's not much new per se to cover about them on this topic (though, as you'll see in a moment, the points next made are generally applicable).

For semi-autonomous cars, it is important that the public needs to be forewarned about a disturbing aspect that's been arising lately, namely that despite those human drivers that keep posting videos of themselves falling asleep at the wheel of a Level 2 or Level 3 car, we all need to avoid being misled into believing that the driver can take away their attention from the driving task while driving a semi-autonomous car. You are the responsible party for the driving actions of the vehicle, regardless of how much automation might be tossed into a Level 2 or Level 3.

Self-Driving Cars And The Fox And Hedgehog Parable

For Level 4 and Level 5 true self-driving vehicles, there won't be a human driver involved in the driving task.

All occupants will be passengers.

The AI is doing the driving.

One aspect to immediately discuss entails the fact that the AI involved in today's AI driving systems is not sentient. In other words, the AI is altogether a collective of computer-based programming and algorithms, and most assuredly not able to reason in the same manner that humans can.

Why is this added emphasis about the AI not being sentient?

Because I want to underscore that when discussing the role of the AI driving system, I am not ascribing human qualities to the AI. Please be aware that there is an ongoing and dangerous tendency these days to anthropomorphize AI. In essence, people are assigning human-like sentience to today's AI, despite the undeniable and inarguable fact that no such AI exists as yet.

With that clarification, you can envision that the AI driving system won't natively somehow "know" about the facets of driving. Driving and all that it entails will need to be programmed as part of the hardware and software of the self-driving car.

Let's dive into the myriad of aspects that come to play on this topic.

We can start this AI-related fox and hedgehog discussion by considering the aspirations of those that work in the field of Artificial Intelligence.

Succinctly stated, the goal of the AI field is to develop machines that exhibit intelligent behavior. The baseline for intelligence is calibrated by the capabilities of human intelligence. This means that the ultimate goal is to devise computer-based systems that seem to be as intelligent if not more so than humans. Of course, there is also a semblance of intelligence within other forms of animals, though the upscale barometer is to attain human levels.

Some would say that the AI field can be divided into two kinds of AI developers.

First, there are strong and quite vocal proponents that believe AI will only be attained by a tremendous breakthrough that reveals an as yet unknown singular and an overarching indication of how intelligence arises in human beings. Once we have cracked that enigmatic secret, we presumably will be able to use that eye-opening divining to then craft AI that will reach human intelligence capacities.

The second camp believes that we aren't likely to come across or ferret out a comprehensive picture of what drives human intelligence. Thus, we will need to do this on a bite at a time basis. We will need to figure out this little corner over here of how an itsy-bitsy piece of intelligence arises in humans. And then find another piece over there in another corner of the human mind. And so on.

Does that kind of characterization of two broadly differing camps or perspectives seem to ring a bell?

I hope so.

It is eerily reminiscent of the fox and the hedgehog parable. You could claim that those AI developers that are pining away to discern the singular Holy Grail of human intelligence are the hedgehogs. They are convinced that without the big picture being derived, the chances of creating AI that is on par with humans are exceedingly low. You might have some minor successes in narrow areas, but overall, the full-blown AI won't be achievable.

The contrasting camp exhorts that you could be waiting until the cows come home if you are stuck on insisting that there must be a singular and comprehensive mapping to get to full-blown AI. Forget it, they say. Sure, life would be a lot easier, but it is a pipedream. The better bet entails making a lot of smaller progressive leaps and piling them on top of each other along the way.

Which do you vote for, namely, would you prefer to be an AI developer that is the hedgehog or the fox?

You might be thinking that surely there is a right or wrong answer to that question. I assure you that the hedgehogs would clamor that they are right, while the foxes are equally adamant that they are right.

Some believe we need to be doing both at the same time. This is akin to the earlier point made that perhaps the hedgehog and the fox are not mutually exclusive and it is feasible to be both at the same time.

Now that we've seen how the parable applies to the overall field of AI, let's next dive into the particular focus on AI-based true self-driving cars.

We are going to once again come face-to-face with two camps.

One camp asserts that the way to best develop AI-based true self-driving cars consists of first devising a singular and comprehensive indication of how humans drive. In essence, uncover all of the human intelligence that goes into driving a car. Once you've got that laid out, you are then best able to craft AI that can drive on par with human drivers.

The other camp eschews that approach. They believe instead that you can incrementally build your way toward self-driving cars. Get an AI driving system devised that can handle the core functions of driving. After that, start adding to the core with all of the myriads of edge or corner cases that arise in driving. Step at a time, construct the AI driving system and achieve self-driving cars incrementally.

Aha, we are back to the hedgehog and the fox.

Which do you think will win, the self-driving car that is driven toward attainment by the hedgehogs or by the foxes?

Time will tell.

Conclusion

The race toward devising self-driving cars has a lot of dough at stake.

With all the business pressures of having to showcase progress in self-driving cars, you can pretty much shunt to the side the notion of trying to do the big divine. Millions and billions of dollars are being poured into the development of self-driving cars. Patience has already worn thin.

The idea that you would be somehow stinted until a comprehensive portrayal was figured out is something few investors have the stomach for. They want results now, not in some wide-eyed future nirvana.

The hedgehog has to lay low right now. They need to appear like the fox. By doing so, they can potentially still be doing their hedgehog thing. The fox, for now, gets the glory.

In the end, it might be that the hedgehog gets the final shining light.

As a final comment, a hedgehog and a fox perchance meet each other in a forest. The hedgehog says that it knows one big thing. The fox disparagingly replies that it knows a lot of small things and the fact that the hedgehog knows only one big thing is abundantly a disadvantage.

Maybe so, acknowledges the hedgehog, which then continues onward, knowing that a big bear is around the bend and that the fox is soon going to have quite an unpleasant surprise.

That's the magnificence of knowing the one big thing.

CHAPTER 10
FREEWAY LANES AND SELF-DRIVING CARS

We have all sorts of dedicated lanes these days on our freeways and highways.

The ubiquitous carpool lane has been around for many years. As you know, the core idea is that people will be voluntarily nudged to ride *together* in a car rather than each using a car *individually*. That's the High Occupancy Vehicle (HOV) concept in contrast to the Low Occupancy Vehicle (LOV) approach.

The justification for carpooling is pretty straightforward.

By having more riders in each car it is naturally presumed that there will be a lesser total number of cars on the roadway. This is simple math.

Whereas four people might be riding in one car due to carpooling, they could have been driving four separate cars if left to their own devices. Miraculously, you've then reduced the volume of cars by a huge margin, going down from a count of four vehicles to merely accounting for that one vehicle on the freeway or highway. Multiply this out by the thousands upon thousands of individual drivers that might have gotten behind the wheel. The scaling factor is significant, for which the reduction in the count of cars is astounding when essentially repacking people into a fewer number of vehicles.

In theory, this translates into less congestion.

Less congestion presumably implies faster speeds and less stop-and-go traffic. People get to their destinations sooner than they would otherwise. Furthermore, those people are less exasperated and less frustrated about having traversed the roadways. There is something to be said about the consternation that arises from being stuck in traffic jams. It can ruin the rest of your entire day and spill over into your work life and your private life.

There is a slew of additional benefits associated with reducing the number of cars on the roadways.

One aspect entails reducing pollution emissions.

A conventional ICE (internal combustion engine) car produces various pollutants, even despite the numerous smog control features built into modern-day vehicles. Fewer cars on the roads mean less pollution generated. Less time on the roads due to lessened congestion means less pollution produced too. It is a win-win.

Another aspect involves roadway surface wear-and-tear.

Cars are pretty rough on the roadways. We all can daily see the results. There are potholes aplenty. The roads are replete with cracks, loose gravel, tire marks, and get worn down over time. This in turn can impact your travel efforts. An everyday drive can become bumpy and possibly dangerous. In addition, cars get damaged via those darned potholes. Fewer cars on the roadways mean less stress and ordinary usage upon those vaunted surfaces.

I don't think you probably need much more convincing about the values of carpooling.

Of course, when you are on a freeway that has a carpool lane, and if you are not eligible to use the carpool lane, you might have a different opinion at that moment about the perceived value of a lane dedicated for that sole purpose.

We've all been sitting in traffic that is adjacent to carpool lanes. The traffic we are faced with as solo drivers can be miserably sluggish. Meanwhile, the carpool lane is zipping along with ease. You watch that speedy pace and lament that the carpool lane is there.

In your mind, you might generally agree that a carpool lane is a handy concept. Nonetheless, if the carpool lane appears to be sparsely used, you begin to think twice about why that dedicated lane exists. You are sure that if that lane was reassigned for conventional traffic, the result would be to reduce the sluggishness you are currently in the midst of.

Seeing a nearly empty carpool lane can be highly maddening. We all get the notion that it is intended for a good purpose and done with the sincerest of hopes. This altruistic viewpoint though comes to the fore when you are crawling along next to the dedicated lane and can clearly observe that it is being vastly underutilized. As such, you doubt that the reasoned basis is valid in light of the reality that you are experiencing.

Aha, some would retort. You are feeling the pain because you are not abiding by the carpool lane aspirations. Rather than thinking in a narrow fashion that the dedicated lane is being misappropriated, you ought to instead be dinging yourself for not aiming to be a carpool using rider. Stop complaining, get your act together, and get more people into your car (or, stop using your car and get into someone else's car).

Ouch, that stings.

The counterargument to that retort is that the person is perhaps in a circumstance of life that makes participating in a carpool prohibitive. Maybe the person is having to drive from place to place for their work efforts and cannot consolidate into one vehicle. Lots of reasons that seem justifiable are floated about why someone is unable to reasonably undertake to carpool.

Excuses, excuses, excuses, the other side says.

You can create excuses all day long. In the end, we have to force people into deciding which is more important to them. They can either take a chance by remaining as a solo driver, which means being unable to use the carpool lane, or they can rearrange their lives so that they can use a carpool and glean the advantages thereof.

In that sense of things, a dedicated lane is oftentimes a form of reward or possibly punishment in a gambit of trying to shape or reshape human behavior.

It goes like this.

Society wants you to carpool, ostensibly for the various reasons earlier listed. Society will not impose upon you a legal requirement that you must carpool. You are free to choose whether to carpool or not. If you do carpool, you get a nifty reward, namely that you can use the carpool lane and garner all those handy benefits thereof. If you don't carpool, you won't have those benefits, and in fact, you are somewhat being punished, due to being relegated to the non-dedicated lanes and the possibility of enduring onerous traffic woes.

I realize it is somewhat outlandish to suggest that the dedicated lane is *both* a form of reward and a form of punishment. Some would say that it is only a rewards-based approach. They would contend that any "punishment" is entirely of your own doing. The dedicated lane is not somehow harming you per se, it is only there to be beneficial to you and all of society.

A contrarian would argue that there is abundantly a punishment involved. That dedicated lane was potentially an existing lane that was repurposed as a dedicated lane. In that case, you have taken away something from those other drivers. You are punishing them by removing an available lane. This in turn is assuredly going to make traffic worse for them.

Even if the dedicated lane was made from scratch, and thus it wasn't taken away from the existing roadway, it still is a form of punishment when set aside for dedicated purposes. Here's why. The new lane could have been used by everyone. Instead, society is restricting the use of the lane. That is decidedly a kind of punishment to other drivers. The added lane could have been beneficial to all drivers, yet it is being focused on just a selected set.

These tit-for-tat arguments are nearly endless and apply to all variants of dedicated lanes.

You can for example say the same thing about bus lanes. A roadway that has a dedicated lane for busses is just as susceptible to the same pro and con arguments as does the carpool lane.

Yes, a bus carries more passengers than a car. Yes, a bus is in theory a more efficient and effective form of transportation than a car. But, we can also note that a dedicated lane for a bus is something that is acting as a reward toward those that use buses, and a kind of penalty or punishment towards those that do not do so.

Toll lanes are another such example.

The creation of toll lanes bring forth added points of contention. A toll lane usually involves a cost for those that use the lane. You pay a fee of one kind or another. Assuming there are no other restrictions or rules about the toll lane, it comes down to money as the key criterion.

That might seem on the face of things to be a fair measure. You either are willing to pay to use the toll lane, or you are not. Unlike a carpool lane, you don't need to change your behavior per se. You don't need to share a ride with someone else. All you need to do is plunk down some dough.

There is though a problem on that end too.

Some decry that toll lanes are predominantly beneficial for those that have money. If you are poor, you aren't readily able to use the toll lanes. Those toll lanes become dedicated lanes that are saying you are rewarded if you have money, and you are seemingly being punished if you don't have money (punished in the sense that you won't be able to use those lanes).

That is eschewed as elitist or at least biased against those in certain socioeconomic categories. There are lots of counterarguments, such as suggesting that the toll lanes might not exist at all except for the fact that people are willing to pay to use them. How else can the toll lanes be put into place? The money has to come from someplace. And so on.

One supposes that the most noticeable outcry about dedicated lanes arises when those lanes are sparsely used.

If you are driving along and not able to use a dedicated lane, you are witness to one of two momentary aspects about the dedicated lane, denoted broadly as either robust use versus bleak use. You might observe that the dedicated lane is being actively used and seems to be fulfilling whatever intention or purpose it claims to have. That would fit into the robust use category. Or you might notice that the dedicated lane has almost no vehicles in it and seems to be wasted space. That's the bleak use classification.

In the use case of the dedicated lane seemingly actively in use and labeled as robustness, you can still feel hurt that you aren't able to use it, but you have to (begrudgingly) admit that the darned thing is being used. You can grumble about the lane. You can whine about the lane. Your own eyes tell you though that the lane is being leveraged.

On the other hand, your blood comes to a boil when a dedicated lane is virtually empty. This is especially beguiling if the other lanes of traffic are all boxed in. In your mind's eye, you envision that the lane could be the reliever for the traffic bottlenecks that you are suffering in. An unused dedicated lane seems to be an utter boondoggle and showcases the grandiose err of the ways of mankind.

A typical response to that kind of bemoaning is that the dedicated lane is perhaps being unfairly judged. Your microscopic glimpse of the use is based on those few minutes that you are driving alongside the dedicated lane. Perhaps overall statistics indicate that the dedicated lane is used quite a bit, and your perception is mistaken by having merely witnessed a brief instance of desolation.

Statistics are hard to swallow though when you can see the dedicated lane with your own eyes and know in your heart of hearts about what you believe that you saw (that's a tongue twister).

Why all this discussion and recounting of the debates about dedicated lanes?

Because we have a new entrant that is earnestly eyeing the notion of having dedicated lanes.

Self-driving cars.

There are proponents for self-driving cars that are clamoring for the use of dedicated lanes that would be set aside specifically for self-driving cars.

By and large, the notion is that only self-driving cars could ride in those lanes. Some pundits would also be willing to include ground-based Autonomous Vehicles (AVs) of any shape or size, such as self-driving trucks, self-driving buses, and so on. For ease of discussion herein, let's go with the simpler core case of being dedicated to self-driving cars (though, acknowledging that a variant involves being a dedicated lane for a wider array of AVs, of which the same general principles still apply).

This necessitates providing a bit of helpful background for you about self-driving or driverless cars.

In brief, the future of cars consists of AI-based true self-driving cars. There isn't a human driver involved in a true self-driving car. Keep in mind that true self-driving cars are driven via an AI driving system. There isn't a need for a human driver at the wheel, and nor is there a provision for a human to drive the vehicle.

Here's an intriguing question that is worth pondering: *What controversy might there be about having dedicated lanes devoted to the advent of AI-based true self-driving cars?*

I'd like to first further clarify what is meant when I refer to true self-driving cars.

Understanding The Levels Of Self-Driving Cars

As a clarification, true self-driving cars are ones that the AI drives the car entirely on its own and there isn't any human assistance during the driving task.

These driverless vehicles are considered Level 4 and Level 5 while a car that requires a human driver to co-share the driving effort is usually considered at Level 2 or Level 3. The cars that co-share the driving task are described as being semi-autonomous, and typically contain a variety of automated add-on's that are referred to as ADAS (Advanced Driver-Assistance Systems).

There is not yet a true self-driving car at Level 5, which we don't yet even know if this will be possible to achieve, and nor how long it will take to get there.

Meanwhile, the Level 4 efforts are gradually trying to get some traction by undergoing very narrow and selective public roadway trials, though there is controversy over whether this testing should be allowed per se (we are all life-or-death guinea pigs in an experiment taking place on our highways and byways, some contend).

Since semi-autonomous cars require a human driver, the adoption of those types of cars won't be markedly different than driving conventional vehicles, so there's not much new per se to cover about them on this topic (though, as you'll see in a moment, the points next made are generally applicable).

For semi-autonomous cars, it is important that the public needs to be forewarned about a disturbing aspect that's been arising lately, namely that despite those human drivers that keep posting videos of themselves falling asleep at the wheel of a Level 2 or Level 3 car, we all need to avoid being misled into believing that the driver can take away their attention from the driving task while driving a semi-autonomous car.

You are the responsible party for the driving actions of the vehicle, regardless of how much automation might be tossed into a Level 2 or Level 3.

Self-Driving Cars And Dedicated Lanes

For Level 4 and Level 5 true self-driving vehicles, there won't be a human driver involved in the driving task.

All occupants will be passengers.

The AI is doing the driving.

One aspect to immediately discuss entails the fact that the AI involved in today's AI driving systems is not sentient. In other words, the AI is altogether a collective of computer-based programming and algorithms, and most assuredly not able to reason in the same manner that humans can.

Why is this added emphasis about the AI not being sentient?

Because I want to underscore that when discussing the role of the AI driving system, I am not ascribing human qualities to the AI. Please be aware that there is an ongoing and dangerous tendency these days to anthropomorphize AI. In essence, people are assigning human-like sentience to today's AI, despite the undeniable and inarguable fact that no such AI exists as yet.

With that clarification, you can envision that the AI driving system won't natively somehow "know" about the facets of driving. Driving and all that it entails will need to be programmed as part of the hardware and software of the self-driving car.

Let's dive into the myriad of aspects that come to play on this topic.

There is an ongoing clamor that we ought to establish dedicated lanes for self-driving cars.

Why so?

One basis for seeking dedicated lanes is ostensibly due to a technological deficiency and being unable to sufficiently attain suitably capable self-driving cars.

Here's the rub.

Getting self-driving cars to operate on public roadways is relatively straightforward, as long as you are willing to toss aside all of the usual complexities that entail being on open roads. Imagine a world in which there weren't any of those pesky pedestrians that might opt to foolishly jaywalk. Imagine a world in which human drivers were entirely out of the way and never pestered a self-driving car. Etc.

The moment that you bring all of those complications into the picture, the advent of self-driving cars is potentially going to be stymied. Developing an AI driving system that can cope with the myriad of wild and crazy antics that can happen on our public roadways is a humongous uphill battle. Some believe we will never be able to overcome that hurdle (see my coverage about edge cases and the long-tail problem at **the link here**).

If we had self-driving cars running only on private closed tracks that prohibited any of the vagaries of the real world, we probably would not find much value in having self-driving cars. The real trick is to figure out how to devise AI driving systems that can handle the same real-world driving that human drivers contend with on an everyday basis.

Okay, given that we are still beyond the reach of that vaunted goal, some point out that we could constrain the real world to make things easier for these less-than-ideal self-driving cars. Voila, set up dedicated lanes that only self-driving cars could utilize.

In short, if self-driving cars can't yet handle the real world, readapt the real world to fit what self-driving cars can do.

The creation of dedicated lanes for self-driving cars would reduce the complexity that the AI driving systems have to deal with. In theory, once in a dedicated lane, the only considerations are dealing with the lane and other self-driving cars.

We could presumably get the self-driving cars to cooperate with each other via appropriate programming of the AI. In addition, it is already anticipated that self-driving cars will communicate electronically with each other via V2V (vehicle-to-vehicle) capabilities. As such, while cruising along in a dedicated lane, the AI driving systems would be conveying traffic-related messaging to each other on the V2V feature.

Wait for a second, some say, why rush to get self-driving cars onto the public roadways if they aren't fully capable?

The usual answer is that self-driving cars offer great promise that we might wish to exploit sooner rather than later. It is hoped that self-driving cars will dramatically reduce the number of car crashes and car crash-related injuries and fatalities that occur each year. Do keep in mind that there are about 2.5 million car crashes annually in the United States alone and produce sadly about 1.2 million injuries and some 40,000 fatalities (see my analysis of driving stats at **the link here**).

For each year and each day that we aren't using self-driving cars, the assertion is that we are allowing those car crashes and related injuries and fatalities to continue to mount up, even though we could be doing something constructive to prevent them. Using self-driving cars in dedicated lanes would be one step toward that rather compassionate goal.

There is a slew of additional benefits expected once we have self-driving cars aplenty. Indeed, there is a mantra that we will enter into a mobility-for-all era. The concept is that those today that find themselves mobility disadvantaged will finally have an opportunity to use mobility that otherwise has been prohibitive to access.

Alright, you can plainly see that the dedicated lanes would be a form of stopgap that could enable self-driving cars to nearly immediately be put into active use. Furthermore, giving self-driving cars those specially dedicated lanes would reduce the complexities facing self-driving cars and essentially protect them the real world.

Not so fast, the counterarguments go.

How would these self-driving cars get onto those dedicated lanes? Presumably, the self-driving cars would have to make their way to the entry onramps, which means they would be likely driving in open-ended areas such as neighborhoods and communities. You can't just have a self-driving magically appear at an onramp out of thin air.

One reply to that concern is that perhaps self-driving cars would be parked at the edge of a freeway or highway that had a self-driving car's dedicated lane. You would get into a self-driving car at that spot and it would whisk you down the highway while only using the special purpose dedicated lane. Upon arriving at some designated exit point, the self-driving car would once again go to a parking lot that was directly adjacent to the highway. This would then ensure that the self-driving cars were only using the dedicated lanes and not having to contend with open-ended driving conditions.

A bellowing objection to this scenario is that we already have something that does just exactly what has been described.

It is a thing called a train.

Yes, trains have train stations that you use to get into and out of the train. The trains go along on laid out and fixed-in-place tracks.

You are essentially recreating a train by using self-driving cars in this equivalent manner. Meanwhile, a train has the advantage that it takes a lot of people all at once as a form of transit, while a car is not even close to that kind of efficiency.

The retort to that reply is that you have to be willing to start somewhere in terms of using self-driving cars on our public roadways. Sure, at first they are going to be used as though they are comparable to trains in the sense of only going from and to predetermined fixed points.

The hope and belief are that eventually the AI driving systems will catch up with the dreamy aspirations and we will then be able to let loose the self-driving cars so that they go beyond just those dedicated lanes.

Around and around we go on these heated debates.

As an additional taste, there are many more monkey wrenches involved.

For example, suppose that there were these dedicated lanes for self-driving cars and we proceed to make use of them.

How would we prevent human-driven cars from intervening?

You might have to build the dedicated lanes in a manner that physically precluded any interlopers, but this is assuredly an extraordinarily costly proposition. Do we want to spend our precious highway dollars on that kind of a singular purpose lane?

Well, perhaps we might just put up signs that tell human drivers that they cannot use those self-driving dedicated lanes. We could impose hefty fines for those human drivers that dared to interject themselves into the self-driving lanes. Yes, that might help, but you can imagine that those rules would still be flouted by some and we could end up with quite a mess on our highways and freeways accordingly.

Here's yet another twist.

Some worry that if we did implement dedicated lanes for self-driving cars at this time, it is as though we are tossing in the towel about their existent technological lack of prowess. We are saying that even though self-driving cars are decidedly not up to snuff in terms of driving on our public roadways, we are going to use them anyway, albeit in a limited fashion via being restricted to using just those dedicated lanes.

Here's why that generates a sour face.

This might reduce the urgency of pressure on the automakers and self-driving tech firms about seeking to make true self-driving cars. The AI developers might choose to ease off that important goal. In short, the impetus toward gaining true self-driving cars would potentially be woefully undercut.

This ironically then does the opposite of what it is said that the dedicated lanes were going to achieve. Rather than spurring the advent of self-driving cars, it might downshift the rushing forward momentum. We could then have a dour and inadvertently adverse consequence of stretching out the time toward true self-driving cars and not meanwhile gleaning many benefits in return.

Dizzying!

Conclusion

This is one of those topics that has numerous layers upon layers of potential unpacking.

One viewpoint is that perhaps at first we might have dedicated lanes for self-driving cars because of technological weaknesses and then, over time, find that self-driving cars have been improved immensely by AI developers as the technology gets improved. At that point, the dedicated lanes have an entirely different significance.

No longer are the dedicated lanes there to make things easier for self-driving cars. Instead, the dedicated lanes are there to allow self-driving cars to run smoothly and avoid the idiocy and foibles of human drivers.

You see, the AI driving systems of that sophistication can cope with human drivers nearby, but it is best to not have them have to do so.

The dedicated lanes become express lanes. They are express-oriented due to the self-driving cars cooperating with each other and ergo aiming to streamline the use of the lane.

We can add more to this matter.

Society might want to encourage people to use self-driving cars. This could seem surprising to you since many believe that everyone will want to use self-driving cars. That is yet to be seen. We might have a vast segment of society that eschews using self-driving cars. It could be that they don't trust self-driving cars. It could be that they insist on driving and don't want to let some machine do the driving for them. And so on.

If self-driving cars had dedicated lanes, it would be the same type of reward as there is for today's carpool lanes. By using a self-driving car, you as a passenger are being rewarded by being able to zoom along in a dedicated lane. Those that aren't using self-driving cars are somewhat being "punished" because they would not be able to use those dedicated lanes.

As a final remark for now on this entangled debate about dedicated lanes for self-driving cars envision a future in which self-driving cars are widely in use. They are daily in your neighborhood and taking kids to school and giving lifts to those that want to visit a local park or go to the grocery store. They are nearly ubiquitous.

When you get onto a freeway and are driving your human-driven conventional car, here's what might happen.

It turns out that nearly all of the lanes are for self-driving cars and there is only just one paltry designated lane for human-driven cars. The dedicated lane is solely for human-driven cars. That lane is always jam-packed and goes at a snail's pace. For those that keep insisting on driving a car, they are now relegated to the bottom of the totem pole, as it were.

Society has thusly reached a point that it won't ban people from driving cars, but will make the driving experience so atrocious and bogged down that the message is being said loud and clear. You ought to stop your stubborn desire to drive and join everyone else in using self-driving cars.

That type of future is darned hard to envision at this time. There are drivers today that insist they will only give up their driving when you pry their cold dead hands from the steering wheel.

Some believe that future generations will have an entirely different outlook, being more avidly *dedicated* to the advent of self-driving cars.

Which lane are you in?

CHAPTER 11
BEAR BUSTS IN AND SELF-DRIVING CARS

Get ready for a bit of a surprise.

Imagine that you've driven up to the mountains to enjoy some fresh air and are relishing the chance of getting back to nature. You proceed to carefully park your vehicle in a handy and seemingly safe parking lot adjacent to a wooded area. Grabbing up your gear, you start your blissful hike into the forest.

Others have forewarned you that bears have been spotted in this region.

So noted.

Throughout your trek, you keep your eyes open and your ears wide to try and detect any indications that bears are nearby. In addition, you are carrying a can of bear spray that you hope you'll never need to use. All in all, though you realize there is a semblance of danger undertaking a hike in this area, you feel like you've done your homework in preparing for any potential encounter with a grizzly bear.

After hiking for many hours, you decide to head back to your car. You continue to be ever vigilant about watching for bears. Is there any evidence of bears being around? On the trails, you've been routinely scanning the ground to detect any bear footprints. You've also been looking for and using your nostrils to potentially detect the sights or odors of bear scat.

Better to be safe than sorry, that's your lifelong motto. All told, there hasn't been any sign of bears and you successfully and uneventfully return to your vehicle.

Easy-peasy.

Just as you start to reach for the door handle of your vehicle, you suddenly see a commotion inside the vehicle. A really big commotion. A giant-sized bear-like commotion.

Well, in fact, it is a bear.

You know how there are those ships in a bottle and you've always wondered how they get that thing into the bottle. This is exactly the same wonderment you are feeling at this grand moment. A bear is inside your vehicle. How it got in there is unclear. Why it is still in there is also unclear.

The amazement instantly turns into fear, angst, dread, confusion, shock, and a myriad of other emotions and reactions. I dare say that nobody in their right mind would seem to want a wild bear inside their vehicle. That isn't *blowing out of those candles* on a birthday cake kind of wish.

Bears getting inside a car and getting stuck inside are more prevalent than you might think.

A recent news story out of Colorado by the Colorado Parks and Wildlife (CPW) service described just such a circumstance. Taking place near the intersection of the Gilpin and Jefferson counties, officials of the CPW service were called to contend with a bear trapped inside a vehicle.

What would you do?

The smarmy answer of course is to say that you would let the bear out.

Sure, that's obvious. The tricky part is how to let the bear out and not get stomped or torn to shreds in the process. It would seem nearly axiomatic that any person that stood at the vehicle door and calmly opened it, perhaps extending a cheerful greeting to the bear and explaining politely that it ought to please exit, would be asking for grave trouble.

Envision a darned angry bear, probably overheated, likely irked to the max, and willing to scamper out while trouncing anything and anybody that might be in the way or that is close enough to be considered a possible threat.

I've shooed a bird out of my car when it one day perchance flew into the vehicle. I wasn't particularly worried that the bird was going to attack me like those birds in the famous Hitchcock movie. I was relatively confident the bird would fly out and be on its merry way.

A bear, though, provides a completely different scenario.

Here's what the CPW officer did.

The officer parked their own vehicle immediately adjacent to the one that had the trapped bear. Being as discretely quiet as feasible, the officer slightly opened the door of the bear-entrapped vehicle, leaving the door just a nudge ajar. The officer then waited inside their own vehicle to see what would happen next.

Sure enough, the bear decided that playtime inside the vehicular playground was over and pushed open the door to get out. According to news reports, the bear tore the car door off its hinges. That makes sense to me. If you have brute strength, might as well use it when the need so arises.

Away scampered the bear.

No humans were hurt in that bear encounter, thankfully. The interior of the vehicle was pretty much thrashed and beaten to a pulp. Windows and the windshield were summarily cracked and shattered. The dashboard was ripped up. Etc.

In looking at posted pictures of the vehicle and its tattered interior (per the Twitter feed of the CPW), I would like to suggest that the bear was actually a lot less impulsive and destructive than you might otherwise assume.

First, let me clarify, the interior was inarguably rather shredded. On the other hand, the seats appear to be relatively intact, the steering wheel looks usable, and other facets are not utterly devastated. I'm not trying to make the case that the bear was frolicking and tried to be tidy. It just seems to me that the bear could have done a lot more to entirely and without question wreak havoc on the interior of that vehicle.

The cost to repair the damages is anyway going to be high and I have sympathy for any car repair shop that takes on that convoluted, or shall I say *unbearable* task (what a great pun, if you don't mind my claiming so).

The CPW officials opted to use this instance as a life hack lesson, namely, always make sure to remove any attractants from inside your vehicle and also ensure that your windows are rolled up and your car doors are fully locked. This is certainly useful advice when parking your vehicle in a region that has bears on the loose.

Okay, then again, maybe it is useful advice all of the time, seeking to ensure that bears and nor car thieves are attracted to breaking into your car.

The National Park Service (NPS) of the federal government provides extensive advice about how to try and avoid encounters with bears. Some of the advice might seem obvious, while other facets could be somewhat surprising to some.

We all generally would hopefully know that leaving food inside a car is not a good idea when there are bears around. The thing is, the common definition or interpretation of the word "food" is usually things like leftover fast-food hamburgers or French fries. You would be overly narrow in your thinking.

Here's what the NPS indicates: "Bears have an insatiable appetite and an amazing sense of smell, and they consider anything with a scent to be "food." This can include canned goods, bottles, drinks, soaps, cosmetics, toiletries, trash, ice chests, sunscreen, bug repellant, fuel, items used for preparing or eating meals, etc." Additional subtle details are mentioned, including: "Remember to clear your car of food wrappers, crumbs in baby seats, baby wipes, and even canned food and drinks."

You might be tempted to believe that the odds of a bear approaching a car are extremely low. It would not seem like something a bear would "naturally" seek to do.

The twist is that bears are smart enough to learn about what cars can potentially contain. A bear that discovers a car with attractants will likely remember the discovery. Over time, the bear begins to form a habit of going toward cars, hopeful that something scrumptious might be inside. They can use both sight and smell to try and figure out if there are any hidden treasures within.

Pretend that you are a bear and put yourself into their shoes, or perhaps more aptly *into* their paws. Which is easier to do, forage throughout a forest and try to scavenge for food, or simply go to a parking lot and roam from car to car? The parking lot is essentially a collection of handy-dandy food containers, all assembled in one convenient place, at least from the perspective of the bear.

Until the day that bears learn how to drive, they merely perceive those parked cars as a free meal, rather than a means of transit.

Speaking of bears that might want to get a driver's license is a reminder that there have been attempts to train dogs to drive a car. Yes, you read that correctly. Some have advised that maybe a dog would be smart enough to be able to drive a car.

Since we've now veered this discussion into the driving of cars, it seems timely for me to mention that the future of cars consists of AI self-driving cars.

There isn't a human driver involved in a true self-driving car.

Keep in mind that true self-driving cars are driven via an AI driving system. There isn't a need for a human driver at the wheel, and nor is there a provision for a human to drive the vehicle.

Here's an intriguing question that is worth pondering: *What can this bear story tell us about the advent of AI-based true self-driving cars?*

I'd like to first further clarify what is meant when I refer to true self-driving cars.

Understanding The Levels Of Self-Driving Cars

As a clarification, true self-driving cars are ones that the AI drives the car entirely on its own and there isn't any human assistance during the driving task.

These driverless vehicles are considered Level 4 and Level 5 while a car that requires a human driver to co-share the driving effort is usually considered at Level 2 or Level 3. The cars that co-share the driving task are described as being semi-autonomous, and typically contain a variety of automated add-on's that are referred to as ADAS (Advanced Driver-Assistance Systems).

There is not yet a true self-driving car at Level 5, which we don't yet even know if this will be possible to achieve, and nor how long it will take to get there.

Meanwhile, the Level 4 efforts are gradually trying to get some traction by undergoing very narrow and selective public roadway trials, though there is controversy over whether this testing should be allowed per se (we are all life-or-death guinea pigs in an experiment taking place on our highways and byways, some contend, see my coverage at **this link here**).

Since semi-autonomous cars require a human driver, the adoption of those types of cars won't be markedly different than driving conventional vehicles, so there's not much new per se to cover about them on this topic (though, as you'll see in a moment, the points next made are generally applicable).

For semi-autonomous cars, it is important that the public needs to be forewarned about a disturbing aspect that's been arising lately, namely that despite those human drivers that keep posting videos of themselves falling asleep at the wheel of a Level 2 or Level 3 car, we all need to avoid being misled into believing that the driver can take away their attention from the driving task while driving a semi-autonomous car.

You are the responsible party for the driving actions of the vehicle, regardless of how much automation might be tossed into a Level 2 or Level 3.

Self-Driving Cars And Bear Lessons

For Level 4 and Level 5 true self-driving vehicles, there won't be a human driver involved in the driving task.

All occupants will be passengers.

The AI is doing the driving.

One aspect to immediately discuss entails the fact that the AI involved in today's AI driving systems is not sentient. In other words, the AI is altogether a collective of computer-based programming and algorithms, and most assuredly not able to reason in the same manner that humans can.

Why is this added emphasis about the AI not being sentient?

Because I want to underscore that when discussing the role of the AI driving system, I am not ascribing human qualities to the AI. Please be aware that there is an ongoing and dangerous tendency these days to anthropomorphize AI. In essence, people are assigning human-like sentience to today's AI, despite the undeniable and inarguable fact that no such AI exists as yet.

With that clarification, you can envision that the AI driving system won't natively somehow "know" about the facets of driving. Driving and all that it entails will need to be programmed as part of the hardware and software of the self-driving car.

Let's dive into the myriad of aspects that come to play on this topic.

First, you'll be undoubtedly happy to know that numerous interesting insights can be gleaned from those bears that are determined to find a meal inside of a car. Of course, the most important and immediate lesson is that you should not be leaving food or any other attractants inside your vehicle. That's already been emphasized herein.

But what about the world once we have self-driving cars aplenty?

Suppose you opt to use a self-driving car to go up to the mountains. Upon arriving at a parking lot nearby a wooded area, you get out of the self-driving car to get underway on a pleasant hike.

Some self-driving car pundits would insist that the self-driving car is not going to park in the parking lot and merely sit there awaiting your return. No, they claim, the self-driving car will drive off, seeking to give lifts to other people.

This seems a bit doubtful in this particular use case.

Sure, if a self-driving car is in a busy city and drops off a passenger, the autonomous vehicle is presumably going to be programmed to start roaming and be ready for the next driving request. Similar to today's human-driven ridesharing vehicles, the AI driving system will be driving around and aims to be in the right place at the right time for the next incoming ridesharing request.

I don't know about you, but if I was hiking in a forest and my ride there was suddenly zipping away to go give someone else a lift, I would not be a happy camper. I would be steamed. I would expect that the self-driving car should be right where I left it. I want to know that I can come back to that parking lot and the vehicle is still there, such that I have a ride out of there.

Now, I might be willing to modify that requirement just a tad. One nice thing about a self-driving car would be that you could instruct it to meet you at the spot that you anticipate exiting the forest from. Thus, rather than having to a roundtrip hike, you can do a one-way trek and the self-driving car will nicely enough end up there too.

You would normally have to hope that somebody would be able to drive your car to that other destination. This would ostensibly require making prior arrangements. With the self-driving car, you can merely on-the-spot send it instructions to meet you elsewhere and make sure to show up accordingly.

Those of you that are sneaky might say that if the self-driving car is going to meet me elsewhere, why not let it be any self-driving car. In other words, it could be that one self-driving car drops me off, and another one picks me up. Ergo there isn't a need for the exact same self-driving car to be sitting around and nor to be roaming around awaiting the conclusion of my forest romp.

The likely concern about this arrangement is whether there would be a sufficient abundance of self-driving cars available to do the type of separate drop-off and pick-up that is being suggested. In a remote mountain area, it might be unlikely that other self-driving cars are perchance there. The one that brought you to the locale is bound to be the only one nearby.

In short, I am contending that there will be some circumstances during which you might want a self-driving car to park and await your return. I acknowledge that this is not always going to be the case and a variety of variant scenarios are all plausible. In that same vein, hopefully, you would concede that having a self-driving car become parked and await your arrival is in fact a reasonable scenario and fully sensible.

Whew, had to work our way through that thorny thicket.

All right, we have a self-driving car parked in a parking lot of a place that has wild bears. The self-driving car is awaiting the return of the hiker that used the self-driving car to get there.

We now reach a startling and mind-bending question: *Does a roaming wild bear particularly care that a car is a conventional human-driven car versus an AI-based self-driving car?*

I'd bet that's a question that no one else has been pondering at great length.

We can gleefully do so.

The initial reaction is that the bear would not care at all that the vehicle is an autonomous vehicle. From the bear's perspective, it is a container of potential food or other attractants. That's about it. The nature of how the container is propelled or steered or whatever, the bear really has no focus on. Food is food, a container is a container.

Case closed.

Wait for a second, maybe there is more to this bearish story than meets the eye.

We usually assume that a car parked in a parking lot is bereft of a driver. Other than when a driver is getting into or out of the parked car or driving the car throughout the parking lot, the rest of the time the car is presumably empty of a human driver. There is no one at the steering wheel.

The AI driving system of a self-driving car is always intact. A parked self-driving car is immediately able to become a moving car. At the snap of the fingers, you can ask the self-driving car to get underway. This can be done from inside the self-driving car as a passenger, and potentially can be done remotely, such as a ridesharing service that electronically transmits a request to the autonomous vehicle.

By the way, this convenient remote activation also bodes for some ominous cybersecurity issues.

A self-driving car might also activate itself into doing a driving act.

Say what?

Yes, depending upon how the AI driving system has been programmed, the self-driving car can engage itself to proceed.

Consider this scenario. A self-driving car is parked in a city parking lot. A human driver is at the wheel of a conventional car and is winding their way through the same parking lot. The human driver inadvertently steers directly toward the self-driving car, seemingly likely to accidentally ram the self-driving car.

If the self-driving car is making use of its object detection system, even though the autonomous vehicle is parked, the AI driving capability would be alerted at the pending crash that is about to occur. Depending upon what the AI developers anticipated, the AI driving system might activate the self-driving car and attempt to quickly drive away from the converging human-driven car.

Nifty!

Some would say eerie. The notion that a self-driving car will suddenly start moving seems unnerving. Maybe so, but if a person was perchance sitting in that parked car and they opted to try and move the car and avert a collision, you would certainly agree that this is a prudent step to take, assuming that getting away was reasonably feasible.

You might be curious why I've dragged you through this telling of the self-activating self-driving car capacity.

Because of those wild bears, of course.

Envision that a self-driving car is parked in a parking lot next to a forest. The human hiker has left the autonomous vehicle and has trekked somewhere deep in the woods. A bear meanders into the parking lot, looking for a free meal.

If the AI driving system is using its object detection features, the bear would likely be detected. When the bear decides to wander directly toward the self-driving car, the AI driving system might activate the autonomous vehicle and drive away from the bear.

It is unclear if the bear will somehow divine that the self-driving car is capable of moving on its own accord. We don't know if bears are able to "know" that cars need a human driver at the wheel for the vehicle to get underway. Maybe they have figured this out, maybe not.

What we can reasonably assert is that the bear might gradually realize that sometimes a car will move away from it. The bear won't necessarily know how this happens. It just happens. One supposes that the bears might realize that this happens when there is no human inside the vehicle (and, obviously, can happen too when a human is present).

After a while, it seems plausible to suggest that bears will be concerned that those free meal containers (on wheels) seem to move away upon the bear approaching. This will possibly discourage some bears and they will steer clear of parked cars.

Other bears might turn this into a game. Kind of hide-and-seek, of sorts. Approach a car, it moves away. Fun! Walk over to the car and see which way it goes next. A grand old time in the parking lot, that's for sure.

Though if the bear never gets the food or other attractant, this will be a game that has little reward, other than idle fun. Expending energies toward not getting food is something a bear would usually do judiciously. When the bear has a full tummy, maybe playtime is okay.

When the bear is as hungry as a bear, which self-referentially seems logical, they probably aren't keen on playing games that won't result in filling their stomach.

Conclusion

With all of that laid out, we don't yet know whether the makers of self-driving cars are going to deal with this kind of a problem.

For most of them, the idea of right now programming the self-driving car to do some evasive actions while parked is considered an edge or corner case. This means that it is ranked as a low priority, see my discussion about edge cases and the long-tail aspects of self-driving cars at **the link here**.

In that sense, a self-driving car that is parked in a parking lot where bears are roaming is a sitting duck, as it were.

That means that a conventional human-driven car and a self-driving car are construed as the same, from the viewpoint of those hungry bears. The bear won't care that tons of high-tech have been infused into that shiny new self-driving car. Food is food, regardless of the geeked-out tech of the vehicle.

This does raise an intriguing question.

The odds are that self-driving cars will be designed differently on the interior than are conventional human-driven cars. For example, there is no need for a steering wheel and nor any need for the pedals. Those will no longer be included. The interior is opened up to allow for perhaps swiveling seats, possibly reclining seats so that you can sleep on a long journey inside a self-driving car.

Given that type of interior, the bear is bound to find things a lot more comfortable inside a self-driving car than a conventional human-driven car.

The next thing you know, bears will fall in love with self-driving cars, doing so because it is a quiet, spacious, and secure place to rest and relax. No need to worry about predators getting at the bear while relishing the plush and roomy interior.

One question is whether any predators of bears would figure out that bears are neatly found "packaged" inside of self-driving cars, and wait outside to grab them at the earliest opportunity (in an ecosystem of fearsome mountain lions, wolves, and other even angrier bears). Kind of a sad face on that.

A second question is whether the bears might figure out how to communicate with the AI driving system. You know, bears are pretty sharp. Perhaps a truly enterprising bear could convince the AI to take the bear for a cozy ride while inside the self-driving car.

Don't be especially surprised if you start to see bears riding around in self-driving cars.

And please remember, you heard about it here, first.

CHAPTER 12
ESCAPED ZEBRAS AND SELF-DRIVING CARS

Get ready for some especially sweet irony.

First, some needed background.

There is a famous saying in the medical field that makes reference to zebras. Turns out that in the 1940s a professor at the University Maryland School of Medicine repeatedly exhorted his newbie medical interns that if you hear hoofbeats behind you, don't expect to see a zebra.

This was sensible advice.

You see, the clever saying alludes to the fact that horses are by far more prevalent in Maryland than are zebras. Statistically, you would be somewhat foolish to guess that you had heard a zebra. In the same vein, as a medical doctor, you are more likely to presumably come across commonplace ailments and diseases more so than rare ones. Thus, when you see symptoms in a patient and want to perhaps immediately leap to a conclusion that the malady is some rare instance, the odds are that it is the common one.

The popular TV series called *House, M.D.* provided a continual stream of examples that fit this sage wisdom. The fictional character that served as a kind of medical genius, Dr. Gregory House, was quick to suggest rather wildly unlikely diseases when doing his rapid-fire diagnoses. Of course, the creative storytelling usually had him shown to be right. You could argue that this was merely feel-good efforts by the producers and writers, aiming to gain audience infatuation with the show.

On the other hand, there is a counterargument to be made that since Dr. House was typically only involved in baffling medical cases, there presumably would be a heightened chance that the medical issue was particularly rare.

A type of pre-selection was taking place at the hospital.

The everyday circumstances ran the usual gauntlet and were seemingly instances of everyday kinds of medical problems. The outliers and offbeat instances would presumably tend toward more complex and unusual medical explanations, and those were being routed to Dr. House. Anyway, the overall mantra is that you are best to consider the usual, and only once you've found a reasoned basis for potentially rejecting or questioning the usual, you can turn your gaze toward the unusual. This inevitably became a popular credo in the medical profession at large.

Hearing hoofbeats while you are walking around Maryland is more likely to be a horse coming toward you than a zebra.

Case closed.

But wait for a second, maybe not.

We are now up to the sweet irony that I earlier promised would be revealed.

Maryland has been in the news recently due to a bunch of zebras that are roaming the streets of Maryland, fancy-free and footloose, as they say.

Yes, some zebras managed to apparently escape from a private farm in Maryland and decided they would take in the sights of the local towns and cities nearby. One can only imagine how much fun those zebras must be having. After being cooped up on the farm and generally semi-restricted in their movement, they have found themselves enjoying the utterly free-range way of living.

Go where you want. See what you want. Freedom at long last.

What a wonderful moment to be a zebra in Maryland!

Admittedly, there are practical realities to be contended with.

Finding food is not that easy to do for a zebra that is wandering the streets. The allure of food is indeed how the striped creatures are likely to ultimately get nabbed by the local authorities. The official animal services department is putting out food at a feeding station and trying to attract the zebras to come there. It is hoped that the zebras will let down their guard at the feeding station and be easily corralled.

No-fuss, no harm, no foul.

I'm sure you are thinking that the animal services officials ought to stridently hunt for the zebras and use tranquilizers to subdue the wild beasts. Per news reports, the authorities say that the zebras are too fast and it is overly dangerous to try and shoot them with the tranquilizers. A preference is to do things the friendlier way, thus gently lure them to the feeding station and corner them there.

Okay, given that latest news story about zebras on the loose in Maryland, I want to ask you a question.

If you hear hoofbeats, should you assume they are horses or that they are zebras?

Aha, we return to the witty saying in the medical field.

That being said, we have to be upfront and acknowledge that the odds are still higher that you'll be hearing hoofbeats of horses rather than zebras. The number of zebras in this *Great Escape* is quite small, less than a half-dozen, and they are pretty much remaining in a confined rural area. So, unless you perchance live or work in that specific locale, you are unlikely to be witnessing footloose zebras anyplace else.

We'll have to remain contented with the famous saying, though relishing the lighthearted irony in this instance is certainly a dollop of grazing fun.

A bit of seriousness does enter into the situation when you consider what could happen if those zebras run around on the highways and byways of Maryland. The zebras seem to have opted to stay in wooded areas and luckily keep off the motorways.

There are though alarming photos of the zebras walking, striding, and galloping on busy avenues and car-using streets.

Imagine that you are driving your car and perchance see up ahead a zebra.

If you didn't know about the zebra breakout, you would swear your eyes were deceiving you. The odds are that you would at first assume the zebras were horses that just so happened to resemble zebras. Or you might guess that the circus has come to town, and they are doing one of those elephants walks whereby they parade a bunch of extraordinary animals down the local streets.

I really doubt that you would instantaneously believe they were zebras.

Shifting gears, what would an AI-based true self-driving car calculate the wiry beasts to be?

Note that there isn't a human driver involved in a true self-driving car. Keep in mind that true self-driving cars are driven via an AI driving system. There isn't a need for a human driver at the wheel, and nor is there a provision for a human to drive the vehicle.

Here's an intriguing question that is worth pondering: *What can these zebras on the loose inform us about the advent of AI-based true self-driving cars?*

I'd like to first further clarify what is meant when I refer to true self-driving cars.

Understanding The Levels Of Self-Driving Cars

As a clarification, true self-driving cars are ones that the AI drives the car entirely on its own and there isn't any human assistance during the driving task.

These driverless vehicles are considered Level 4 and Level 5, while a car that requires a human driver to co-share the driving effort is usually considered at Level 2 or Level 3. The cars that co-share the driving task are described as being semi-autonomous, and typically contain a variety of automated add-on's that are referred to as ADAS (Advanced Driver-Assistance Systems).

There is not yet a true self-driving car at Level 5, which we don't yet even know if this will be possible to achieve, and nor how long it will take to get there.

Meanwhile, the Level 4 efforts are gradually trying to get some traction by undergoing very narrow and selective public roadway trials, though there is controversy over whether this testing should be allowed per se (we are all life-or-death guinea pigs in an experiment taking place on our highways and byways, some contend).

Since semi-autonomous cars require a human driver, the adoption of those types of cars won't be markedly different than driving conventional vehicles, so there's not much new per se to cover about them on this topic (though, as you'll see in a moment, the points next made are generally applicable).

For semi-autonomous cars, it is important that the public needs to be forewarned about a disturbing aspect that's been arising lately, namely that despite those human drivers that keep posting videos of themselves falling asleep at the wheel of a Level 2 or Level 3 car, we all need to avoid being misled into believing that the driver can take away their attention from the driving task while driving a semi-autonomous car. You are the responsible party for the driving actions of the vehicle, regardless of how much automation might be tossed into a Level 2 or Level 3.

Self-Driving Cars And Striped Zebras Afoot

For Level 4 and Level 5 true self-driving vehicles, there won't be a human driver involved in the driving task.

All occupants will be passengers.

The AI is doing the driving.

One aspect to immediately discuss entails the fact that the AI involved in today's AI driving systems is not sentient. In other words, the AI is altogether a collective of computer-based programming and algorithms, and most assuredly not able to reason in the same manner that humans can.

Why is this added emphasis about the AI not being sentient?

Because I want to underscore that when discussing the role of the AI driving system, I am not ascribing human qualities to the AI. Please be aware that there is an ongoing and dangerous tendency these days to anthropomorphize AI. In essence, people are assigning human-like sentience to today's AI, despite the undeniable and inarguable fact that no such AI exists as yet.

With that clarification, you can envision that the AI driving system won't natively somehow "know" about the facets of driving. Driving and all that it entails will need to be programmed as part of the hardware and software of the self-driving car.

Let's dive into the myriad of aspects that come to play on this topic.

Self-driving cars are outfitted with a variety of sensors. The sensor suite is used to examine the driving scene. Sensors can include video cameras, radar, LIDAR, ultrasonic units, thermal imagining devices, and the like. The choice of which sensors to utilize is something that varies from automaker to automaker and depends upon the preferences of the self-driving tech firm involved.

The sensors are used to collect data about the driving environment. Within the AI driving system, there are various algorithms and techniques used to detect objects that exist in the driving scene. The use of Machine Learning (ML) and Deep Learning (DL) are frequently being used for image processing and other object detection capacities.

Envision that a true self-driving car is driving along and up ahead there are some zebras.

Presumably, the sensors are feeding gulps of data into the AI driving system. The object detection facilities are mathematically analyzing the data to figure out what objects are being detected. For example, there might be other cars nearby, all of which are objects that hopefully the AI can discern. Likewise, pedestrians standing on the sidewalk are objects that need to be detected.

The first aspect entails discerning the objects are in the driving scene. It would be like you taking a picture with your smartphone camera and then circling all of the objects that you can spy. I'm sure you've played the popular child's game of *I Spy*, wherein you glance outside of the car and try to spot or detect various objects.

Once the objects have been generally delineated, the next step involves classifying the objects. Those blobs over on the sidewalk that seems to have two legs and two arms are likely pedestrians. Those large contraptions on four wheels seem to be cars. And so on.

It can be harder than you might assume to try and categorize detected objects.

Humans generally do a nifty job of categorizing or classifying objects. You see an object and almost immediately are able to classify what it is. Rarely are you be up in the air about the thing you've seen. A light pole is a light pole. A fire hydrant is a fire hydrant. Anybody used to being in an everyday setting is likely to know what the objects represent.

You can get a semblance of how hard classifying can be if you chat with a toddler about what they see around themselves. A young child will be able to tell you what some objects are, and be at a loss for words about other objects. This is the proverbial "what is that?" question that kids will bombard adults with. They are curious to know what unknown objects signify.

Part of the reason to classify objects is so that you'll be aware of what those objects portend.

Once you've ascertained that a light pole is a light pole, you right away can rest easy about the object. I say that because you would normally anticipate that a light pole will remain steady and upright. It isn't going to suddenly and shockingly run out into the street. By classifying an object, you associate a bunch of potential actions and events that can arise related to that object.

Take for example pedestrians. The moment that you realize a pedestrian is a pedestrian, you can gauge a lot of nuances about what might occur in the driving scene. A pedestrian can jaywalk, doing so at any time and for any reason. You need therefore to keep your eye on pedestrians. If they are seemingly staying on the sidewalk, all is okay. Meanwhile, a pedestrian that turns toward the street or darts along is a potential danger that might require an evasive driving maneuver in the quick.

Sometimes you aren't completely sure about the classification that you assign to an object.

Suppose there is a crowd of people at the corner of the street. They are bunched up. Can you be absolutely sure how many people are in there? In fact, someone that has a stroller is obscuring another child standing behind the parent and the stroller. You cannot be fully sure about what you see in this circumstance.

In the case of AI driving systems, the objects are usually assigned a probability associated with whether the object exists or not, along with a probability of what the object represents. We kind of assume that people do the same type of thing.

Let there be no doubt that uncertainty plays a notable role in our world.

Humans need to deal with uncertainty and this rears its ugly head when at the wheel of a car. A car is a multi-ton vehicle with a great deal of power. Misjudgments by human drivers can readily produce car crashes. In the United States alone, there are an estimated 6.7 million annual car crashes, of which produce approximately 2.3 million injuries and sadly 40,000 fatalities.

I've dragged you through this discussion about objects so that you'll be ready to grasp the delicate matter of dealing with footloose zebras.

Earlier, I mentioned that a human driver would be surprised to see zebras whilst driving along a roadway. Unless you lived in a country or locale that had an abundance of zebras and that were commonly meandering around, you would be caught entirely off-guard to suddenly spy some zebras up ahead of you.

The odds are that most of today's AI driving systems would likewise be caught somewhat by surprise, though I don't want to suggest or imply that the AI is "surprised" in an anthropomorphic manner. The surprise is really based on the lack of programming by the developers of the AI driving system being utilized.

Allow me to explain.

Things are quite hectic for those devising AI driving systems and self-driving cars. The primary goal is to make self-driving cars that can drive in our everyday neighborhoods and communities. As such, the AI is shaped around detecting the type of objects you would expect to see on city streets.

Anything else is likely rated as an outlier, oftentimes referred to as an edge or corner case. The notion is that the first place to get the AI figured out involves the core aspects of driving. The oddball or rarer situations can be dealt with later on. Some fervently believe that we are never going to turn the corner on true self-driving cars because there are always more edge cases to be dealt with, as per the so-called long-tail problem.

Bottom-line is that zebras are not likely a fully recognizable or classifiable object by most of today's AI driving systems.

Let me clarify that assertion.

A zebra is certainly detectable as an object, and likely so as an object that has four legs and moves around. But that object is not matchable to its aligned virtual representation if there isn't a defined aspect of zebras inside the AI driving system and its object recognition software.

In essence, act as though you had never seen a zebra in your life. You hadn't seen any pictures of zebras. You hadn't seen them in movies or on TV. Nor did you see any zebras when you visited your local zoo. A zebra is a completely unknown creature to you.

That's what happens when the AI developers decide that getting the AI to recognize zebras is not something worthy of attention right now. The same could be said about recognizing elephants. These are animals that a U.S. traversing AI self-driving car is highly unlikely to encounter and ergo the AI object detection is not trained to gauge.

This though doesn't mean that the AI will ignore the detected object.

There is an object up ahead, and it has four legs. It appears to be moving. The shape of the object and its motions are akin to those of a horse. Most of the AI driving systems are programmed to recognize horses, which makes sense because the chances of at some point encountering horses while driving a car are relatively assured.

I'm not just talking about when driving in remote farmlands where you are bound to come across a horse. There are horses even in the bustling heart of New York City. Some of the horses are used to take tourists around for a festive ride in the major parks via horse-drawn carriages. There are also horses being used by police.

It makes inarguable sense to be able to categorize objects that are discernable as horses.

This takes us back to the medical profession and the catchphrase about horses and zebras.

When it comes to the crafty saying that if you hear hoofbeats then assume they are horses rather than zebras, most of the existing AI driving systems have no other option but to assume that the object is a horse. In that manner of consideration, there is pretty much zero chance of categorizing the object as a zebra.

This will continue to prevail until the developers of AI driving systems decide it is time to incorporate a familiarity about zebras into their wares.

Conclusion

Here's something that you might have been pondering.

Would it make a difference that an AI self-driving car misconstrued a zebra as being a horse?

In the Maryland scenario, the odds are that this faulty categorization would not make any notable difference. The AI driving system probably is programmed to anticipate that a horse could suddenly move this way or that way. As such, the AI is attempting to predict what this kind of object might do next. Whether this is classified as a horse or a zebra is not of substantive consequence, as long as the horse classification comes to bear.

We could reasonably guess that the actions of a horse and the actions of a zebra are approximately the same when it comes to considering how they will react on roadways. The two types of animals might have other fundamental differences such as dietary or other facets, but that isn't especially significant to the act of driving when near them.

Let's wrap up this discussion with some handy lessons learned.

Being at the steering wheel and upon hearing hoofbeats, you can allow yourself some latitude and make a reasoned guess that those are the sounds of a horse.

When you get home and your family asks you if you saw those escaped zebras, you'll undoubtedly be a bit ashamed and chagrined to report that you thought they were horses. You missed your big chance, perhaps once in a lifetime, to drive nearby escaped zebras (please do so cautiously!).

For peace of mind, I'd bet that by the time you read this article, the Maryland zebras will have been adroitly returned to their farm. They will have had an adventure they can delightfully tell their offspring about.

For medical doctors that are working in Maryland, they are probably having a good laugh about those footloose zebras. As a medical professional, after all those years of medical school and being knocked over the head about the zebra aspects, they now had a modicum of insider mirth about it all.

Well, if I somehow end up visiting Maryland and gosh-forbid have something adverse occur such that I need to be hospitalized, I still want them to be thinking about horses, though I'm fine with them also considering zebras to make sure that whatever ails me is getting covered on all the bases. Calling Dr. House, stat.

We've covered this topic extensively and I'd loath to beat a dead horse on it. But I was wondering if those zebras are happy that we are potentially mistakenly classifying them as horses. This might greatly irk them. How in the heck can we not notice those awe-inspiring stripes?

Hey, humans and AI, wake up and get your act together, they collectively exhort. Zebras have a right to be recognized..

CHAPTER 13

ROAD ARGUMENT AND SELF-DRIVING CARS

Two men argued themselves to death.

That phrasing is not meant to be pejorative but serves somberly as a sad indication of what can happen when you remain on the freeway while in or near active lanes after a car crash has occurred.

Here are the details as per the recently reported news story.

Two cars collided while driving on a major freeway in the San Francisco Bay Area. One of the vehicles was a Chevrolet Malibu and the other was a Dodge Durango. For those of you that are familiar with the Northern California freeways, the incident occurred on the I-80 near the Berkeley area.

Both of the cars were stridently damaged, though the drivers and passengers seemed to survive the crash without any substantive injuries. That's something to be thankful for.

To me, any car crash that you can walk away from and not have to immediately go to the emergency room is a cause for relief. Sure, there will be a hassle about the insurance and getting your car repaired, but that pales in comparison to severe injuries or outright fatalities.

Anyway, the drivers of the respective two cars decided to argue about the crash. Their banged-up vehicles were still in an active lane, plus the resultant mashed together mangled mess extended into an adjacent lane. All told, two lanes of this active freeway were now entangled in the collision aftermath.

I'm sure that you must know that the advice by the highway patrol and nearly all motor vehicle agencies is that you should get out of the active lanes as soon as practical. If you can safely move your cars, that's certainly welcomed. On the other hand, even if the cars are unmovable, at least ensure that you and any passengers step clearly out of the active lanes and seek the safety of the shoulder.

This is sound advice that is repeatedly hammered away on the driver licensing tests and that is oftentimes displayed on billboards bordering the freeways. The thing is, sometimes the shock and unnerving reaction to a car crash can cause people to not think fully about what the best course of action might be. Whatever they might have been prior trained on or perhaps previously exhorted to do is not at the top of their minds.

They become fixated on the matter at hand.

In this case, a bit of road rage ensued. The male driver of the Chevrolet Malibu and the male driver of the Dodge Durango opted to argue about the crash. They could have readily gone over to the shoulder to argue to their heart's content. Unfortunately, in the heated passion of the moment, they stood in the active lanes, nearby to the wrecked vehicles.

One supposes that it is readily possible for someone to assume that wrecked cars would be a sufficient form of forewarning to other traffic. You might be looking directly at the battered vehicles and believe that nobody could somehow fail to see the morass. Furthermore, it is conceivable that you might believe that the meshed steel and vehicular parts are a sturdy barrier, such that even if some wayward car comes along and strikes the now-stalled vehicles, you would be protected from harm.

Let's be totally frank about this.

Do <u>not</u> ever assume that other drivers will notice your shattered vehicle.

That type of assumption is a surefire recipe for disaster. You see, there are plenty of drivers on the roadways that are driving while distracted, such as watching cat videos when they should be watching the traffic. Some drivers are intoxicated. They might see the wreck and yet do absolutely nothing to avoid it. And so on.

We can add to the aforementioned advice.

Do not ever assume that your car wreckage will act as a shield and protect you from oncoming traffic.

I know it seems like a logical idea that a smashed vehicle would seem like a useful and sturdy barrier, but this is faulty thinking. You've got to realize that the oncoming cars are moving at high rates of speed. If one of those oncoming vehicles strikes your ball of steel, the odds are that all heck is going to break loose.

By breaking loose, I mean to suggest that the seemingly unmovable wrecked car is bound to be pushed around like a soccer ball. The velocity and impact of a car moving at say 65 miles per hour are tremendous. It can easily scoot that wreck a hefty distance. You must also consider that the steel entanglement is likely to splinter apart, shooting shards in every direction.

Your human body is going to be completely exposed to all of that horrendous and killer-like fragmentation. To recap, you will either get struck by the steel ball that is pushed into you, or you will get splatted with sharp pieces of steel and glass, or you will get run over by the car that has rammed into the car wreckage.

All of those are unpleasant outcomes.

Period, full stop.

I trust that any of you that were otherwise unconvinced are now convinced that the best bet involves getting out of the active lanes. Try to find a safe spot on the shoulder. Admittedly, standing even on the shoulder can be dangerous, especially if you do so within just a few feet of the wrecked cars. Look around and find the safest nearest spot that allows you to remain at the accident scene and yet does not imperil you.

Some people feel guilty about their wrecked vehicle being in an active lane. They worry about other cars ramming into it. Not so much because of their own car getting further busted, but due to a genuine concern for their fellow humans.

This is admirable.

It still does not though justify standing in an active lane. If you can somehow wave or flag oncoming traffic while being safely on the shoulder, yes, this is likely helpful. Generally, you ought to be trying to call for emergency roadway assistance that can come and set up flares or will place their emergency vehicles in a posture to block off the wreckage.

Let the professionals do what they do daily.

Now that we've covered those overall aspects, I have some rather unsettling aspects to tell you about this particular incident and the two arguing men. Maybe skip the next paragraph or so, if you don't want to know the dreadful results of what happened.

A driver in a Mini Cooper came upon the wrecked cars and tried to avoid hitting the wreckage. In so doing, the driver swerved in such a manner that he struck both of the arguing men. Both men were killed. As an aside, per the news, apparently, there was no intoxication involved on the part of the Mini Cooper driver. The follow-on crash of the original crash was seemingly an unfortunate domino effect, as it were.

We can reasonably speculate that if the arguing men had taken refuge on the shoulder, they would still be alive today.

Shifting gears, suppose that the cars involved in the initial crash were not being driven by humans. I know that seems like an odd concept. Anyway, under that scenario, there wouldn't be two human drivers that got out of the vehicles, and nor would there be those two standing in an active lane and arguing about the crash.

What I'm referring to is AI-based true self-driving cars.

Note that there isn't a human driver involved in a true self-driving car. Keep in mind that true self-driving cars are driven via an AI driving system. There isn't a need for a human driver at the wheel, and nor is there a provision for a human to drive the vehicle.

Here's an intriguing question that is worth pondering: *What can the news story of the two arguing men inform us about the advent of AI-based true self-driving cars?*

I'd like to first further clarify what is meant when I refer to true self-driving cars.

Understanding The Levels Of Self-Driving Cars

As a clarification, true self-driving cars are ones that the AI drives the car entirely on its own and there isn't any human assistance during the driving task.

These driverless vehicles are considered Level 4 and Level 5 while a car that requires a human driver to co-share the driving effort is usually considered at Level 2 or Level 3. The cars that co-share the driving task are described as being semi-autonomous, and typically contain a variety of automated add-on's that are referred to as ADAS (Advanced Driver-Assistance Systems).

There is not yet a true self-driving car at Level 5, which we don't yet even know if this will be possible to achieve, and nor how long it will take to get there.

Meanwhile, the Level 4 efforts are gradually trying to get some traction by undergoing very narrow and selective public roadway trials, though there is controversy over whether this testing should be allowed per se (we are all life-or-death guinea pigs in an experiment taking place on our highways and byways, some contend).

Since semi-autonomous cars require a human driver, the adoption of those types of cars won't be markedly different than driving conventional vehicles, so there's not much new per se to cover about them on this topic (though, as you'll see in a moment, the points next made are generally applicable).

For semi-autonomous cars, it is important that the public needs to be forewarned about a disturbing aspect that's been arising lately, namely that despite those human drivers that keep posting videos of themselves falling asleep at the wheel of a Level 2 or Level 3 car, we all need to avoid being misled into believing that the driver can take away their attention from the driving task while driving a semi-autonomous car.

You are the responsible party for the driving actions of the vehicle, regardless of how much automation might be tossed into a Level 2 or Level 3.

Self-Driving Cars And Crashes On Active Roadways

For Level 4 and Level 5 true self-driving vehicles, there won't be a human driver involved in the driving task.

All occupants will be passengers.

The AI is doing the driving.

One aspect to immediately discuss entails the fact that the AI involved in today's AI driving systems is not sentient. In other words, the AI is altogether a collective of computer-based programming and algorithms, and most assuredly not able to reason in the same manner that humans can.

Why is this added emphasis about the AI not being sentient?

Because I want to underscore that when discussing the role of the AI driving system, I am not ascribing human qualities to the AI. Please be aware that there is an ongoing and dangerous tendency these days to anthropomorphize AI. In essence, people are assigning human-like sentience to today's AI, despite the undeniable and inarguable fact that no such AI exists as yet.

With that clarification, you can envision that the AI driving system won't natively somehow "know" about the facets of driving. Driving and all that it entails will need to be programmed as part of the hardware and software of the self-driving car.

Let's dive into the myriad of aspects that come to play on this topic.

First, it is important to realize that not all AI self-driving cars are the same. Each automaker and self-driving tech firm is taking its own approach to devising self-driving cars. As such, it is difficult to make sweeping statements about what AI driving systems will do or not do.

Furthermore, whenever stating that an AI driving system doesn't do some particular thing, this can, later on, be overtaken by developers that in fact program the computer to do that very thing. Step by step, AI driving systems are being gradually improved and extended. An existing limitation today might no longer exist in a future iteration or version of the system.

I trust that provides a sufficient litany of caveats to underlie what I am about to relate.

Probably the most obvious aspect to first address is the ongoing and utterly ridiculous claim by some pundits that self-driving cars will be uncrashable. As crazy as it might seem, there are those inside and outside of the self-driving industry that believes there will never be car crashes involving self-driving cars.

Nutty thinking!

I've repeatedly covered instances of self-driving cars that have gotten into car crashes. It happens. It will continue to happen.

Some assert that once we have our roadways filled with only self-driving cars then we will never have car crashes. Well, that's wishful and falsely fairytale conjecture. In their envisioned Utopia, all self-driving cars will communicate with each other, likely via V2V (vehicle-to-vehicle) electronic communication, and adroitly share our highways and byways. This coordination and cooperation will ensure that no car crashes ever occur again, they contend.

That speculation can be poked full of holes, quite easily. Let's assume that V2V is implemented, doing so for all self-driving cars (no exceptions). You still have the possibility of a self-driving car that suffers a sudden tire blowout. Unless the self-driving cars nearby have kept an appropriate distance, they will get caught off-guard. A car crash could ensue.

Dreamers seem to forget that cars are cars. They have tires. They have mechanical parts that can falter or fail. Etc. Those same dreamers also forget that roadways can have all kinds of misfit actions take place. A boulder topples from a cliff onto the highway. A chair falls off the back of a truck. Zillions of things can go awry.

We also need to consider the practicality (or impractical notion) of somehow having only self-driving cars on our roadways. There are about 250 million conventional cars in the United States today. Those human-driven cars are not going to be summarily and overnight junked when self-driving cars come along. In fact, we don't know that human driving will be brought to a halt. Some resolute drivers insist you will take away their driving privileges the day that you pry their cold dead hands off the steering wheel.

I don't want to wrangle any further herein on this zany proposition that there won't be car crashes involving self-driving cars.

There will be self-driving cars that get into car crashes.

I would tend to agree that this is more likely to happen in the entanglement between a human-driven car and a self-driving car. For example, the somewhat common instance nowadays is that a human driver rear-ends a self-driving car. This can occur because the human driver is following the self-driving car in too close a manner.

It can also happen when a human driver gets exasperated with a self-driving car, which is generally programmed to follow the speed limit and obey the rules of the road. A human driver that is behind a self-driving car is tempted to go around or otherwise try to inspire the self-driving car to get going.

Go ahead and assume that we will have self-driving cars that get into car crashes with human-driven cars. Set aside the matter of which vehicle is at fault. That's a different consideration and one I've covered elsewhere in my columns.

We might first contemplate what the status of the vehicles involved in the car crash consists of. Consider these two distinct circumstances:

- The human-driven car might be movable or might be unmovable due to being severely damaged.
- Likewise, the self-driving car might be movable or might be unmovable due to the damages incurred.

For the human-driven car, a human would need to get into the car and try and drive it out of the way. This is the customary way of doing things today. In the case of the self-driving car, there is unlikely to be any human driver accessible driving controls inside of the autonomous vehicle. This means that no person can simply get into the self-driving car and directly drive it away from the impact zone.

If the AI driving system is still intact, you could potentially try to convince it to move the self-driving car. This is bound to be problematic. You might not have any means to communicate with the AI driving system, assuming that the audio input capabilities got smashed or that the electronic communication via your smartphone is no longer functioning.

You might try contacting the fleet operator that is responsible for the self-driving car and ask them to help out. They too though might not be able to electronically communicate with the crashed self-driving car.

The overall odds are that a self-driving car that has gotten into a car crash is going to be unable to readily self-move itself along. Chances are that the autonomous vehicle will need to be towed or somehow dragged or pushed out of the roadway.

I am about to ask you a simple question and I am hoping upon hopes that I already know your answer.

If you were a passenger inside a self-driving car that got into a car crash and the wrecked autonomous vehicle was stuck in an active lane of traffic, would you stand outside next to the self-driving car?

As per the same advice about a conventional human-driven car, the answer ought to be that you would not stand next to the wreckage and would instead find a safe spot off the freeway and entirely out of the peril of the active lanes. I realize a smarmy person is bound to argue that there might be some rare instances that justify remaining with the self-driving car, including staying inside the vehicle, and though I grant that there probably are some arcane situations warranting this, it is not a viable general rule-of-thumb.

One thing to make abundantly clear is that people can still do things they shouldn't do, albeit during an era of self-driving cars.

For example, let's reuse the arguing men scenario in an updated fashion. A human-driven car rams into a self-driving car. The driver of the conventional car gets out and confronts the passenger that was inside the self-driving car, for which the passenger also gets out and earnestly seeks to confront the human driver.

The passenger of the self-driving car and the driver of the conventional car decide to heatedly argue about the collision. They both stand next to the wrecked vehicles.

What could happen next?

A human-driven car could come along and smash into them. Or smash into the wreckage which then smashes into them.

I'll add a twist that will make your hair stand on end.

A self-driving car comes along that smashes into the arguing humans. Or the self-driving car strikes the wreckage which smashes into them.

I know that this last suggested scenario will immediately be rejected by some pundits. They would exclaim that no self-respecting self-driving car would ever ram into wrecked vehicles on the freeway. Nor would the self-driving car ever strike humans standing on the freeway.

Sorry to say that those pundits are once again entirely out-to-lunch. There is a demonstrative chance of the self-driving car striking the wreckage or possibly directly striking the humans. It all depends upon how fast the self-driving car is going, the roadway conditions at the time, the timing of when the car crash occurred, and so on.

I would be willing to concede that the odds are likely less than the equivalent odds of human drivers that are subject to human foibles such as driving while drinking, driving while distracted, and the like. Those kinds of faulty forms of driving would not be something an AI driving system is going to imbue.

Conclusion

There are a lot more twists and turns on this topic.

Space limitations allow me just a few final remarks for now.

We could have two self-driving cars that crash into each other. I purposely chose earlier to focus on a human-driven car that crashes into a self-driving car. That's a more likely possibility. Nonetheless, there is also a chance of two self-driving cars colliding with each other.

I've got something to say that will undoubtedly raise your eyebrows.

Imagine that there are passengers in each of the two self-driving cars. You would kind of assume that the passengers of the respective vehicles would not try to argue with each other. I mention this because none of them were driving the two autonomous vehicles. We can kind of see the logic of why a human driver wants to argue about a car crash, but the matter of passengers arguing seems nonsensical since none of them had anything to do with the driving itself.

With a heavy heart, I must point out that humans are humans. They often argue. They argue when it might not be sensible to do so.

I can readily envision the passengers of the two self-driving cars deciding to stand outside of the wrecked self-driving cars and have an impassioned and heated debate. Perhaps they are arguing about which self-driving car is at fault. They might be arguing about which of them has the more severe injuries.

They might be arguing about nothing in particular and just darned angry about being in the self-driving cars crash.

My hope is that they would have enough presence of mind to get away from the wreckage and retreat away from the active lanes. This does bring up a potential new feature for self-driving cars.

It would be handy to have a feature built within self-driving cars that tries to warn any humans to step away from a wrecked self-driving car. This might consist of an Alexa or Siri kind of vocalization, telling you to find a safe place to wait for assistance.

Obviously, this feature might have gotten damaged and won't function when the time comes for it to do its thing. I'd wager it would still be handy to have available and ergo be usable in some minor fender benders. Yep, AI ought to do more than just driving the self-driving car. We should be devising AI to be an all-around aid to preserving and protecting mankind, including telling humans to stop arguing when they are neck-deep in peril.

CHAPTER 14
DOOR CRUSH
AND
SELF-DRIVING CARS

A recent news story is nearly unfathomable.

On the other hand, the sadly dire incident is something that could happen to just about any of us and proffers some important hindsight lessons.

First, imagine that you are in your car and decide to fulfill your growling stomach by a quick drive-thru at a local fast-food eatery. It seems like there are drive-thru options galore these days. You can get a hamburger and fries, or a delicious bucket of chicken wings, or scrumptious tacos, etc.

No need to even get out of your vehicle.

All you need to do is drive up to an ordering screen, place your order, drive forward to make payment, and then get your food. After that, you are on your way and only used up perhaps five minutes of your precious time to obtain some desired nourishment (research indicates the average time waiting in line at a drive-thru is about 4.5 minutes).

I'd bet that many of you have found yourself in a somewhat awkward predicament at times when you might be in the drive-thru line and something drops out your driver's side window. It has happened to me numerous times.

For example, when the eatery food server hands me my meal, there is occasionally a faulty handoff involved. The person might drop packets of ketchup or taco sauce that land on the ground, sitting just between my car and the edge of the drive-thru window building. Or at times a straw is dropped. I am usually tempted to open my car door and retrieve the fallen items, especially if it is perhaps my fault for not having grasped them firmly when they were handed over to me.

Usually, the food server says not to worry and that I shouldn't be bothered to try and grab up the fallen items. The person hands over another set and the matter is concluded. You can oftentimes see fallen debris when you are waiting in line and ready to approach the food-providing window. Obviously, these same handoff issues occur with some frequency.

Another variation on this notion is the circumstances involving a car that has a driver-side window that won't open. You might not have seen this in action. On rare occasions, I'll be in line and notice that the car ahead of me is opening its car door. I overhear the driver explaining to the food server that their car door window won't roll down. I'm sure this is a source of embarrassment and certainly makes using a drive-thru a contortionist effort.

Part of the difficulty of opening a car door while in a drive-thru line is that you are usually pinched for space once you get up to the payment or food service window. At that juncture, your car is just a few inches away from the wall of the building. You probably have the most marginal of latitude about opening your car door.

I know this too because I tried to reach out and get some fallen secret sauce packets one time. The food server seemed to be in a rush and I wasn't sure that they would bring me any replacement packets. So, I figured it would be a simple matter of opening my car door to retrieve them.

Darned if my car door slightly banged against the wall. Scratching my car for a few packets of secret sauce was not very astute on my part. Also, I then observed that a pole was situated at the window. I hadn't especially noticed this before. Upon reflection though, I realize that likely others had tried to open their car doors and the manager of the eatery realized it would be prudent to put a post there.

This made things abundantly clear that you would not have sufficient clearance to fully open your car door. The logic was likely too that if a car veered toward the building, the post would prevent the building from getting damaged. The cost to replace a post would assuredly be less than the cost of repairing the wall of the building (and be a much sturdier guard, as it were).

Here's a question for you.

When you reach the payment window or the order receiving window at a drive-thru, do you put your car in Park or do you remain in Drive?

As far as I can tell, it seems like most people continue to keep their car in Drive. You have your foot on the brakes to make sure you remain in a firm position. No need to shift the car into the Park position since you know that momentarily you will be driving away from the eatery. Of course, if it seems that the wait time is going to be excessive, you might decide to prudently put your vehicle into Park.

I suggest this is a prudent action because you can inadvertently readily lift your foot from the brakes and have your car creep or lurch forward. Any long waiting time can increase the odds that you might relax your leg or foot. The safest approach would be to shift into Park. You can then be less anxious about any untoward sudden movement forward.

The normal course of things is that you keep your car in Drive the entire time of the drive-thru trek.

You use your brakes to momentarily come to a halt at the ordering screen. You then continue forward by releasing the pressure on the brake pedal. The car proceeds forward by the axiomatic act of being in Drive. The brakes are used again to come to a stop at the payment window. Easing up on the brakes, you proceed to the order pick-up window. While there, you continue to keep the brakes depressed and await your food.

That's the on-and-off-again effort of driving in a drive-thru, whereby you leave the car entirely in Drive and judiciously use your brakes to come to those periodic and temporary stops or halts. The car is ready to move ahead at all times. Only your overt efforts are keeping that movement in check.

What sometimes catches my eye are those people in line that feel they need to back up for one reason or another. A driver might overshoot the payment window and decide that they need to put their vehicle in reverse. They back up a foot or two. This aligns their vehicle and their car door window with the window of the eatery.

This catches my eye due to the potential danger of the person forgetting that they have their car in reverse. You probably know what I mean by this. The driver is so anxious about backing up that once they get aligned, they merely have their foot on their brakes. Meanwhile, the reverse or backup lights on the rear of their car are still illuminated.

You can plainly see that they are in reverse. What you don't know is whether they realize they are still in reverse. The angst is that they will try to move forward by rapidly using the accelerator pedal, which in turn will cause the car to zip backward towards you.

It is an ominous freak accident just waiting to happen.

Anyway, all told, you can perhaps understand that driving in a drive-thru has a lot more nuances to it than you might otherwise have considered. Believe it or not, some driver training classes include the act of navigating a drive-thru in their on-the-road exercises. This makes abundant sense. A newbie driver ought to learn the ropes of how to best maneuver in a drive-thru.

Using a drive-thru becomes secondary in nature to all of us after a while.

I admit that I've done more than probably my share of eatery drive-thru journeys, though my excuse is that for most of my working career I've made extensive use of my car. Long commutes and having to make vital visits all across town means that there is a lot of time spent inside the vehicle. To minimize any lost time for merely getting food, those fast-food drive-thru operations are a handy-dandy option, that's for sure.

A quirk of fate though led to a recent heartbreaking incident at a McDonald's that is shocking and nearly unimaginable. Though it took place at a McDonald's, the manner of what occurred could happen at nearly any drive-thru anywhere and at any time. For that reason, I am not playing up the McDonald's aspect, which some news reports did.

Consider this as something that any kind of drive-thru operation might incur.

Also, please prepare yourself accordingly for what I am about to describe.

A man was driving in the drive-thru of a McDonald's and came up the payment window. Apparently, his payment card dropped as he was extending it to the clerk. This is certainly unlike dropping a ketchup packet or a straw. Your first inclination would be that you need to pick up your payment card, right away.

He opened his car door and started to reach out to retrieve the payment card that was now laying on the pavement. Unfortunately, as he made this outreach, his foot must have come off the brake pedal.

The car was still in Drive. The vehicle lurched forward.

Skip past the next few paragraphs if you are already queasy about what occurred.

The exterior of the partially open car door rubbed up against the structural portion of the eatery. The car door then sought to swing shut due to the dual shoving forces entailing the car wanting to move forward and being pinned against the eatery. Meanwhile, the driver was leaning out the partially open car door. He ended up getting crushed by the car door as it is being shoved closed by the forces of the structural pinning and the vehicle wanting to move forward. He passed away at the scene.

Words cannot convey the maddening and mindbending consequence of the matter.

A police spokesperson later articulated something that we all know in our hearts, namely that this was a tragic scenario and beyond everyday comprehension. The man was 42 years old. His widow and their son and daughter have set up a fundraising page online. Friends and relatives indicated that he was a doting father and loving husband. He worked as an elevator mechanic.

Some of the news reports pointed out the unusual circumstance of essentially getting killed by one's own car. This was described variously as an extraordinary outlier or as a freak accident.

Though it is decidedly highly unusual, similar instances have been reported in the past. Plus, when you consider how this can happen, it would almost seem surprising that it hasn't happened more often. There you are, in line at a drive-thru, and the tendency is to keep your car in gear the entire time. Anyone that opts to open their car door could do so almost reflexively and not consider the need to put their vehicle in Park.

I suppose none of us expects though to somehow get pinned if their foot does slide off the brake pedal. You would likely assume that you could immediately lean back into your car seat and step on the brakes. It just doesn't seem feasible that you would be unable to prevent the car from moving forward and at the same time get utterly jammed in the partially open car door passageway.

Suppose though that there was no one in the driver's seat. In theory, this would imply that no driver could get themselves into such an untoward posture.

What I'm referring to is AI-based true self-driving cars.

Note that there isn't a human driver involved in a true self-driving car. Keep in mind that true self-driving cars are driven via an AI driving system. There isn't a need for a human driver at the wheel, and nor is there a provision for a human to drive the vehicle.

Here's an intriguing question that is worth pondering: *What can the news story about the unfortunate drive-thru incident inform us about the advent of AI-based true self-driving cars?*

I'd like to first further clarify what is meant when I refer to true self-driving cars.

Understanding The Levels Of Self-Driving Cars

As a clarification, true self-driving cars are ones that the AI drives the car entirely on its own and there isn't any human assistance during the driving task.

These driverless vehicles are considered Level 4 and Level 5 while a car that requires a human driver to co-share the driving effort is usually considered at Level 2 or Level 3. The cars that co-share the driving task are described as being semi-autonomous, and typically contain a variety of automated add-on's that are referred to as ADAS (Advanced Driver-Assistance Systems).

There is not yet a true self-driving car at Level 5, which we don't yet even know if this will be possible to achieve, and nor how long it will take to get there.

Meanwhile, the Level 4 efforts are gradually trying to get some traction by undergoing very narrow and selective public roadway trials, though there is controversy over whether this testing should be allowed per se (we are all life-or-death guinea pigs in an experiment taking place on our highways and byways, some contend).

Since semi-autonomous cars require a human driver, the adoption of those types of cars won't be markedly different than driving conventional vehicles, so there's not much new per se to cover about them on this topic (though, as you'll see in a moment, the points next made are generally applicable).

For semi-autonomous cars, it is important that the public needs to be forewarned about a disturbing aspect that's been arising lately, namely that despite those human drivers that keep posting videos of themselves falling asleep at the wheel of a Level 2 or Level 3 car, we all need to avoid being misled into believing that the driver can take away their attention from the driving task while driving a semi-autonomous car.

You are the responsible party for the driving actions of the vehicle, regardless of how much automation might be tossed into a Level 2 or Level 3.

Self-Driving Cars And Opening Of The Car Doors

For Level 4 and Level 5 true self-driving vehicles, there won't be a human driver involved in the driving task.

All occupants will be passengers.

The AI is doing the driving.

One aspect to immediately discuss entails the fact that the AI involved in today's AI driving systems is not sentient. In other words, the AI is altogether a collective of computer-based programming and algorithms, and most assuredly not able to reason in the same manner that humans can.

Why is this added emphasis about the AI not being sentient?

Because I want to underscore that when discussing the role of the AI driving system, I am not ascribing human qualities to the AI. Please be aware that there is an ongoing and dangerous tendency these days to anthropomorphize AI. In essence, people are assigning human-like sentience to today's AI, despite the undeniable and inarguable fact that no such AI exists as yet.

With that clarification, you can envision that the AI driving system won't natively somehow "know" about the facets of driving. Driving and all that it entails will need to be programmed as part of the hardware and software of the self-driving car.

Let's dive into the myriad of aspects that come to play on this topic.

First, it is important to realize that not all AI self-driving cars are the same. Each automaker and self-driving tech firm is taking its own approach to devising self-driving cars. As such, it is difficult to make sweeping statements about what AI driving systems will do or not do.

Furthermore, whenever stating that an AI driving system doesn't do some particular thing, this can, later on, be overtaken by developers that in fact program the computer to do that very thing. Step by step, AI driving systems are being gradually improved and extended. An existing limitation today might no longer exist in a future iteration or version of the system.

I trust that provides a sufficient litany of caveats to underlie what I am about to relate.

Let's go ahead and assume that there isn't a human at the wheel of a true self-driving car.

This implies that we could never again have an incident involving a human driver that opened a car door whilst at a drive-thru and then inadvertently allowed the car to move ahead, pinning them injuriously or fatally so.

Yes, by definition, that would seem to be the case and we would not ever have that kind of an occurrence.

Case closed.

But wait for a second, other considerations come to the fore.

There could be passengers inside the self-driving car. Those passengers might ask the AI driving system to route the self-driving car through a drive-thru. I've repeatedly predicted that this is going to be a commonly requested driving task and that the programming of the AI driving systems will inevitably and inexorably need to include this particular driving chore (see my column coverage).

Few of today's self-driving cars have this specific driving action capability programmed into them.

As an aside, you might be tempted to assume that if a self-driving car can drive down a neighborhood street and take you to the local grocery that it should ergo be able to navigate a drive-thru operation, easy-peasy. I can see why you might make that assumption.

It is not an assumption though that is worth betting on.

There is a lot of driving finesse involved in a drive-thru.

As earlier mentioned, newbie human drivers can have difficulty at first with this type of driving effort. AI driving systems are not yet able to generalize and use their driving capabilities for a variety of driving settings. By and large, the AI driving systems are programmed for the classic point A to point B kind of driving. This involves using conventional roads and abundantly apparent pathways.

Revisit the prior aspects about driving at a drive-thru.

The autonomous vehicle would need to determine where to stop the car in terms of allowing a passenger to vocalize their order. The AI driving system would need to ascertain when to continue forward. It would need to stop at the right spot at the payment window. It would need to proceed and then stop at the order receiving window. Once the order has been handed over to the passenger, the AI driving system would need to proceed onward with the driving journey.

A smarmy retort is that the passenger could simply tell the AI driving system to start and stop. Yes, that is a possibility. This might be used as a quick-and-dirty stopgap, but will be quite unsatisfying in the long term.

You can almost in your mind envision a comical stage play that this could produce. The passenger says stop and the AI driving system instantaneously does so, perhaps a few feet still away from where the person really wanted the halt to occur. Move ahead a few inches, the person says. The AI driving system complies. Turns out that now the self-driving car is further ahead of the window and the person has to ask the AI driving system to back up.

This would be exasperating.

Now, the smarmy retort to this quandary is that the AI ought to be more flexible and be able to detect where it needs to place the self-driving car. The video cameras of the self-driving car could be used to detect where the ordering screen is. The AI driving system ought to be programmed to position precisely in front of that screen. And so on.

You are absolutely right about that. But realize that the AI needs to be programmed for that purpose. It is either directly programmed by AI developers or might be "taught" via the use of Machine Learning (ML) and Deep Learning (DL).

None of that is an especially high priority for today's automakers and self-driving tech firms. The public and society at large want self-driving cars that can go from point A to point B, safely, and that is the top priority. Dealing with a drive-thru is a low priority in comparison. Some would classify it as an edge or corner case, meaning that it is not at the core of what needs to be put together and can wait until someday in the future to be dealt with.

Set aside for the moment this tangent about getting AI driving systems to cope with drive-thru navigation. Concentrate instead on something related to the entire matter and that has larger importance.

Allow me a moment to properly set the scene.

Suppose a self-driving car is able to drive in a drive-thru and has been prepared for that specialized task. Upon entering the drive-thru line, the self-driving car comes up to the payment window. Who will pay for the food? I know that some of you are yelling aloud that there should be no need to extend a physical payment card to someone at the window. All of this ought to be done electronically. The passenger should order via a smartphone app. The passenger should pay via the app. The only instance of having to open a window would be to receive the food.

I could argue that not everyone is going to convert entirely over to electronic ordering. For many years to come, likely decades, there will still be the manual effort of handing over a payment card. That's reality.

I'll somewhat put that aside and shift attention to getting the food.

I trust that we all agree that this is a moment when the window is going to be opened on the self-driving car. Unless we, later on, have other means to handle the handover of the food, this is the way things will be. As an aside, I've discussed that we will have drones that deliver fast food to self-driving cars, in which case there might be another car-provided portal through which the food would be handed to the passengers.

What I am trying to drag you toward is the possibility that a passenger might want to open the door of the self-driving car.

During the handover of the food, imagine that the mustard packets fall to the floor. The passenger decides they will open the car door to retrieve the fallen packets.

Could this then endanger the passenger?

One supposes that if the self-driving car is still in Drive, and the passenger opens the door, we have a dicey situation in hand. Untoward things could happen.

The obvious solution is that the moment a passenger opens the car door, the AI driving system shifts into Park and stops the autonomous vehicle from moving ahead. Some would even insist that the car doors can never be opened by a passenger unless the AI driving system allows the person to do so.

In essence, some believe that you ought to be locked inside a self-driving car and only be able to open the doors if the AI permits you to do so. This is equivalent to those child locks that are on some of today's cars.

I realize that for many AI developers this is the easiest and best way to solve the problem of the open-the-door issue facing the advent of self-driving cars. Just always keep the doors locked and closed. Only when a person requests will the AI unlock the doors and allow the doors to be opened.

Do you really think that passengers inside self-driving cars are going to be delighted at this kind of stringent approach?

I doubt it.

Being locked inside a self-driving car and having no means of ready exit other than by pleading with the AI driving system is not something that gives much confidence to the average person. The AI might refuse to unlock and allow the doors to be opened. Maybe the AI is right, maybe the AI is wrong. It has no semblance of sentience or common-sense.

Okay, pundits say, the passenger can invoke a remote agent of the fleet that is overseeing the self-driving cars. The remote agent would be able to command the AI to unlock and open the doors.

Whoa, this assumes that an electronic remote communications capability will flawlessly work in any conditions whenever someone wants to get out of the self-driving car. You also need to include the amount of time that this would take. In an emergency, and if you were in dire straits, this option would seem untenable.

Conclusion

I'm using this drive-thru topic to bring up a rather puzzling problem that we are all going to grapple with due to the advent of AI-based true self-driving cars.

Passengers are customarily allowed to open car doors when they are in a human-driven ridesharing vehicle or whenever a human is at the wheel. We take for granted that the human driver will know when passengers ought to be opening doors and when they should not. Presumably, the behavior of passengers is somewhat modulated due to the presence of the human driver.

For an AI self-driving car, there isn't a human at the wheel. This means that there is no longer an obvious and always "supervising" influence inside the self-driving car.

When adults go for a ride in a self-driving car, what latitude should be allowed about being able to open a car door? Some assert that there should be no restrictions whatsoever. Others argue that the lack of some constraints on opening the car door could lead to terrible situations involving passengers that tried to get out when they should not be doing so, such as while on a freeway, etc.

A ton of twists and turns exist on this thorny topic.

For example, what will we do about children that ride alone in a self-driving car and for which no adult is present? I'm sure you are leaning toward insisting that the car doors remain locked and closed. This seems right on the surface of things, but it does have some adverse consequences.

Dealing with car doors is gradually going to become a big thing. We don't give it much thought nowadays. The emergence of true self-driving cars will bring forth this vexing conundrum.

We should be thinking about it now and not wait and act surprised that no one thought of such issues. I am thinking about the matter, as are other insiders, and we need a wider array of input and discussion that will make sure that we do not get caught unawares on what needs to be done.

What seems like a potential outlier matter can have quite alarming consequences.

CHAPTER 15
SNOWBIRDS AND SELF-DRIVING CARS

They migrate seemingly en masse yet distinctly in a onesie-twosie fashion, dong so from the northern colder areas of the U.S. and Canada down into the southern parts of America during the winter months.

You might be thinking that I am talking about some migratory animals such as flocks of birds. Actually, I'm referring to human beings. Yes, people opt to escape the freezing temperatures and scoot down to southern locations in the Sun Belt once the harsh and frigid winter begins to rear its chilly head in ice-cold northern locales.

Snowbirds.

That's the moniker given to this brand of person. The name certainly befits their actions. They fly, drive, walk, and run to get away from the snowy climates of their hometowns. For the otherwise unbearably icy months of winter, the snowbirds set up camp in warm places such as parts of Arizona, Texas, California, and Florida.

When I say that they establish themselves temporarily in southern locations, this widely ranges in terms of formality versus informality.

Some people have a second home in their favored snowbird destination. During the rest of the year the house is pretty much boarded up and unused. They typically have a local contact watch over the property for them. Hopefully, their secondary home remains in a proper and preserved dormant state until the snowbird comes to roost during the winter.

Rather than owning a second home, some snowbirds book a lengthy stay at a resort in their targeted warm spot. Of course, the cost for this luxury can be a bit high. In some cases, the resorts are happy to have the bookings. You see, resorts that usually rely almost entirely on summer bookings and making money only in the hottest months are at times pleased to charge a reasonable rental cost for winter use. On the other hand, there are enough snowbirds and other business-related bookings during the winter that the daily, weekly, and monthly rental fees can often be kept at sky-high rates.

The traditional snowbird is a retiree, often subsisting on a rather constrained budget.

As such, one of the most popular forms of snowbird living consists of using an RV (recreational vehicle). The RV might be kept at home in the northern location for the bulk of the year and then used as a means of transit down to the southern warmer climates. It is a twofer. The RV can be used to get to the desired destination, plus the RV becomes the secondary home while staying in the more accommodating weather.

Massive RV communities of snowbirds can be readily seen in the south during the winter periods. There are RV parks that purposely try to attract snowbirds. The snowbirds are treated like royalty. The influx of the RVs and the spending by the snowbirds can make or break some of these RV housing businesses. In some cases, the RV parks are on wide-open desert or wilderness-like lands that would not have many other money-making possibilities other than serving the RV snowbirds.

In other cases, conventional year-round RV parks get themselves ready each winter for the added arrival of the snowbird RVs. One qualm is that this can lead to RVs packed together like sardines. Those that are always at the RV park are apt to resent the interlopers. That being said, many of the permanent RV residents are overjoyed to have the snowbirds arrive, providing a semblance of quaint freshness and newness for a while (and, then, the perm RVers are comforted by the fact that those interim visitors will ultimately head back out).

These RV communities can seemingly appear and later disappear as though miraculously occurring via the waving of a magic wand. The matter is typically a dramatically seasonal activity. During the time that the snowbirds are in town, all kinds of associated economic benefits get kicked into gear. Restaurants do brisk business. Entertainment venues flourish. And so on.

For many snowbirds, there is a tendency each year to reside in the same place for their escape from the wintry north. This creates familiarity and a type of bonding, sometimes alluded to as being a member of the snowbird family or imbuing the snowbird community spirit. People get to know each other in their warmer locale and become buddies. Snowbird buddies, as it were. This can be exciting. You have the joy of getting reacquainted during those winter months. Familiar faces can make the extended time away from your primary home a lot easier and make for an all-out fun time.

In some sense, the desire to avoid the cold weather is almost an excuse to have a kind of extended vacation. Sure, no one probably prefers having to shovel snow and deal with the problems of those overbearing winter months, but at the same time, they are drawn to the snowbird destination delights as much as getting away from the cold.

I should perhaps also mention that living in cold weather can be adverse to one's health. Retirees are often more susceptible to the dangers of getting overly cold or finding themselves slipping while trying to walk on iced-up sidewalks and streets. A bona fide case can be made that you are potentially doing the right health-related effort when scooting down to a warmer locale for the winter.

Not everyone is entirely elated about those snowbirds. Residents that live in the snowbird destinations are at times quite disturbed by the perceived intruders. Snowbirds are apt to cause local traffic congestion to worsen. This is partially due to the added volume of vehicles on the road in those areas during those packed-in months. It can also arise because the snowbirds do not know their way around the local byways and streets. In short, those snail-paced drivers that make radical turns and seem to do oddball driving are labeled as those darned intrepid snowbirds that ought to go back to where they came from.

Even snowbirds themselves are apt to eschew the snowbird moniker.

When someone in a local area asks if you are a snowbird, you are tempted to insist that you aren't one. A clever relabeling is to refer to yourself as simply a winter visitor. This provides an immediate indication that you acknowledge your visitor status and want to emphasize that you respect the locals and consider yourself fortunate to be amongst them during the winter months.

I mentioned earlier that snowbirds tend to be retirees. This is somewhat a misleading portrayal if you think of retirees as sedate and just lolling around at their snowbird destination. The baby boomers that are in that classification today of retirees are often very active. They want to play golf, tennis and do lots of outdoor walking and hiking. Some like to take on part-time jobs in their snowbird destinations, either to make some added dough or to be active and give back to the local community.

There has also been a rising amount of blogging and vlogging by snowbirds. They are social butterflies that want to share their experiences with the masses. This can be helpful to newbie snowbirds. Many lessons learned from being a snowbird are being conveyed across social media. Out of this comes more snowbirds and likewise more informed snowbirds that are better equipped to be a snowbird.

The latest trend is the emergence of the zoombirds.

You've probably not heard about them. The naming is a clever readaptation of the snowbirds moniker and applies to those that are able to work remotely and that travel to warmer climates during the winter. As you know, the use of Zoom has become associated with being able to do your job remotely and online. Employers are less concerned about where you are living and mainly focused on having online access to you.

If you can arrange to work remotely, you might as well live in a locale that befits your preferences. Thus, many that are not retirees are now finding themselves lured into the snowbird existence. For most of the year, these remote workers are living in the northern areas. Upon the onset of winter, they head down to southern locales just as snowbirds would do.

A key criterion for the zoombirds is that they must end up in a place that has really good Internet connectivity and will allow them to carry on their online work efforts seamlessly. Some RV parks have been caught off-guard by this requirement. Those behind-the-eight-ball RV parks were previously not especially worried about providing top-notch online access and broadband capabilities. Now they are.

On a lighter side about snowbirds, they frequently bring their pets along on their journey.

It would ostensibly be hard to imagine leaving behind your beloved dog or cat while you were frolicking in a warmer climate. Some like to refer to these snowbird accompanying pets as snowdogs and snowcats. I guess if you take your pet bird with you, it would be a *snowbird snowbird* (a droll piece of humor on my part, I must say).

The preponderance of snowbirds (the human ones) tends to be at the wheel of a car or RV for a lot of their snowbird efforts.

They drive a long distance from their primary home to the snowbird destination that they have chosen. Once they've gotten settled in at the destination, they drive around extensively in their new local area. This includes trips to the grocery store, visits with friends at nearby snowbird encampments, touristy types of trips, and the like. Eventually, they have to make that same long drive back to their primary home. Miles upon miles are racked up.

Driving, driving, driving.

The constant and ongoing ordeal of driving can be an onerous chore. You need to keep your wits about you and avoid getting into any car crashes or other maladies. Lots of driving woes can arise. A common aspect is inadvertently going faster than the speed limit and getting ticketed for the transgression. Plus, as earlier stated, your local driving might infuriate other drivers and confound the existing traffic situation.

It sure would be nifty to find a solution for dealing with all that needed driving.

Wait for a second, there is a potential solution that will gradually emerge. I'm referring to AI-based true self-driving cars.

Note that there isn't a human driver involved in a true self-driving car. Keep in mind that true self-driving cars are driven via an AI driving system. There isn't a need for a human driver at the wheel, and nor is there a provision for a human to drive the vehicle.

Here's an intriguing question that is worth pondering: *How might the advent of AI-based true self-driving cars be a sizable benefit and a boon to the snowbirds and the zoombirds?*

I'd like to first further clarify what is meant when I refer to true self-driving cars.

Understanding The Levels Of Self-Driving Cars

As a clarification, true self-driving cars are ones that the AI drives the car entirely on its own and there isn't any human assistance during the driving task.

These driverless vehicles are considered Level 4 and Level 5 while a car that requires a human driver to co-share the driving effort is usually considered at Level 2 or Level 3. The cars that co-share the driving task are described as being semi-autonomous, and typically contain a variety of automated add-on's that are referred to as ADAS (Advanced Driver-Assistance Systems).

There is not yet a true self-driving car at Level 5, which we don't yet even know if this will be possible to achieve, and nor how long it will take to get there.

Meanwhile, the Level 4 efforts are gradually trying to get some traction by undergoing very narrow and selective public roadway trials, though there is controversy over whether this testing should be allowed per se (we are all life-or-death guinea pigs in an experiment taking place on our highways and byways, some contend).

Since semi-autonomous cars require a human driver, the adoption of those types of cars won't be markedly different than driving conventional vehicles, so there's not much new per se to cover about them on this topic (though, as you'll see in a moment, the points next made are generally applicable).

For semi-autonomous cars, it is important that the public needs to be forewarned about a disturbing aspect that's been arising lately, namely that despite those human drivers that keep posting videos of themselves falling asleep at the wheel of a Level 2 or Level 3 car, we all need to avoid being misled into believing that the driver can take away their attention from the driving task while driving a semi-autonomous car.

You are the responsible party for the driving actions of the vehicle, regardless of how much automation might be tossed into a Level 2 or Level 3.

Self-Driving Cars And Snowbirds

For Level 4 and Level 5 true self-driving vehicles, there won't be a human driver involved in the driving task.

All occupants will be passengers.

The AI is doing the driving.

One aspect to immediately discuss entails the fact that the AI involved in today's AI driving systems is not sentient. In other words, the AI is altogether a collective of computer-based programming and algorithms, and most assuredly not able to reason in the same manner that humans can.

Why is this added emphasis about the AI not being sentient?

Because I want to underscore that when discussing the role of the AI driving system, I am not ascribing human qualities to the AI. Please be aware that there is an ongoing and dangerous tendency these days to anthropomorphize AI. In essence, people are assigning human-like sentience to today's AI, despite the undeniable and inarguable fact that no such AI exists as yet.

With that clarification, you can envision that the AI driving system won't natively somehow "know" about the facets of driving. Driving and all that it entails will need to be programmed as part of the hardware and software of the self-driving car.

Let's dive into the myriad of aspects that come to play on this topic.

First, it is important to realize that not all AI self-driving cars are the same. Each automaker and self-driving tech firm is taking its own approach to devising self-driving cars. As such, it is difficult to make sweeping statements about what AI driving systems will do or not do.

Furthermore, whenever stating that an AI driving system doesn't do some particular thing, this can, later on, be overtaken by developers that in fact program the computer to do that very thing. Step by step, AI driving systems are being gradually improved and extended. An existing limitation today might no longer exist in a future iteration or version of the system.

I trust that provides a sufficient litany of caveats to underlie what I am about to relate.

When I refer to self-driving cars, you can reasonably include in that rubric the advent of self-driving RVs.

By and large, the AI driving systems for a car are approximately the same as those for an RV. There are some subtle and yet notable differences, particularly related to the oversized aspects of an RV. You could say that a car is nimbler. For an RV, you have to be more judicious about making lane changes, taking those sharp turns, and otherwise take into account the lumbering nature of being a larger-sized vehicle.

Anyway, the beauty of an AI driving system for snowbirds is that they can sit back and let the AI do the driving for them.

On that lengthy cross-country trip to get to your snowbird destination, the AI will be dealing with all the driving-related stress and angst for you. You can be having fun and start partying right away. No need to be attentive to the roadways. Sleeping or taking a nap is a fully allowed action.

This brings up one potential spurring effect of AI self-driving cars for snowbirds. Whereas a snowbird might be reluctant to drive extended distances when having to sit at the wheel, the AI driving system will go for as far as the snowbird wants to go. This means that the southern locale for your snowbird destination can be even further away than it might otherwise have been.

If you were going only to Arizona for example because the drive to Florida seemed far distant, you can now try out the Florida snowbird destination with ease. Just instruct the AI driving system where you want to go and then let the AI take care of the rest of things for you. No-fuss, no worries.

Snowbirds are likely to be willing to try greater distance locales. They might also find it easier to stay at one place and then try another one. This might normally be exhausting. After having made a tiresome drive from your primary home, you want to get off the road and not make another long drive. With the AI driving system at your command, you can merely select another location and then see how things look once you get there.

In brief, snowbird migration is bound to go up in terms of lengthier distances, along with potentially doing switchovers during the snowbird migration period as a result of the self-driving capabilities.

There will also be an increase in people opting to be snowbirds since the hurdle of having to drive is taken out of the equation. Non-drivers and people that generally have a distaste for having to drive at length will be comforted by the notion that the self-driving vehicle will do that dirty work for them.

Another advantage will be the local driving facets.

A human driver is often unfamiliar with local roads and how to best traverse across town. The AI driving systems are likely to be specially trained for local driving nuances. Upon seeking to go to a local grocery store, the AI driving system will figure out how to get you there and do so with the least amount of disruption to local traffic. Locals will relish this capability.

Furthermore, you don't need to necessarily go along for the ride on those local trips. You can send your self-driving vehicle to do an errand for you. Have it to go to the grocery store and preorder online, such that the clerks at the store will merely load your groceries into the autonomous vehicle and the food will be delivered back to you. Meanwhile, you are out hiking or hitting some golf balls.

We should though include some of the downsides or gotchas that might arise too.

For example, if you are living in your RV, it would seem pretty tough to send it out on a driving errand without you being inside. Your entire secondary home could become possibly errant and wayward, as it were. Of course, the RV should go do the errand and come right back, though this would seem a dicey situation to be in. Anything that happens to your RV means that you are suddenly without a place to live as a snowbird.

Another consideration is that some people love to drive. Yes, some snowbirds are eager to get into the driver's seat and do the driving. Perhaps it is the thrill. Maybe it is the idea of being in command. Regardless of the reason, the point is that there are going to be snowbirds that don't want to have the AI do the driving and will instead insist on doing the driving themselves.

That is a bit of a thorny thicket.

True self-driving cars will likely not have any driving controls that are accessible for a human driver. The belief is that if you include driving controls, people will be tempted to use them. This then suggests that a true self-driving car would sometimes be AI-driven and other times be human-driven. For those that want to reduce the number of car crashes and resultant injuries and fatalities, you need to get humans out of the driver's seat entirely. No waffling about that.

There are some drivers today that exhort you will never get them to give up their driving. You will need to pry their cold dead hands from the steering wheel before they stop driving. Snowbirds that have that mindset are probably not going to be especially enamored about self-driving capabilities.

One supposes that you might have a human-driven RV and tow along with a self-driving car that you would use during your winter stay at a snowbird park. Or, maybe the reverse of that. You might have the RV be self-driving and then tow along a human-drivable car that you would use at your snowbird park.

Generally, it assuredly seems that most snowbirds would welcome the self-driving capabilities and be happy to not have to do any of the driving themselves. I'd bet inevitably this will be the predominant viewpoint.

Conclusion

We should also ponder the interests of the zoombirds.

They would seemingly relish the self-driving aspects. I say this because they can be working while amid a driving journey.

Instead of "wasting" time at the wheel, the zoombirds can be using their laptops, smartphones, and otherwise engaged in work activity during any of their road trips. The odds are that self-driving cars will be outfitted with high-speed connectivity. Passengers can tap into that facility and undertake Zoom-like live interactions at any time, including while on lengthy highways and byways.

There are a lot more twists and turns on this overall topic.

For example, I earlier mentioned that snowbirds often bring along their pets. Having a self-driving vehicle is handy when you think about the myriad of pet-related chores. You can put your beloved animal in a self-driving car and have them taken to the local vet. You might decide to send your dog to visit with nearby friends while you are on a golf outing. And so on.

There's more.

While on your snowbird trek, relatives and acquaintances might want to come and visit you. They would seemingly be more inclined to do so if self-driving cars were available. They load the family into a self-driving car and head over to see the snowbird encampment that you are at.

Endless possibilities.

All of this showcases how mobility will change due to self-driving and autonomous vehicles. Pundits are describing a new era known as mobility-for-all. Once mobility becomes cheaper, easier, friction-free, and plentiful, our behavior as to how we live, where we live, and what we do is bound to be changed too.

Perhaps I've whetted your appetite about becoming a snowbird or a zoombird.

Now, all we need is the self-driving advent to emerge.

CHAPTER 16
TODDLER SAVED AND SELF-DRIVING CARS

A driver did the right thing the other day and saved the life of a meandering toddler.

Per recent news reports, a driver in Virginia noticed that a little girl was getting dangerously close to the roadway. The toddler was pushing a child's toy stroller and had a stuffed animal inside the petite carriage. She and her comforting companion (the stuffed animal) appeared to be in their own playful world, enjoying a casual frolic outdoors and not mindful of the cars, buses, and trucks whizzing nearby.

There didn't seem to be any parental supervision in the proximity of the unfolding and altogether ominous calamity.

The cute youngster might have been so distracted by her stroller and her beloved stuffed animal, and equally unaware of the perils of being in traffic that she might have veered directly into the pathway of lumbering vehicles. We don't know if other drivers would have noticed her. The worst outcome could have occurred, namely, an unthinkable collision could have arisen.

Let's not go there.

Instead, we can relish that a driver decided to stop his vehicle and take quick action. He was already wearing a neon vest since he was driving a bus. Upon stopping the bus to try and block traffic, he then scooted out and waved at oncoming drivers to maneuver over and out of the way. Meanwhile, he scurried over to the girl and guided her to safety.

He and another good Samaritan proceeded to walk with the girl on a door-to-door basis in the neighborhood to see if they could reunite the wayward girl with her family. They were able to do so.

A happy ending ensued in that the toddler and her stuff animal with stroller were all preserved and averted a serious and somber outcome. One can only hope that the parents will take this as a blissful lesson and ensure that the toddler does not get into such a predicament again.

Would you have stopped your vehicle to aid the youngster?

I'm assuming that nearly all of us would absolutely do so.

Perhaps that is overly optimistic. I realize that you can argue about whether or not taking such action was entirely warranted per se.

I mention this because the child wasn't yet fully into the street. She was nearing that dire position. It would be easy to have assumed that she would not go directly into the roadway. Perhaps her instincts would prevent her from doing so. She might have also been taught to stay out of the street. All of those are distinct possibilities.

The question entails when do you decide that enough is enough. Is it sufficient that the child appeared to be aiming toward the roadway? Or do you believe that until an actual entry into the street occurs is there nothing out of the ordinary to be done?

You can't seemingly stop at all points in time and places that you suspect someone is going to potentially mistakenly go into the street. You would never make any driving progress. That doesn't seem like a practical everyday solution.

Whoa, the retort goes, this was just a toddler, perhaps around no older than 3 years old (per the estimate of the heroic driver). If you see a toddler that is wandering on their own, diverging toward the street, and assuming that you don't observe anything that will prevent a doomsday outcome, you have to take action. Come on, the lament goes, show some compassion and common sense. This is ostensibly a rather unique situation that necessitates that type of boldness.

Let's recast the scenario and pretend that a parent had been nearby.

In that case, you might have frantically waved at the parent or honked your horn to alert the presumably distracted or otherwise preoccupied adult. That would be the first step of action. You would not have anticipated that you would need to get out of your vehicle entirely. Assuming that the parent still seemed to be lacking in care, you might certainly bring your vehicle to a complete stop.

And at that point, as a final act of heroism, possibly get out to somehow more directly get the parent to watch out for the child, only as a final step of exasperation and concern.

Maybe the parent would be irritated and upset that you intervened. The toddler was just fine, the parent might insist. This is none of your darned business. Of course, had you not stopped and not proffered assistance, and if the toddler had gotten into the street and injured, you would forever be alarmed that you didn't take overt action. Perhaps the parent might even accuse you of not having made an attempt to alert them about the impending catastrophe.

But returning to the actual situation, we know that there wasn't a parent or any adult within reach.

In that circumstance, another question that arises is whether you would notice that the child was indeed alone.

Think about that for a moment. You are driving your car, minding your own business. You are watching the other cars. You are watching the trucks and buses. You are watching bike riders. There is a lot to keep your attention riveted to the roadway.

You glance at the sidewalk and take notice of obvious instances of endangerment. For example, a dog that is on the loose and running directly for the street. That would probably catch your eye. You might spy a jogger that is wearing a headset and seems oblivious to the traffic conditions. If that person, even if an adult, suddenly turns as though they are going to enter into the street, I'd bet that would cause you consternation and you would definitely notice the adverse action.

There are zillions of instances of pedestrians on the sidewalk that might not especially put you on alert. You cannot be watching and mentally tagging every nuance of the sidewalk activity. Doing so would seem to distract you from the traffic itself. No sense in ramming into another car simply because you are preoccupied with whatever is happening up on the sidewalk.

In short, we have some drivers that might not have noticed the little girl at all.

Yes, that's totally feasible.

Envision that we somehow did an experiment and stopped those cars further down the street. We might ask the drivers; did you see that toddler on the sidewalk? Some percentage will say that they didn't, and some of those might insist that there wasn't a child anywhere in the vicinity (claiming, defensively, that you are making it up, trying to fool them).

That is one segment of drivers.

Another segment might have noticed the little girl but had not noticed the absence of an adult being present. Again, envisioning a kind of experiment, we would likely find that those drivers assumed that a parent must be nearby. In their minds, a child on the sidewalk is almost always accompanied by an adult. The adult must have been there. Some of those drivers will *reluctantly concede* that they didn't see an adult, while others might exhort that there was an adult there and you are lying that an adult wasn't present.

This is all the stuff of human behavior.

Let's try another variant.

There might be drivers that noticed the little girl, plus observed explicitly that no parent was around, but these drivers did not deduce that the girl was heading toward the street. It would be easy to merely have subliminally acknowledged the toddler and yet not placed the matter onto any kind of driving priority list in your noggin. The toddler wasn't acting outrageously or doing anything that would create abundant attention.

Those drivers would probably, later on, reflect upon the situation and kick themselves for not having stopped. They would replay the moment in their minds, revisiting the aspect that the child was alone and nearing the street. Most of those drivers would probably feel sick to their stomach about not having done anything. Some would proffer an excuse that they were preoccupied with some work-related matters or personal troubles that allowed them to let the toddler situation seem distant and inconsequential at that moment.

Well, welcome to just another day of driving. You never know what drivers are going to notice. You don't know what is on their minds. Some drivers are highly attentive. There are drivers that are distracted. You've got all kinds of drivers, good and bad, considerate or abrasive, and so on.

The list is nearly endless.

Furthermore, the act of driving is one that plays out over time. This means that a driver might not be distracted at one instant of time, and then seconds later be deep in thought and become distracted. You would be hard-pressed to say that a driver was always one way or another.

That being said, let's be honest and agree that there are drivers that are more prone for example to being distracted drivers. Someone that routinely glances at their smartphone while at the wheel of a car is more likely to be predominantly and continually distracted. A driver that almost never looks at their smartphone would be less so a distracted driver (at least with respect to the smartphone aspects), though they too might become distracted when the smartphone rings and suddenly draws their awareness.

Are there ways to cope with the human foibles of drivers?

Yes, there are.

Perhaps the most all-encompassing solution is to obviate the need for human drivers all told. In other words, excise the role of human driving and you presumably and by definition no longer have to cope with the failings of human drivers since there aren't any human beings sitting in the driver's seat.

Seems pretty straightforward and indisputable.

This is a perfect segue into talking about those emerging AI-based true self-driving cars.

Note that there isn't a human driver involved in a true self-driving car. Keep in mind that true self-driving cars are driven via an AI driving system. There isn't a need for a human driver at the wheel, and nor is there a provision for a human to drive the vehicle.

Here's an intriguing question that is worth pondering: *What can the heroic tale of the driver that saved the toddler and the stuffed animal inform us about the advent of AI-based true self-driving cars?*

I'd like to first further clarify what is meant when I refer to true self-driving cars.

Understanding The Levels Of Self-Driving Cars

As a clarification, true self-driving cars are ones that the AI drives the car entirely on its own and there isn't any human assistance during the driving task.

These driverless vehicles are considered Level 4 and Level 5 while a car that requires a human driver to co-share the driving effort is usually considered at Level 2 or Level 3. The cars that co-share the driving task are described as being semi-autonomous, and typically contain a variety of automated add-on's that are referred to as ADAS

(Advanced Driver-Assistance Systems).

There is not yet a true self-driving car at Level 5, which we don't yet even know if this will be possible to achieve, and nor how long it will take to get there.

Meanwhile, the Level 4 efforts are gradually trying to get some traction by undergoing very narrow and selective public roadway trials, though there is controversy over whether this testing should be allowed per se (we are all life-or-death guinea pigs in an experiment taking place on our highways and byways, some contend).

Since semi-autonomous cars require a human driver, the adoption of those types of cars won't be markedly different than driving conventional vehicles, so there's not much new per se to cover about them on this topic (though, as you'll see in a moment, the points next made are generally applicable).

For semi-autonomous cars, it is important that the public needs to be forewarned about a disturbing aspect that's been arising lately, namely that despite those human drivers that keep posting videos of themselves falling asleep at the wheel of a Level 2 or Level 3 car, we all need to avoid being misled into believing that the driver can take away their attention from the driving task while driving a semi-autonomous car.

You are the responsible party for the driving actions of the vehicle, regardless of how much automation might be tossed into a Level 2 or Level 3.

Self-Driving Cars And The Toddler With The Stroller

For Level 4 and Level 5 true self-driving vehicles, there won't be a human driver involved in the driving task.

All occupants will be passengers.

The AI is doing the driving.

One aspect to immediately discuss entails the fact that the AI involved in today's AI driving systems is not sentient. In other words, the AI is altogether a collective of computer-based programming and algorithms, and most assuredly not able to reason in the same manner that humans can.

Why is this added emphasis about the AI not being sentient?

Because I want to underscore that when discussing the role of the AI driving system, I am not ascribing human qualities to the AI. Please be aware that there is an ongoing and dangerous tendency these days to anthropomorphize AI. In essence, people are assigning human-like sentience to today's AI, despite the undeniable and inarguable fact that no such AI exists as yet.

With that clarification, you can envision that the AI driving system won't natively somehow "know" about the facets of driving. Driving and all that it entails will need to be programmed as part of the hardware and software of the self-driving car.

Let's dive into the myriad of aspects that come to play on this topic.

First, it is important to realize that not all AI self-driving cars are the same. Each automaker and self-driving tech firm is taking its own approach to devising self-driving cars. As such, it is difficult to make sweeping statements about what AI driving systems will do or not do.

Furthermore, whenever stating that an AI driving system doesn't do some particular thing, this can, later on, be overtaken by developers that in fact program the computer to do that very thing. Step by step, AI driving systems are being gradually improved and extended. An existing limitation today might no longer exist in a future iteration or version of the system.

I trust that provides a sufficient litany of caveats to underlie what I am about to relate.

We can use the toddler situation as fodder for discussing what today's AI driving systems are seemingly capable of. This is a useful means of gleaning the weaknesses and potential strengths of using AI driving systems, albeit with my earlier caveats still being kept in your mind.

Would a true self-driving car detect a toddler on the sidewalk that is pushing a stroller of which contains a stuffed animal?

That's an interesting question.

Self-driving cars are outfitted with a variety of sensors. The choice of sensors to be included is up to the automaker and self-driving tech firm. Generally, you can expect that the sensor suite would include video cameras, radar, LIDAR, ultrasonic units, thermal imaging devices, and the like.

I'll go out on a limb and declare that it is likely the sensors would indeed detect an object on the sidewalk that was the toddler. There would be a blob of a child-like shape, along with a blob that is the stroller. The chances of determining that the stroller is a stroller are less likely. The odds of figuring out that the child is a child is somewhat higher, all else being equal.

My point is that the data collected by the sensors is merely data. The AI driving system has to try and analyze the data to find recognizable patterns. Of those patterns, the AI driving system can then categorize or classify what is found by the sensors. One would reasonably assume that most of the self-driving cars are doing sufficient pattern matching via Machine Learning (ML) and Deep Learning (DL) to determine that the blob that has two little legs and two little arms and a head is a child.

This is actually a lot harder to computationally calculate than you might assume.

A misclassification could easily be performed. There are potential false positives and false negatives that can be computed.

Also, a classification usually has a probability associated with the matter. For example, the blob might be categorized as a child, based on a probability of 85% chance that this is a correct estimation. Note that means that the classifier is not absolutely affirming the categorization and instead basing the result on probabilities and uncertainties.

Okay, we will focus on the toddler, and for now, we'll ignore the stroller. The stroller is likely considered an unknown blob that seems to be attached to or somehow associated with the categorized blob of the child. The nature of this unknown blob is unknown, but it appears to accompany the child wherever it goes.

I'll toss a bit of a twist at you. A human would presumably instantly realize that the stroller is a stroller. Also, it is a reasonable assumption that a human adult driver would know what a stroller is and what can be done with it.

Allow me a tangent to explain.

The toddler could presumably push the stroller toward the street and let go of the stroller as she does so. In that case, the child might remain on the sidewalk. Meanwhile, the child has sent the stroller as a kind of unguided missile into the traffic. A human would know that this could happen. Few of the existing AI driving systems have that kind of "reasoning" capability.

You see, one of the biggest challenges and qualms about being able to achieve true self-driving cars is that we have a huge unresolved form of human reasoning that commonly is referred to as common sense. Numerous efforts have been made to devise AI that can reason in a common-sense fashion. These unfortunately are not anywhere close to attaining human levels.

Back to the mainstay of the elicitation.

The AI driving system has likely calculated that the child is a child, but has no particular semblance about the blob that is the stroller. Via the sensors, we'll suppose that the pace and direction of the child are being observed as moving toward the street. The prediction portion of the AI driving system is likely to calculate that the child is on a dire course toward the street and a potential intersecting path of the self-driving car.

Here's the part that might get your goat, as it were.

By and large, most of the AI driving systems are focused on whatever might be an endangerment to the self-driving car. Does the child pose a danger to the self-driving car in terms of possibly colliding with the self-driving car?

If the answer is yes, the AI driving system will begin to perform whatever evasive maneuvers have been programmed for avoiding striking objects, including and in specific a person as a type of object in this instance.

If the answer is no, namely that the child would not be an endangerment to the self-driving car, the AI driving system is likely to be programmed to simply carry on with the driving task. In essence, suppose that the AI driving system computed that at the speed of the autonomous vehicle and its direction, it was not feasible for the child to end up in the street and be in front of the self-driving car.

That means that there isn't any danger associated with a potential collision. Thus, keep driving. There is nothing else here to be done. It is like the famous *Star Wars* aspect of Yoda saying look away since there is nothing here to be seen.

I assume you realize the gaping problem with that kind of assumption. Sure, the self-driving car might scoot on past without any troubles. At the same time, the child might veer into the street just after the self-driving car has passed by, and the car behind the self-driving car might strike the wayward child.

In one sense, you could argue that some human drivers would do exactly the same thing in that they would opt to drive past the child and do nothing about the matter unless they believed that their car was going to collide with the toddler.

I don't think we would hold such a person up as a model citizen per se.

Do we want our self-driving cars to drive in that manner?

That's the million-dollar or more like a billion-dollar question, based on the millions and billions of dollars so far expended toward the attainment of self-driving cars.

Conclusion

There are a lot more twists and turns on this topic.

Due to space limitations, I'll just offer a few closing remarks for now.

Suppose that the AI driving system did opt to stop the autonomous vehicle. This might be done to try and avert striking the child. It might also be done to try and block upcoming traffic that is behind the self-driving car. All in all, the self-driving car could be a kind of shield.

That's what the bus driver did.

Of course, the bus driver also got out of his vehicle, flagged at other traffic to get those other drivers to slow down and move over, plus he then guided the child away from the street.

There isn't any driver in a self-driving car to do any of those actions. Until the day that we end up with robots that can drive, which is something

One supposes that the AI driving system could alert authorities by sending out an electronic message. The police might then arrive to aid in the situation. That seems sensible, though consider the time crunch involved. By the time the authorities arrive, it could already be too late, sadly so.

Another possibility is that if a passenger is inside the self-driving car, the passenger might realize what is taking place and rush out of the autonomous vehicle to take care of things. But we don't know that a passenger will always be inside a self-driving car, and indeed the expectation is that self-driving cars will be roaming around a lot of the time with no passengers.

Having a human at the wheel is pretty handy in a situation of this nature. The human can be both a driver and act in other ways too, such as a hero that rescues an unaware and unsupervised toddler. Not all drivers would do this, of course, and you could therefore argue that the AI self-driving car fits into that percentage of circumstances.

We also have the foibles of human drivers that need to be taken into account. Humans are both a benefit and a drawback when residing in the driver's seat. Getting rid of human driving and replacing the driving action with an AI driving system will provide some benefits but will also engender some drawbacks.

Let's end this on a pleasing and altogether happy note.

We now know that there is a toddler that is alive today due to the heroism of a driver that opted to do the right thing. This particular toddler might be our future, *as it were*, growing up and someday be perhaps the inventor, discoverer, or AI developer that devises a level of AI that can embody common-sense reasoning and perform amazing acts that only humans today can do.

She and her stuffed animal could make the world a better place. Thank goodness that she survived that moment of dire consequences as a toddler and lived to achieve such greatness.

I assuredly like that outcome.

CHAPTER 17
APPLE HITS CURB AND SELF-DRIVING CARS

Have you ever been driving and perchance struck a curb?

I'm sure that you've experienced that gut-wrenching sorrowful moment.

So did an Apple self-driving car that was recently out and about in Silicon Valley during an autonomous driving journey.

To clarify, the AI autonomous driving system was presumably not gut wrenched and nor sorrowful, which would be an over-the-top anthropomorphic overlay (i.e., attributing human emotions to the AI), but it did indeed strike a curb and it did indeed lead to some minor vehicular damage (note that the damage was just to the self-driving car itself and reportedly not to any other vehicles or obstacles).

The Apple self-driving car curb strike occurred on a Monday.

I suppose we all know that Mondays seem to be the one day of the week upon which adverse driving incidents seem to customarily rear their ugly head. For human drivers, it is usually due to having had a ruckus of a weekend and being a bit mind-dulled upon heading back to work for the week ahead. That doesn't seem to befit the Apple self-driving car instance and we can perhaps put to the side any Monday blues considerations.

Before getting further into the Apple self-driving car run-in with the curb, let's take a moment to reflect upon the classic matter of curb striking. Some also internationally refer to this as "kerb" striking, but I prefer the more conventional use of the word curb per se.

Envision yourself at the wheel of your car.

Imagine that you are coming up to make a tight right turn and you miscalculate the positioning of your car. As you begin to round the turn, all of a sudden the rightmost tires rub up against the curb. The car shudders as it skims across the edge of the curb. You probably feel the steering wheel slightly go ajar as the vehicle is getting pinned between a rock and a hard place.

The impact with the curb will be stridently felt depending upon such factors as the speed of the car, the angle of the striking posture, the stiffness and resiliency of the curb, the height of the curb, and so on. These all come to play regarding the physical forces that will jolt you and your vehicle.

After completing the turn, you know in the recesses of your mind that you might have caused some untoward damage to your car. The vehicle is still moving along and you don't hear any dreadful sounds coming from the side of the tires. That means that you probably didn't shred the tires and nor completely knock out the side panels or otherwise cause grievous harm to your precious vehicle.

Nonetheless, the odds are that you've done some amount of damage to the car. There could be some lacerations to the sidewall of the tires that came in harsh contact with the curb. The tire valve stem might have been hammered and now is slowly leaking air.

Assuming that the tires survived without much harm, the likeliest next concern is that your steering facility and suspension components are demonstrably askew.

Think of misaligned tire rods, struts, and the like. When you have such issues, including wheel misalignments, you might not immediately realize the dangers that lurk within. You could end up further down the road and surprisingly find that you cannot properly steer the car, thus upon taking a subsequent turn the vehicle is nearly uncontrollable or at least is not well responding to your steering efforts and could become deviously and insidiously problematic.

You would be wise to have your car examined by a versed mechanic to identify any vehicular internal damages. Make sure to get the car repaired as needed.

Besides the potential harm to your car, there is something else that you might need to consider but that I doubt you would normally have put much thought toward.

Here in California, the DMV (Department of Motor Vehicles) has stipulated via their stridently published Vehicle Code (VC), a provision known as VC 22100 that imposes a penalty for making improper turns. Yes, that's right, you can get into trouble for striking a curb since doing so is construed as an improper turn.

You see, the Vehicle Code says that drivers need to make a right turn as close as possible to the right-hand curb or the right edge of the roadway. That being said, there is a difference between being close to the curb and actively striking the curb.

A driver that manages to do a tight right turn and perchance sweeps into the curb is making an improper turn. You can get a ticket for this infraction. Even though you didn't hit anyone or otherwise cause any outward damages, this can still get you a point against your driving record and you risk ultimately scoring enough points to come under the negligent motorist license suspension. There is also a modest financial penalty, typically around $238 or so for the making of an improper turn.

I mention the legal mumbo jumbo about hitting a curb to proffer a bit of an explanation for why the Apple self-driving car that struck a curb was then somewhat compelled to be reported upon by Apple. I bring this up because some pundits have been surprised that Apple owned up to the incident. Those pundits figured that if the Apple self-driving car did not hit anything else other than the curb, this is a get out of the jail-free situation and Apple could have just pretended that it never happened.

Thus, those (with all due respect) ill-informed or ill-outspoken pundits that speculate on such matters were dumbfounded that Apple officially reported the matter. Just don't say anything and nobody would know, that's what some have been suggesting.

Hide the matter under the rug.

That would be pretty stupid and have inevitably undermined the totality of the Apple self-driving car efforts.

Here's why.

You need to have some context about the self-driving realm.

The California DMV Autonomous Vehicles branch established an Autonomous Vehicle Tester (AVT) Program in 2014. This allows for the testing of autonomous vehicles on active public roadways and doing so with or without having a human driver in the driver's seat.

As background, there are essentially two major ways to test a self-driving car on public roadways.

One is via having a so-called safety driver that is at the wheel of the self-driving car during the entire time that the autonomous vehicle is driving around. The backup human driver is supposed to be closely monitoring the driving effort and be ready to instantly takeover the wheel as needed (these are typically referred to as "disengagements" in the parlance of this industry).

Those that want to test their autonomous vehicles on the public roads in California, usually file for and get granted a permit to do so while also ensuring that a human driver is at the wheel as a means of taking over from the AI driving system. There are 53 such AVT "with driver" permits currently issued.

Meanwhile, once an automaker or self-driving tech firm believes their self-driving car is ready to advance into the next stage, they apply for and potentially receive a permit to do AVT on the public roadways without the use of a human backup driver at the wheel. There are currently only 8 such "without driver" or driverless permit holders here in California.

A stated requirement for all of those autonomous vehicles is this important proviso: "Manufacturers need to report any collision that results in property damage, bodily injury, or death within 10 days of the incident."

If an automaker or self-driving tech firm that is operating under a permit fails to comply with this provision, they presumably would have their permit revoked. This would indicate that they can no longer legally proceed to have their self-driving cars on public roadways. They would have to reapply. But it seems doubtful that a reapplication would receive ready approval if the automaker or self-driving tech firm had failed to earlier and properly report an incident that required reporting.

You would likely have quite an uphill battle to try and get reinstated.

In short, it would be like shooting your own foot. By having failed to report an incident, you risk not just getting knocked out of the game, for now, you might find it arduous if not impossible to, later on, get back into the game. For anyone seriously trying to advance their self-driving car project, being unable to actively practice having your autonomous vehicles on the public roadways would ostensibly put your project out of sorts and potentially at a kind of dead-end (well, at least to the extent of tryouts in that particular state).

Though striking a curb might seem like an innocuous matter, a decision to not report such an incident when there was in fact property damage done (in this case, damage to the autonomous vehicle) would have larger repercussions far beyond the mere incident itself. The prudent thing to do would be to go ahead and file an official report.

Not wanting to beat a dead horse, but if the pundit's advice was followed, namely do not report the rather bland or inoffensive circumstance, here's what could arise. First, someone would likely have seen the incident and possibly report it. Or, there is a chance that an internal whistleblower might bring it to light.

Once word leaked out about the matter, you can bet that the whole thing would be blown entirely out of proportion. Any company caught in such a perilous mode would be accused of hiding a material fact about their self-driving car operations. A scandal would certainly brew. Finger-pointing would take place. Who knew and when did they know? The story would blossom and become as big as if something truly outrageously dastardly had occurred.

Not a pretty picture.

The astute thing to do is report the incident and move on. Few would likely notice it. Of those that noticed it, they would have to note that the situation was no more than a curb strike. And, on top of that, the incident was dutifully reported and the rules of the AVT Program were abided with.

End of story.

Well, that's the end of the story portion about reporting the incident.

We can though perhaps glean some fascinating aspects from the curb strike. Before doing so, I'd like to set some foundation for what I mean when referring to self-driving cars.

Understanding The Levels Of Self-Driving Cars

As a clarification, true self-driving cars are ones that the AI drives the car entirely on its own and there isn't any human assistance during the driving task.

These driverless vehicles are considered a Level 4 and Level 5 while a car that requires a human driver to co-share the driving effort is usually considered at a Level 2 or Level 3. The cars that co-share the driving task are described as being semi-autonomous, and typically contain a variety of automated add-on's that are referred to as ADAS (Advanced Driver-Assistance Systems).

There is not yet a true self-driving car at Level 5, which we don't yet even know if this will be possible to achieve, and nor how long it will take to get there.

Meanwhile, the Level 4 efforts are gradually trying to get some traction by undergoing very narrow and selective public roadway trials, though there is controversy over whether this testing should be allowed per se (we are all life-or-death guinea pigs in an experiment taking place on our highways and byways, some contend).

Since semi-autonomous cars require a human driver, the adoption of those types of cars won't be markedly different than driving conventional vehicles, so there's not much new per se to cover about them on this topic (though, as you'll see in a moment, the points next made are generally applicable).

For semi-autonomous cars, it is important that the public needs to be forewarned about a disturbing aspect that's been arising lately, namely that despite those human drivers that keep posting videos of themselves falling asleep at the wheel of a Level 2 or Level 3 car, we all need to avoid being misled into believing that the driver can take away their attention from the driving task while driving a semi-autonomous car.

You are the responsible party for the driving actions of the vehicle, regardless of how much automation might be tossed into a Level 2 or Level 3.

Self-Driving Cars And A Curb Strike

What can we infer from the aspect that an Apple self-driving car managed to recently strike a curb?

In one sense, it is quite a telltale clue, perhaps surprisingly so. We shall take a moment to explore the nature of the reported matter and then seek to unpack it.

According to the officially self-reported indication, the incident occurred on Monday, September 27, 2021, at 10:53 a.m. in the morning. The Apple self-driving car being used was their sensor-laden Lexus RX 450h and was a 2017 model. If you've not seen these vehicles, they are chockful of an avid outcropping of sensors such as video cameras, radar devices, LIDAR devices, and the like.

I see them quite often, roaming around the Silicon Valley area, along with the numerous other self-driving cars by other competing makers. You might think it would be shocking to see a self-driving car, but after a while, their presence almost seems mundane. I've reported previously that local human drivers have gotten so accustomed to self-driving cars that some drivers aim to bully or play tricks on the self-driving cars.

Don't do that. You are playing with fire and could cause quite untoward results. Enough said.

Let's continue our exploration.

The Apple self-driving car was in the city of Sunnyvale and relatively nearby to various Apple buildings and an Apple campus site. There was some mild atmospheric cloudiness but otherwise, it was daylight, the roadway was dry, and no other unusual roadway conditions existed (such as if there had been loose gravel, or debris, or potholes, etc.).

It is worthwhile to keenly note the *driving context* (per the parlance of the self-driving industry, this is akin to the Operational Design Domain or ODD aspects).

For example, suppose the roadway was slick from rain. That could assuredly affect how the self-driving car would perform. Likewise, suppose it was nighttime and the darkness might somewhat "hide" the appearance of a curb or other roadway structures. Suppose the roadway was torn up and the tires were unable to have suitable traction. And so on.

In this case, it was pretty much a normal day here in late September in the Bay Area, relatively sunny with some cloud cover, predominantly dry roads (we don't get much rain at this time of the year), and the like.

The Apple self-reported description of the incident is this: "A test vehicle, operating in autonomous mode in Sunnyvale and turning right from Mathilda Avenue onto Del Ray Avenue, made contact with a curb at approximately 13 miles per hour. While there was no tire or wheel damage, the contact resulted in misalignment. No other agents were involved, no injuries were reported, and law enforcement was not called to the scene."

I decided to drive over to the scene and make that same right turn, going from Mathilda Avenue onto Del Ray Avenue. Admittedly, I did so a few weeks after the incident, and therefore the driving scene could be quite different than it was at the date of the actually reported matter.

It would though seem reasonable to suggest that there is nothing extraordinary about the right turn at that corner. All in all, it appears to be an everyday kind of corner.

As you are coming down Mathilda Avenue, there are four lanes of traffic. The rightmost lane can either make the right turn onto Del Ray Avenue or continue ahead on Mathilda Avenue. When nearing the right turn, there is a fire hydrant on the sidewalk, just a bit before the corner. As you come around the corner, there is a lamppost on the sidewalk just as you start to straighten out. Upon straightening out of the turn, there is room for cars to be parked on the right side of the street, though the street is wide enough that there is ample room between those parked cars and navigating further down Del Ray Avenue.

Allow me to explain why I am dragging you through those details.

If the corner was tricky in some fashion, it would lend toward the possibility that any kind of driving by either a human or an AI driving system might be befuddled by the turn. In this case, the corner appears relatively normal. The curb height is normal. The curb is the usual color. It does not seem to be obscured or in any manner undetectable. We also know that the matter occurred in daylight, though I suppose some shadows from nearby trees might have been cast (we'll come back to that aspect in a moment).

Given the particulars, there is no obvious basis for striking the curb.

I can readily speculate that human drivers though might sometimes strike this curb.

I observed that as you drive down Mathilda Avenue, it is quite possible that other traffic behind you might be trying to push you along. When seeking to make that right turn at Del Ray Avenue, if perchance a hectic driver is behind you, and if the hectic driver is intending to proceed straight ahead, you could feel the pressure from that driver as you make the right turn.

You've probably experienced that before.

While making a turn off of an active roadway, a car behind you gets irked that you are slowing down to make the turn. They want to continue forward at the pace of prevailing traffic. You want to slow down to make the turn. They don't want to slow down. This is a recipe for potential problems or disasters.

Sometimes, the driver from behind will ram into the car making the turn. That's bad. Sometimes the hectic driver will switch lanes at the last moment and cause traffic in the adjoining lane to have to swerve. That's bad.

The hectic driver is upset that the other driver is slowing down to make the right turn. This though is a legally allowed aspect, and the hectic driver should be adjusting to allow for the turning car to safely make the turn. That being said, if the turning driver does the turn by completely coming to a stop or doing something oddball-like, this could be said to be inappropriately disturbing the traffic that is on the active roadway.

We are all supposed to dance together collegially and civilly when driving our cars.

There is something about this right turn that does stand out though.

There is a ton of space to make the right turn. You could easily swing wide and have lots of room to do so. That is because there is a bit of a painted roadway diamond that separates the other side of Del Ray Avenue and for which there is only an allowed right turn when leaving Del Ray Avenue onto Mathilda Avenue.

Complicating the driving scene is the possibility of cars on Mathilda Avenue being able to make a semi-protected left turn onto Del Rey Avenue. In essence, cars going up Mathilda Avenue could decide to try and make a left onto Del Rey Avenue.

I'd say the odds are you've encountered this type of driving setting too. You want to make a right turn. You can do so without coming to a full stop since there isn't any Stop sign or light controlling the turn. There is though a chance that someone might make a left and come onto the same street or avenue that you are making a right turn into.

You need to eye that left turn since a driver might decide to abruptly cut you off as you make your right turn. Or, you make the right turn, and the left turn driver darts into the same lane area as you are now immersed in. I could definitely see that a war of road warriors could arise at this turning point. The right turn driver going to battle with a left turn driver.

I realize you can use the right-of-way rules to figure out how this traversal should occur. But I dare say that right-of-way and the actual daily driving antics are not necessarily one and the same. A driver making this right turn needs to protect themselves and anticipate that a driver intending to make a left into the same roadway is going to be a threat. Whether the left turn driver is in the right is somewhat immaterial. The point being that the left-turn driver might be careless, might be distracted, might be drunk, or whatever.

Okay, in recap, a human driver could inadvertently strike the curb if they felt pressured by the traffic behind them when making the right turn. They might oversteer in their "panic" of making the right turn and be trying to avert getting rammed from behind by some crazed following driver.

Another means of striking the curb would be if you were making the right turn and were somewhat startled to see that a car making a left turn has decided to enter into the roadway at the same point of your turning activity. You might try to avoid the interloper car by oversteering into the curb.

Per the Apple self-reporting succinct description, we do not know whether or not that there was traffic directly behind the self-driving car as it made the right turn. We also don't know if a car was making a left turn onto the same roadway at the time of the incident.

We do know that the self-driving car was moving at a relatively slow speed, namely at 13 miles per hour.

The speed is slow enough that we might infer that the self-driving car was making the right turn at a reasonable pace. In other words, if the self-driving car had been going say 35 to 40 miles per hour on the active roadway, and then tried to take the turn without reducing speed, we would seemingly question why the AI driving system had not slowed to make the turn.

We do not know if the self-driving car was trying to make any evasive maneuvers. One doubts that it was doing so. This would seem like something that ought to have been mentioned if indeed it was related to the curb strike. We'll assume that there was no evasive action underway.

My overarching point is that we can come up with lots of potential underlying reasons that a human driver might strike that curb. This would partially arise due to the design of the corner and the roads that intersect there. The mainstay would be that oversteer might occur by a human driver based on the perceived angst due to a driver behind them or a driver trying to make a left turn into the same roadway path.

As far as we know, there were no other drivers nearby that somehow led to or were amidst this incident. No other human-driven cars seemed to parlay into the situation. Likewise, no other self-driving cars seemed to parlay into the situation (that's a bit of a new notion, namely that we nowadays have the added possibility of a self-driving car that might be nearby another self-driving car while both are actively underway on a public roadway).

Shift for a moment into a generalized perspective about self-driving cars.

Keep in mind that some AI driving systems might not especially note that a driver in a human-driven car that is behind the autonomous vehicle is getting upset and tailgating the self-driving car. Some AI driving systems basically do not take into account such actions. The programming of the AI driving system is focused on making the turn and it is little or no coding that deals with cars behind the self-driving car during that maneuver.

Humans of course do tend to take that into account (not all, but many do).

Many AI driving systems tend to focus their sensors and multi-sensor data fusion (MSDF) on what is ahead or in front of the self-driving car, rather than giving much credence to what is behind the autonomous vehicle. In that case, there is a chance that a left-turning car that might impede the self-driving car would be detected.

I say that there is a chance because there is also a chance that such a left-turning car might not be detected. It all depends upon how well seen or detectable the left-turn car is. If there was a lot of traffic at the time of making the right turn, it is conceivable that being able to detect a car that is several lanes away and entering in real-time into the left turn would be somewhat difficult to discern. Of course, once it proceeded to make the left turn, the odds are that the right turning self-driving car would get a strong sensory detection of the interloping vehicle.

This brings up a whole slew of other aspects. For example, if a self-driving car was making a right turn and another car suddenly made a left turn that imperiled the self-driving car, what would the AI driving system do?

It all depends upon the programming.

The AI driving system might try to slam on the brakes and come to a halt. Or, it might try to stay as close to the curb as possible, aiming to stay away from an interloper, and still proceed to make the turn. In theory, the AI driving system could even calculate whether to go up onto the sidewalk, avoiding the interloper as much as possible, if it seemed that staying in the roadway was going to highly likely produce a collision.

None of those considerations appear to be a factor in this instance.

For unexplained reasons (per the Apple self-report), the self-driving car struck the curb. That's all we know.

Given that we are currently in the month of October and nearing Halloween, you could lightheartedly dismiss the circumstance by saying that a ghost might have caused the curb strike (the spooky apparition having jumped the gun on celebrating Halloween, as it were).

Keeping our heads in the serious game of real-world self-driving cars, consider something not quite so supernatural.

One of the foundational aspects of any AI driving system is the programming required for properly navigating the roadways. This involves detecting the drivable road space. Humans do so with ease, most of the time. You glance up ahead and can readily see that the road goes this way or that way, and you can readily see that the curbs are here or there.

Curbs can be tricky.

Some places have no discernable curb. Some places have a curb that runs along and then no longer continues. There are breaks in curbs. Curbs can be cracked and in piecemeal. Some curbs are painted red and you aren't supposed to stop there. Curbs are a vital aspect of being a driver, though we tend to give little explicit regard to the importance of curbs.

For many of the AI driving systems in use today, a herculean effort is made to pre-map where the autonomous vehicle is going to go. Besides purchasing or making digital maps that showcase the roads and their structures, including the curbs, another additional aspect involves driving around a given area and further enhancing the digitized maps.

Some fervently believe that the future of self-driving cars is tied to having those kinds of strictly detailed pre-mapped and pre-driven datasets. Others decry this as a sad reliance that, notably, humans do not need for driving purposes. When you go to drive in a locale that you've never driven before, you don't need to have detailed maps per se. You merely start driving. You observe the roadway as the roadway arises. This is what a true self-driving car and a true AI driving system ought to be able to do, some argue voraciously.

Returning to the Apple self-driving car matter at hand, we would likely expect that this locale would have been pre-mapped and pre-driven, a logically reasonable assumption given that it is in Sunnyvale and nearby a complex of Apple facilities. It seems entirely unimaginable that this corner was an unknown corner and that the AI driving system would not have already had lots of data about the corner.

Put on your sleuth-like thinking cap.

Somewhat like a Sherlock Holmes detective scenario, we seem to have eliminated the car-behind theory, the left-turning car theory, and the "never seen this" theory about the location of the curb strike.

Just for sake of discussion, we will also eliminate the "steering problems" theory that perhaps the mechanics of the steering on the self-driving car were already afoul. The basis for asserting that the steering was likely working and not somehow askew is that by and large the self-driving cars in these tryouts are being pampered beyond belief. Each night, the self-driving cars throughout the Silicon Valley area are usually brought back into their respective maintenance and repair facilities and are given a careful inspection. They are then maintained and repaired. Furthermore, when starting on a trip the next morning, usually a complete inspection is done again to make sure that the autonomous vehicle is suitable to go on a driving journey.

We are left with the notion that the AI driving system presumably had sufficient data about where the curb was. The weather and roadway conditions did not seem to be a factor since it was a clear day and during daylight that this occurred. No other cars apparently were involved. The roadway surface was not a seeming factor. The condition of the self-driving car itself was not a seeming factor (we are assuming it was physically operating as normal).

It would appear that the only thing remaining to deduce is that the butler did it.

The AI driving system might have miscalculated the right turn and ran into the curb.

Perhaps the right-turn programming had been recently updated or modified, and a bug or error was now included that led to the turn being taken overly so.

There is also a chance that the sensors detected something that is not apparent now but was considered a concern at the time by the AI driving system. Some nearby object was misinterpreted as an issue and thus the AI driving system directed the self-driving car to take as tight a turn as feasible, including rubbing against the curb.

Striking a curb is pretty much a simple matter and maybe not worthy of giving any undue attention. On the other hand, navigating a turn and properly avoiding striking a curb is considered the Self-Driving Car 101 kind of stuff. You would be extremely hard-pressed to claim that an everyday curb is an outlier or edge or corner case.

One of the biggest and most common refrains about developing AI driving systems is the qualms about addressing those outliers, edge cases, and corner cases. Some believe that the long-tail aspects of zillions of such unusual cases will demonstrably delay the advent of self-driving cars, and there are even skeptics that say it will forever delay safe self-driving cars.

Anyway, it is a bit of a head-scratcher that a curb strike of this nature occurred. Maybe some additional AI programming and coding nourishment is needed.

As they say, an apple a day can keep the curb strikes away.

CHAPTER 18
DEAD ENDING AND SELF-DRIVING CARS

Sometimes, you can be quite surprised by what you might see on the sunny streets of San Francisco.

For example, this proverbial City by the Bay is a Silicon Valley favorite right now, allowing an abundance of self-driving cars to crisscross the steep hills and teeming streets, doing so in a visionary flurry of experimental tryouts for emergent driverless cars.

If that isn't enough of an unusual scenery for you, there is something else that San Francisco also is known for, namely houses that from time-to-time are rolling throughout the avenues and keep afar from the fabled cable cars. Though some have jokingly said that these slinking along homes have a mind of their home, the reality is that there is a long history of putting treasured houses up on giant dollies and moving them to other parts of town.

To be clear, there are humans at the wheel of those moving homes (not ghosts and nor any venerated AI-based driving systems).

In this latest case, a picturesque Victorian home that is popularly known as the Englander House was moved to make way for a proposed apartment complex. One supposes the easiest path would have been to simply demolish the now outdated and somewhat dilapidated house, crushing it to the bone and carting away the remains.

Instead, the more than five-thousand square-foot structure was carefully and gently rolled to a new spot, which though admittedly only six blocks away, nonetheless constituted a heck of a distance to cart an entire two-story home (you might think of this as the celebrated notion of having seen *it* on Mulberry Street, though in this case, the street names differed).

By lifting the home onto rollable wheels, the affair became one of trying to navigate the winding and hilly streets of famed San Francisco, known as being one of the hilliest cities in the world. Fortunately, no need, in this case, to try and shove the house across the Golden Gate Bridge. The local streets that would witness the inching along house were prepared beforehand to make way. This included cutting back overstretched tree limbs, removing parking meters, temporarily taking down road signs that were potential obstructions, and the like.

You might be wondering whether the posted speed limit sign was perhaps also removed, and in which case, could the house opt to sprint its way to the new location. Sorry to disappoint, the speed limit still applied, though it wasn't a consideration since the rolling process had a top speed of about 1 mile per hour anyway. No sense in laying out rubber on the roadway from doing any kind of tire screeching starts or donuts, and just make sure that the house safely reached its ultimate destination.

Here's a question for you.

Suppose you were driving your car in San Francisco on that particular day, and also assume that you did not know beforehand that a house was being moved. In that scenario, you would have been quietly driving along, minding your own business, and upon turning a corner on some ordinary street there would suddenly be looming ahead of you a house.

Mind you, not a house that was on the sides of the street and sitting still, nailed to the perch, but instead a home smack dab in the middle of the street. Perhaps you would end-up going head-to-head with this menacing figure. In a street duel involving going face to face with a house versus a car, consider the likely winner of this driving battle. The house weighs a lot more and has quite a hefty size advantage, while your car is nimble and can make circles around the snail-paced home.

I'd bet that most drivers would have let the house win.

The odds are that you would have been caught off-guard at seeing a house coming down the street toward you. Since this was happening in slow motion, you would have plenty of time to take in the sight and mentally calculate what was taking place. Other than a mild surprise and perhaps giving you a bit of a chuckle, it seems likely that you would have taken the matter in stride.

That being said, it is not every day that you manage to observe a house in the middle of the roadway and that is moving along too. Someone visiting San Francisco as a tourist might immediately assume it was a touristy act being undertaken by the authorities that run Frisco, possibly attempting to gain renewed attention to the Golden Gate City. I suspect that it would be easy to shrug off the experience and maybe make a posting on social media in a nonchalant manner, doing a trendy insta-bragging or a so-called humble-brag about what you just saw.

The odds are that you would have made a U-turn and made your way beyond the reach of the iceberg-slow moving house. Of course, the reality is that you probably would not have gotten especially close to the being-moved home anyway. There were plenty of barricades and road closures, along with bright and flashing warning signs and police enforcing the right-of-way for this Victorian-style masterpiece.

All told, a human driver would have presumably remained calm and at most been curious about how a house managed to get onto the street. Despite never having seen such a roadway condition before (how many of us have ever experienced a rolling home coming down the street?), a person witnessing such a spectacle can readily make a mental sense of what they are seeing.

It is a house. It is on the street. It is slowly moving. It poses no immediate danger. I can drive away without difficulty. That's the extent of the driving mental contortions, and the remaining cognitive action can entail the why and how of the story behind a house confronting you while on a normal driving journey.

Shifting gears, the future of cars consists of self-driving cars. The AI-based *true* self-driving cars are driven entirely by an AI driving system. There isn't a human at the wheel, and in fact, the expectation is that most self-driving cars will not provide any provision of human-accessible driving controls. The AI will be the sole driver and no human will directly be involved.

This gives rise to today's intriguing question: *What would a self-driving car do when suddenly facing a house that was moving down the middle of the street?*

Let's unpack the matter and see.

Understanding The Levels Of Self-Driving Cars

As a clarification, true self-driving cars are ones that the AI drives the car entirely on its own and there isn't any human assistance during the driving task.

These driverless vehicles are considered Level 4 and Level 5 while a car that requires a human driver to co-share the driving effort is usually considered at Level 2 or Level 3. The cars that co-share the driving task are described as being semi-autonomous, and typically contain a variety of automated add-on's that are referred to as ADAS (Advanced Driver-Assistance Systems).

There is not yet a true self-driving car at Level 5, which we don't yet even know if this will be possible to achieve, and nor how long it will take to get there.

Meanwhile, the Level 4 efforts are gradually trying to get some traction by undergoing very narrow and selective public roadway trials, though there is controversy over whether this testing should be allowed per se (we are all life-or-death guinea pigs in an experiment taking place on our highways and byways, some contend).

Since semi-autonomous cars require a human driver, the adoption of those types of cars won't be markedly different than driving conventional vehicles, so there's not much new per se to cover about them on this topic (though, as you'll see in a moment, the points next made are generally applicable).

For semi-autonomous cars, it is important that the public needs to be forewarned about a disturbing aspect that's been arising lately, namely that despite those human drivers that keep posting videos of themselves falling asleep at the wheel of a Level 2 or Level 3 car, we all need to avoid being misled into believing that the driver can take away their attention from the driving task while driving a semi-autonomous car.

You are the responsible party for the driving actions of the vehicle, regardless of how much automation might be tossed into a Level 2 or Level 3.

Self-Driving Cars And Those Rolling Houses

For Level 4 and Level 5 true self-driving vehicles, there won't be a human driver involved in the driving task.

All occupants will be passengers.

The AI is doing the driving.

One aspect to immediately discuss entails the fact that today's AI is not sentient. In other words, the AI is altogether a collective of computer-based programming and algorithms, and most assuredly not able to reason in the same manner that humans can. For example, current AI lacks any semblance of common sense and nor has any kind of common-sense reasoning.

This is important to keep in mind when considering the matter of a house coming down the middle of a street on a driving trek.

Humans comprehend that the object ahead of them is a house. Houses are usually not in the middle of the street. Houses rarely move, other than perhaps shifting here and there due to earth movement or seismic activity. Overall, a human would readily grasp that this is an unusual situation and would realize that this Victorian house is in the wrong place and doing something it should not be doing, namely cruising along on a presumably active street meant for cars, bikes, motorcycles, vans, and the like.

The house is altogether out of place. A human would reason that there must be some logical explanation for this oddball circumstance. How could a house get into the street? It is not as though a house is like a pet dog that got off its leash and sneaked out to play in the middle of the roadway. A house is not a dog. Houses do not customarily of their own volition opt to stray.

A quick visual scan of the driving scene would undoubtedly showcase the special roadway and moving crews that were shlepping along with the house. The street would be barren of all of the usual trappings that you'd expect to see on a typical everyday roadway. Thus, even if you somehow did not notice the blizzard of warning signs and somehow avoided getting stopped by those esteemed guardians securing the route, you nonetheless would reason about what you are seeing and be able to turn the extraordinary setting into something sensible and understandable.

What would an AI driving system do?

As mentioned, today's AI is not sentient. It cannot "reason" in the manner that humans can. Let's trace the technological aspects of what might occur.

The odds are that the sensors would detect that things were amiss. Self-driving cars are loaded with various sensors such as video cameras, radar, LIDAR, ultrasonic devices, and the like. You can certainly assume that all of those sensors are pretty much going to detect a house that is sitting in the middle of the street.

Realize though that the various sensors each have their own range of detection. This means that some of the sensors would sooner detect the object than others. Within the AI driving system, there is a function or component that undertakes Multi-Sensor Data Fusion (MSDF). This capability is programmed to compare and contrast the results of the sensor data collections and try to resolve any differences and also amplify any similarities. The visual imaging interpretations would be indicating that a large object is blocking the roadway. The radar and LIDAR would likewise be reporting that a large object is straight ahead. Etc.

The AI driving system maintains a virtual world model, essentially an internal frame of reference about what the outside world of the surrounding driving scene seems to consist of. Based on the sensor data and the algorithmic interpretation of the sensor indications, the AI driving system likely would make a mark in the virtual world model that something rather monstrous in size is blocking the roadway ahead.

Notice that I have carefully worded that description to refer to the thing as an object and not refer to it as a house.

We don't know that the AI driving system would necessarily classify the massive object as a house per se. For some AI driving systems, a house is considered an object that sits outside of the roadway. It could be the case that the AI driving system would be trying to compare the house to objects that are usually found within the path of the street, such as other cars, trucks, moving vans, pedestrians, and the like.

The AI doesn't "know" that a house is a house, at least not in the manner that you and I understand the meaning of the word. Any programming related to the object that is being called a "house" would likely have simple attributes associated with it. There is no semblance of realization that a house can have a family that grew-up within the home and lived a wonderful life there, enjoying the company of others and the raising of children, and so on.

Consider for a moment all of the memories and thoughts you might embody about the nature of houses and homes. Essentially, none of that robust wealth of knowledge and understanding is within the reach of today's AI systems.

Okay, we hopefully all agree that the AI driving system is unaware of what a house per se is (and, please avoid anthropomorphizing AI). At this juncture of the step-by-step exploration, the AI driving system has detected a large-sized object, taking up the majority of the ahead driving scene. This is beyond the size of a tumbleweed. It is beyond the size of a piece of furniture that might have dropped off the back of a truck.

All told, the odds are that the AI driving system would feed this indication about a colossal blockage up ahead into the portion of the driving system that plans what to do next. The routing algorithm would potentially have various digital maps and would refer to the maps. If the street ahead is unavailable for traversal, the AI driving system would be seeking to identify an alternative path.

We can assume that the self-driving car would seemingly aim to make a U-turn, and head some other way, utilizing other streets to avoid getting blocked by the object on this particular street.

In that case, consider this matter from the perspective of a car. A human driver would likely have made a U-turn and found some other path to proceed. An AI driving system would also have likely made a U-turn and opted to take a different route to proceed on its driving journey. If you were standing on the street and watching a car that came up to the situation, you would see the car make a U-turn and try to navigate away from the house coming down the roadway.

Could you immediately discern whether the car was being driven by a human versus being driven by an AI driving system?

Not really.

Sure, if you could see into the car, you would obviously have seen a human sitting in the driver's seat in the case of the human-driven car, and you would presumably have observed that there wasn't anyone sitting in the driver's seat of the self-driving car. In that manner, you could readily tell the difference.

But suppose you couldn't see into the car or the car was far enough away that you couldn't discern the nature of what might or might be inside the car. From the external behavior of the car, you would not seemingly be able to discern whether it was being human-driven or being driven by an AI driving system.

Is that good or bad?

Well, you have now reached a vociferous question that many are scratching their heads about.

On the one hand, yes, the AI driving system seemed to do the same thing that a human driver would have done. That seems reassuring.

Per my aforementioned depiction about the AI driving system, you undoubtedly realize that the AI didn't know anything at all about a house or a home, at least in comparison to a human. In this specific setting, it would seem that not "knowing" about houses or homes did not make a notable or discernible difference. The resulting driving actions were the same.

Not all driving actions are of the same ilk.

There are driving actions that entail human thinking that AI driving systems are not yet able to attain, and for which it is unclear if such AI will ever be possible. As such, the AI driving systems are going to be quite rudimentary and lacking in the depth of comprehension that humans have and that humans seemingly leverage when driving a car.

Some worry that as a society we are going to piecemeal allow ourselves into having self-driving cars on our roadways that seem or appear to be driving as though a human was at the wheel, and yet the AI driving system is not even in the same ballpark as human cognition.

The other side of that coin is that humans have all kinds of human foibles that come to play when they are driving. There are about 40,000 car crash-related fatalities each year in the United States alone and approximately 2.5 million related injuries. Much of those statistics are due to drunk driving and distracted driving. The AI driving systems won't be driving while drunk and will not be watching cat videos when driving the vehicle.

Are we willing to trade off the advantages of AI driving systems over the foibles of human drivers, though also realizing that the AI is not sentient?

We will need to accept the notion that the AI will be of a merely mechanical and programmatic capability, and overcome a false sense that the AI is of caliber with human thinking and intrinsic human capabilities.

Conclusion

You might have been surprised to discover that the mere presence of a slowly rolling house in the middle of a street could spur this kind of illustrious discussion.

Turns out fortuitously that the quirkiness and mystery of a house existing where it is not expected serves as a marvelous foil upon which to reveal the oft unspoken aspects about AI and the capabilities of today's AI driving systems. The day-to-day acts of self-driving cars starting to roam our streets can inadvertently lull us into assuming that AI driving systems are the same as human drivers, embodying the same cognitive capacities, and meanwhile excising the adverse role of human emotions and human faults that occur while driving a car.

There is no free lunch.

The AI driving systems are limited in what they can do. A tough tradeoff is going to occur as society has to decide between the advantages of self-driving cars versus the advantages of human drivers. If driving a car is relatively routinized, and some sufficient range of driving scenarios are programmed to be handled, this might be enough to weigh the scales toward those AI driving systems and avert the downsides of human-driven cars.

Time will tell.

Meanwhile, I am determined to put some sturdy wheels onto my house and take it for a spin, including refining my homegrown AI driving system to be able to drive a house rather than a car. One thing seems pretty sure, my AI driving house can stomp on any of those pesky AI self-driving cars, in a heartbeat.

CHAPTER 19
HARVARD POLICY PAPER AND SELF-DRIVING CARS

Are our cities and urban areas ready for the advent of Autonomous Vehicles (AVs) such as public roadway roaming self-driving cars, sidewalk-going self-driving delivery bots, campus-based self-driving shuttle buses, and a plethora of other assorted driverless vehicles?

Maybe yes, or maybe not (more likely not so).

A newly released research report entitled "Developing Urban Mobility Policy in Response to Autonomous Vehicles" has been posted by the Harvard Kennedy School (HKS) via the Taubman Center for State and Local Government. Doing so under the auspices of their Autonomous Vehicles Policy Initiative (AVPI) program, this latest paper is part of an ongoing and overarching analysis that explores the practical and pragmatic considerations underlying the implementation of AVs at the city, state, and federal government levels.

I'm honored to indicate that this is a report that I've co-authored with esteemed colleague Mark Fagan, lecturer at the Harvard Kennedy School and head of the AVPI program there.

Avid readers of my column are well-aware of my persistent calls for making sure that we are all looking at the self-driving forest and not just the trees alone. In essence, it is easy to get caught up in the day-to-day excitement of having numerous driverless pilots and prototypes underway in a given municipality. That being said, retaining a big picture perspective will be vital toward ensuring that AV adoption is a balanced and satisfactory entrant into your urban area.

With that said, let's take a quick look at some of the highlights of this new report.

First, as mindful background, the AVPI program has been actively engaged for several years in conducting research, teaching, and working with policymakers that are grappling with how to prepare for and sensibly cope with the burgeoning testing and fielding of all kinds of Autonomous Vehicles, especially ground-based self-driving vehicles.

In addition to the in-depth research and instructional efforts, the AVPI is also known for undertaking intense policy scrums that bring together governmental policymakers with AV experts, policy analysts, and legal experts. These are exhilarating face-to-face interactive sessions that immerse the participants into candid and quite fruitful dialogue about how to prudently and proactively cope with emerging AVs and self-driving efforts within their respective communities.

This most recent report contains an innovative scenario-based setting or simulation-oriented backdrop that can be used for energizing AV-related policy scrums all told.

In a sense, there is a foundation provided in the report to enable the undertaking of an AV-exploring policy simulation of sorts. Participants in a policy analysis session can take on various roles within the simulation and then see how things go when interacting with their fellow participants that have momentarily also assumed particular roles.

For example, you've got a mayor that is being besieged on all sides, whereby some local constituencies favor the arising use of AVs and meanwhile other local actors express notable concerns. Meanwhile, the AV vendors are pressing ahead earnestly to expand their local self-driving efforts.

But what about the impacts on the people of the city?

Some studies suggest that self-driving cars are tending to increase traffic congestion in already clogged city streets. That's a problem worthy of anticipating and not getting blindsided with.

Some of the fleets of self-driving automobiles are only currently available in certain areas of the city. Does this deny fuller and more balanced access toward suitable mobility equity throughout the urban landscape?

There are AV vendors that are beginning to charge for use of their driverless vehicles. Is the pricing creating a kind of divisiveness as to those that can afford to use this new transportation option versus those that cannot?

And so on it goes.

You see, a robust scenario is laid out that depicts a typical city caught in the midst of the relatively widespread adoption of self-driving vehicles. It can be a nightmare for those that have allowed events and efforts to proceed on a pell-mell basis alone. Though admittedly only a few cities are at this juncture or nearing it, right now, you can bet that in the next several years there will be many more localities that find themselves in this same boat.

Rather than waiting until the horse is already out of the barn, this multi-party policy development simulation can open the eyes of those that want to be ahead of the game. By anticipating the soon-to-be-upon-us future, policymakers have a crucial opportunity to guide their locality in a direction that will either avoid or at least mitigate many of the inadvertent *adverse consequences* that can arise with widespread and possibly uncontrolled AV use.

As stated in the report: "This simulation enables policymakers and stakeholders to develop the operating environment and regulations that position a municipality to tap the opportunities that AVs offer while minimizing the adverse consequences. This exercise is based on an anticipated scenario of how AVs may arrive in cities in the coming few years. It details the players and their interests. Using the descriptions provided, participants engage in a three-round simulation to reach a consensus on the best path forward. The simulation is designed as a facilitated simulation for use by both practitioners and students. It concludes with a framework for how policymakers can migrate from their current position to their desired state."

A framework containing a curated set of potential policy actions is also provided.

Policymakers can consider which of the policy actions seem suitable for the scenario portrayed. More importantly, these are then intended to become active handy-dandy tools for the participants, allowing a leveraging of these same tools and techniques within their own respective localities.

A range of tools is proffered. These include fostering a cohesive mobility-as-a-service approach across the otherwise disparate transport options in a modern-day municipality. Local residents and visitors in today's cities are overwhelmed with multi-modal transportation capabilities. Which should they use? How will the self-driving options fit within the transport fabric or landscape of the locality? Etc.

Another looming issue is going to be the question of data-sharing (note that in my columns, I've referred to this as the data collected via the "roving eye" of self-driving vehicles). If a fleet of self-driving cars is collecting copious amounts of data about where locals are traveling, when they travel, and so on, who owns that data? Suppose the AV operator decides to use or sell the data, could this be a privacy intrusion?

Also, this collected data could be valuable information for local policymakers that wish to plan for and adjust transportation and infrastructure elements in their municipality. Will the AV vendors provide the data openly or insist that it is their own proprietary data and refuse to share it?

One other handy indication in the report consists of a matrix for guiding where a city sits currently on the scale of AV adoption and where it is heading.

As per the report: "The results of the simulation provide a point-in-time view of how a city wants AVs to support mobility. Rarely will the desired outcome be the current state. The results of the simulation can be used to help the city migrate from its current position to the desired state. A propensity matrix may be helpful in facilitating the transition. When examining urban mobility policies in the context of AV deployments, two major factors are useful to consider: (1) The pervasiveness of AVs in the municipality; and (2) The maturity of urban AV mobility policies."

Where is your municipality in terms of its existing readiness for AV adoption considerations?

Many are behind the eight ball.

They are either relatively untouched as yet by self-driving efforts, or they have allowed self-driving efforts to arise organically or sporadically (doing so in a benevolent but rather unplanned manner).

Conclusion

As alluded to earlier, the emergence of self-driving options is taking place in a somewhat semi-random or haphazard manner in our cities.

This makes sense when you consider that AVs are a new form of transportation and there is a staggered start-stop phenomenon involved. One AV vendor makes solid progress. Another one perhaps finds themselves stymied and has to regroup. Some of the AV vendors are utterly focused on the technological facets and either unaware or not versed in the societal impacts that the introduction of self-driving options imbues upon an urban area.

I've said it before, and I'll say it again, namely that it takes a village to bring to proper fruition the plethora of driverless transportation options. I continue to implore policymakers, AV vendors, AV experts, legal experts, policy analysts, and every stakeholder to get up-to-speed, begin your preparations now (don't wait), and make sure that your city is not caught off-guard.

An ounce of preparation is worth a pound of cure.

CHAPTER 20
FOLLOW-ON ROBBERIES AND SELF-DRIVING CARS

The news these days is filled with quite appalling reports of follow-home robberies.

As a quick background, a follow-home robbery consists of criminals that sneakily target someone while the innocent victim is out and about. The evildoers begin to surreptitiously trail the person or persons, including while the unaware prey is driving home in their car. The target is completely unaware that they are being followed. Upon reaching the normally perceived safety of getting home, and whence the targeted victim is now most vulnerable, the robbers then surprise the target and seek to rob them.

The robbery act might occur the moment that the target pulls into their driveway. The miscreants are likely to pull their car directly up behind the victim's vehicle and block any possibility of retreat. Quickly surrounding the now parked car of the target, the crooks confront the victim while just getting out of their vehicle. Whatever cash, jewelry, wallets, or other valuables can be jacked from the target are snatched up. The criminals then jump back into their awaiting getaway car and speed away.

In a scant few seconds, you can find yourself dangerously threatened and have key possessions stolen from you.

It all happens so fast that you are nearly in a state of shock as to what just transpired. The kicker is that you think and naturally assume that you were perfectly safe having gotten home and parked in your own driveway or private garage. The usual need to be on your toes is likely reduced.

For those that are customarily on alert while out and about, the assumption is that reaching their home is akin to being nestled in a fully safe environment (i.e., using a baseball sports-like analogy, you made it safely to home base).

Of course, sadly things could go even worse.

The criminals might be armed and decide to use a weapon upon their victims. Or the scoundrels might beat up the targets. In addition, if perchance someone comes out of the house that was otherwise merely intending to welcome home the driver or passengers, they too are encompassed into the villainous act. The whole matter is repulsive and horrific.

I regret to add that there is even more worseness to be had.

The evildoers might decide to wait until the target gets into the house. When the timing seems right, the robbers burst into the domicile. This gives them the added advantage of not being readily seen during their criminal acts, which else were being done out in the open at the front yard of the house. Being inside the home also opens up the chance to steal other valuables.

In any case, I think you get the idea about the sordid nature of follow-home robberies.

The crux involves identifying a target at some point during an excursion by the person. The crooks usually are randomly selecting a considered viable target. They don't know anything about the person beforehand (in essence, having a predetermined target is a different kind of crime, as it were).

Here's how a follow-home robbery might typically work.

Let's say that a man and a woman decide to go shopping at their local mall.

Having been somewhat trapped indoors during the pandemic, the couple decides to gleefully get dressed up for a visit to the fancy mall that has some nifty upscale stores. The woman wears pricey jewelry that has been simply sitting unused in a jewelry box for the last many months. The man proudly wears his expensive watch that has rarely been on his arm for the last year or so.

They drive over to the mall. Turns out that the mall is somewhat busy with lots of seasonal shopping occurring. After driving around the parking lot for a while, they finally find a parking spot on the outskirts of the lot (but that doesn't spoil the joy of being out shopping!). They walk with delight into the mall and enjoy a bit of a shopping spree, something they have only done these last months online and has been unable to do so in person at a decked-out mall.

Okay, we are now at a vital point in the saga.

Carrying several shopping bags filled with purchased goods, the two happily walk back out to their car. It was an exciting time for them as they relished once again being able to shop at stores. They place their shopping bags into the backseat and then get settled into the front seats for a pleasant ride home. During the drive home, they chat about the fun of being out and about.

You might have guessed that they are about to be victims of a follow-home robbery.

Yes, regrettably, this is the case.

Unbeknownst to them, some criminals sitting in a parked car in the parking lot were eyeing shoppers that came out of the mall. There are particular characteristics of interest to the scoundrels. In this case, the woman is clearly wearing jewelry and the man is wearing what seems to be a posh watch. They are carrying bags filled with items, and the bags are handily labeled as to the store names, of which these names are the pricier stores.

Next, the couple gets into a high-end luxury car. This is icing on the cake. The odds are that between the clothing and accessories they are wearing, and the shopping bags, plus the fancy car, it would seem worthwhile to go after these as potential prey. Another important factor is that the couple seemed to be utterly engrossed in their own conversation and had not looked around to see if anyone was observing them.

All in all, this is a high probability target for a decent score.

The criminals opt to follow the couple as they drive out of the mall parking lot. Staying sufficiently behind the targeted car, the crooks try to not tip their hand that they are following the vehicle. If the driver of the targeted car gets wise to what is going on, the gig might be up. The driver might start driving in a more animated fashion, going slow, going fast, and thus suggest that they are testing to ascertain whether they are being followed.

At that juncture, the crooks would need to decide whether to proceed or instead call off the pursuit. They could try to cut off the car and do the evil deed right away. This is likely problematic, and it might be better to let this fish swim away into the sea.

Assuming that the target is not somehow able to figure out they are being followed, the trap is nearly set. The crooks will continue to follow the targeted car and will make a decision in real-time about what to do once the vehicle arrives at a house. They will need to take immediate action if they want to do the quicker smash-and-grab kind of robbery. If they want to do the home invasion robbery, they might need to wait a bit, or possibly call their criminal cohorts to come there too (amassing more evildoers to aid in the more pronounced effort of an in-home robbery).

That pretty much sums up the conventional version of a follow-home robbery (there are lots of variants).

What can someone do to prevent themselves from becoming a target of a follow-home robbery?

The usual advice given by law enforcement involves being supremely aware of your surroundings. Be watching for anyone eyeing you as you exit from the mall. The driver of the car heading out from the mall should be looking in the rearview mirror to see if anyone seems to be following the car. And so on.

There is also the suggestion that it might be wisest to try and not showcase any semblance of flashy or pricey goods. As noted earlier, the instance of having eye-catching jewelry and a watch, plus the loaded bags of high-priced items, stirred the crooks into adding the couple to their prospective target list.

Some bemoan the idea that there should be a need to be watching around you and seemingly on edge of being potentially targeted for a crime. Surely, none of us wishes to be that preoccupied with such concerns. On the other hand, as they say, better to be safe than sorry.

A follow-home robbery is usually undertaken by following one car with at least one other car. There is the prospective target car that is the vehicle to be followed. Then there is a car containing the crooks, or sometimes they work in packs of vehicles, wherein there might be several cars doing the tailing.

This tailing activity might seem to be sophisticated as though it is a secret agent kind of task, but the reality is that it merely requires the use of smartphones and keeping each other alerted as to where the target seems to be heading. No special skills are required. Easy-peasy.

Recall that the driver of the targeted vehicle has a potential opportunity to discover they are being followed. If that happens, the driver could potentially drive directly to a police station and seek help. The driver might call 911 and report that they are being followed. Essentially, the driver or the passenger could likely attain some modicum of safety if they only knew that they were being followed.

Side note: Do not decide to confront the crooks, as this is highly risky and the outcome is bound to be dire. Your better bet is to seek safety and report the matter to law enforcement right away.

Now that we've covered the fundamentals of follow-home robberies (an admittedly dour topic), what else is there to say?

A lot.

You see, consider that the advent of AI-based self-driving cars is gradually going to emerge.

Note that there isn't a human driver involved in a true self-driving car. Keep in mind that true self-driving cars are driven via an AI driving system. There isn't a need for a human driver at the wheel, and nor is there a provision for a human to drive the vehicle.

Here's an intriguing question that is worth pondering: *What impact if any will there be on follow-home robberies due to the advent of AI-based self-driving cars?*

I'd like to first further clarify what is meant when I refer to true self-driving cars.

Understanding The Levels Of Self-Driving Cars

As a clarification, true self-driving cars are ones that the AI drives the car entirely on its own and there isn't any human assistance during the driving task.

These driverless vehicles are considered Level 4 and Level 5 while a car that requires a human driver to co-share the driving effort is usually considered at Level 2 or Level 3. The cars that co-share the driving task are described as being semi-autonomous, and typically contain a variety of automated add-on's that are referred to as ADAS (Advanced Driver-Assistance Systems).

There is not yet a true self-driving car at Level 5, which we don't yet even know if this will be possible to achieve, and nor how long it will take to get there.

Meanwhile, the Level 4 efforts are gradually trying to get some traction by undergoing very narrow and selective public roadway trials, though there is controversy over whether this testing should be allowed per se (we are all life-or-death guinea pigs in an experiment taking place on our highways and byways, some contend).

Since semi-autonomous cars require a human driver, the adoption of those types of cars won't be markedly different than driving conventional vehicles, so there's not much new per se to cover about them on this topic (though, as you'll see in a moment, the points next made are generally applicable).

For semi-autonomous cars, it is important that the public needs to be forewarned about a disturbing aspect that's been arising lately, namely that despite those human drivers that keep posting videos of themselves falling asleep at the wheel of a Level 2 or Level 3 car, we all need to avoid being misled into believing that the driver can take away their attention from the driving task while driving a semi-autonomous car.

You are the responsible party for the driving actions of the vehicle, regardless of how much automation might be tossed into a Level 2 or Level 3.

Self-Driving Cars And Those Dastardly Follow-Home Robbers

For Level 4 and Level 5 true self-driving vehicles, there won't be a human driver involved in the driving task.

All occupants will be passengers.

The AI is doing the driving.

One aspect to immediately discuss entails the fact that the AI involved in today's AI driving systems is not sentient. In other words, the AI is altogether a collective of computer-based programming and algorithms, and most assuredly not able to reason in the same manner that humans can.

Why is this added emphasis about the AI not being sentient?

Because I want to underscore that when discussing the role of the AI driving system, I am not ascribing human qualities to the AI. Please be aware that there is an ongoing and dangerous tendency these days to anthropomorphize AI. In essence, people are assigning human-like sentience to today's AI, despite the undeniable and inarguable fact that no such AI exists as yet.

With that clarification, you can envision that the AI driving system won't natively somehow "know" about the facets of driving. Driving and all that it entails will need to be programmed as part of the hardware and software of the self-driving car.

Let's dive into the myriad of aspects that come to play on this topic.

First, it is important to realize that not all AI self-driving cars are the same. Each automaker and self-driving tech firm is taking its own approach to devising self-driving cars. As such, it is difficult to make sweeping statements about what AI driving systems will do or not do.

Furthermore, whenever stating that an AI driving system doesn't do some particular thing, this can, later on, be overtaken by developers that in fact program the computer to do that very thing. Step by step, AI driving systems are being gradually improved and extended. An existing limitation today might no longer exist in a future iteration or version of the system.

I trust that provides a sufficient litany of caveats to underlie what I am about to relate.

We can now turn our devoted attention to the follow-home robberies scheme.

Envision that the couple that went to the mall had opted to use a self-driving car rather than using a conventional human-driven car. Here's how things might have gone.

The self-driving car would likely pull up to the curb at the mall, such that the couple would not need to walk out to their car as though it was parked out in the parking lot. This is advantageous for the couple in the sense that it gives less exposure time for the crooks that might be eyeing people coming out of the mall.

Assuming that the self-driving car arrives without any waiting time, the couple would come out of the mall and nearly enter immediately into the self-driving car in one fell swoop. All in all, this reduces the risks of those waiting crooks that aren't going to have much of an opportunity to scrutinize the couple and figure out whether they are worthy of being a target for the follow-home robbery.

That being said, this is not a cure-all. The crooks could station themselves at the doors of the mall and relay to a waiting cohort in a parked car as to whether the couple seems a handy target.

Sorry, but there is no free lunch in life.

Continuing the tale, during the journey home the couple does not need to pay attention to the roadway. Why? Because the AI driving system is doing all the driving. The couple can merely settle into their comfortable seats and idly chat to their heart's content about the wonderous trip to the mall.

This is where things, unfortunately, turn south, of a sort.

Because neither member of the couple is driving the car, they are almost certainly going to have a zero chance of spotting a vehicle that is following them. To clarify, the couple could of course be looking out the back window and aim to spot any cars that seem suspiciously following them. Yes, that is absolutely doable.

What I'm suggesting is that they are not especially on alert to do so. A person that is driving a car is usually eyeing their rearview mirror and periodically looking behind them. If a car is obviously stalking your vehicle, the odds are that you would detect this. Again, for clarification, not every human driver is that alert, but I am saying that at least there is a viable chance of making that detection.

All told, the couple in the self-driving car is bound to be lulled into letting the AI do the driving and they are not going to be spying all around the driverless vehicle to try and find evildoers behind them. It just wouldn't be something on your personal radar to do.

The journey is about to get ugly, so prepare yourself accordingly.

I'll perhaps surprise you with an added insight. The act of following or stalking a self-driving car is somewhat easier than trying to do the same to a human-driven car. The reason for this is multifold.

First, most self-driving cars are being programmed to strictly obey the rules of the road. No speeding. No running of yellow or red lights. Make full stops at all stop signs. You get the idea.

Trying to follow a vehicle with that kind of driving action or driving behavior is pretty straightforward.

When trying to follow a human driver, there is a lot more chancy activity involved. A human might suddenly make a radical left or right turn, doing so simply because they weren't watching the roadway and realized after the fact they need to make a turn. They might do all kinds of driving shenanigans.

The lack of predictability of a human driver makes the effort of tailing a conventional human-driven car a bit more challenging. I'm not saying that human drivers are all experts at kicking tails off their trail. The point is that by their very inherent nature, human drivers are likely more erratic than self-driving cars and this wild driving can be difficult to deal with when seeking to quietly and unobtrusively follow another car.

Second, a self-driving car of today's ilk has a set of exterior features that makes the vehicle stand out. As I've explained in my column, self-driving cars do indeed look like self-driving cars (for the time being). From the perspective of trying to stalk a self-driving car, it is somewhat made easier since the profile of the autonomous vehicle is especially distinctive (in contrast to the everyday conventional-looking car).

The gist is that following a self-driving car is probably easier for the evildoers, unfortunately so.

Once the self-driving car arrives at the home of the couple, we might reasonably assume that the self-driving car will pull up to the curb of the house (rather than parking on the driveway or in a garage, assuming that this is a so-called robo-taxi and not a self-driving car owned by the couple). The couple will get out of the streetside self-driving car, grab up their shopping bags, and walk up to their domicile.

This is the moment that the criminals could undertake the outdoor robbery. They stop their car in front of the house or possibly pull into the empty driveway. They jump out and accost the couple. After doing so, they take their ill-gotten loot and drive away from the crime scene.

Notice that there wasn't probably a need to block the self-driving car. That's another difference between driving a human-driven car versus using an AI-based self-driving car.

Here's the deal.

A human seated at the steering wheel of a conventional car can always start the car and try to desperately drive away. Heck, the human driver might even steer the car in a manner intended to convince the robbers to disperse. I'm not at all saying that anyone should ever do this, and only noting the possibility of it.

With a self-driving car, you are highly unlikely going to be able to suddenly scream at the AI driving system and command it to speed away. That's not in the cards right now. Instead, you would have to use either your smartphone or maybe a verbal command to ask the AI driving system to proceed. In addition, the AI would want to know where you wish to go.

Yelling out the exclamation that you want to go anywhere but where you are right now is going to be of little value. The AI would likely repeatedly ask you to provide a destination address. I know this sounds somewhat comical and robotic-like as though from a sci-fi movie. Pretty much, that's the state of the art today (but presumably not of the future).

Any hope of using the self-driving car for purposes of escape or protection is a slim proposition at this time.

To recap, the good news was that the self-driving car picked up the passengers at the mall and reduced the potential risk of being spotted by the follow-home robbers. The bad news, which is lamentably bad, the self-driving car is easy to follow and provides little or no aid upon arriving at the destination domicile.

It is for those reasons that I suggest that things will get worse regarding follow-home robberies upon the *initial advent* of self-driving cars.

Conclusion

Yikes, this seems to be a bummer for the emergence of self-driving cars.

Do not despair.

The future is brighter than it might seem at first glance.

I'll hopefully brighten your day by pointing out what could happen with self-driving cars, depending upon how they are devised and their rising popularity over time.

Remember that I mentioned the importance of a human driver paying attention to the vehicle behind their car and potentially discovering that they are being followed. We know that not all human drivers are that self-aware. You might not think of doing so. You might normally do so, but on one particular drive neglect to do so, and perhaps that's the time that the curse of fate has you being followed by a follow-home robbery crew.

The beauty of self-driving cars (if we can ascribe beauty to them) is that they can be programmed to consistently and reliably take various desired actions. If we want self-driving cars to be spotting any cars that might be following the self-driving car, this can be done. And it would be programmed to always take place (if that's what we want to have happened).

The AI isn't going to forget or whine about having to once again look behind the autonomous vehicle to see if anyone is following. I'm not ascribing sentience to AI. I am merely emphasizing that is a potentially well-programmed task and it can be done over and over again, with a likely high level of consistency and reliability.

Okay, so the self-driving car can be a constant lookout. That's a handy aspect.

Assuming that the AI is able to use the sensors to detect a suspicious stalking vehicle, the same kinds of potential remedies can be applied as prior mentioned. The AI might let the passengers know and then automatically call 911, plus alert the operator of the fleet of self-driving cars. The AI could potentially reroute the self-driving car to the nearest police station. Even trickier, the self-driving car could potentially coordinate electronically with the nearest police car and rendezvous with that police vehicle.

You get the idea, I'm sure.

We can add some steroids to this capability of detecting a stalking car.

Self-driving cars are generally going to be equipped with V2V (vehicle-to-vehicle) electronic communications. This is useful for aspects such as one self-driving car that alerts another self-driving car that there is debris on the roadway up ahead. The AI driving system of the receiving message can change routes, slow down, or otherwise take evasive action by this kind of electronic heads-up.

Imagine then that a self-driving car has detected the possibility of another car stalking it. Assuming that there are other nearby self-driving cars, the AI can use V2V and ask those other self-driving cars to also be watchful of the suspected follow-home robbery vehicle. Now, just to mention, this is not what the existing V2V approach is specially designed to do, but the concept is something that could be adopted if so needed.

There is a likewise possibility of using V2I (vehicle-to-infrastructure) electronic communications. The idea here is that a self-driving car could electronically get messages from the roadway infrastructure, such as an intersection traffic signal indicating that the light will be going red shortly or that a bridge ahead is temporarily unavailable for use.

An AI driving system could request via V2I for added data about the traffic history of the suspected stalking vehicle. This might assist the AI in figuring out whether the crooks are likely following or maybe just by happenstance it is a car that momentarily appears to be on the trail of the self-driving car.

Overall, the widespread adoption of self-driving cars will accordingly increase the facet that the self-driving cars can identify and potential single out a follow-home robbery activity that is in the midst of being plotted. Besides the V2V and V2I, another factor is that self-driving cars won't stick out anymore. When there are thousands of them on our roadways, they will actually blend in and be harder to likely follow.

The future then appears to be that follow-home robberies will have a devil of a time taking place in an era of widespread use of self-driving cars.

As a quick aside, there are also some tangential downsides to all these V2V and V2I and the avid sensors of driverless cars, which I've denoted as the "roving eye" and entails a plethora of privacy intrusion qualms.

In any case, you might be having a contemplative thought about an added twist, namely if the criminals were trying to use a self-driving car as the stalking vehicle (versus using a human-driven car), what would happen? For various reasons, this would likely be prohibitive as a crime undertaking approach and not a viable means to do the trailing (see my column for further explanation).

That about wraps up things on this topic for now.

There is a grandiose myriad of reasons to seek the rollout of true self-driving cars (there are plenty), you can now add to the impressive list that those dastardly follow-home robbery crooks will find themselves unable to readily carry out at least this type of repugnant crime.

Score one for us all and self-driving cars.

A noteworthy happy ending.

CHAPTER 21
NEWBORN BABY AND SELF-DRIVING CARS

'Tis the season for a feel-good news item.

Please find a comfortable and cozy place to relish this heartwarming account.

A worried husband was rushing his pregnant wife to the hospital in their car when all of a sudden the baby seemingly decided it was time to arrive into this world. The woman began to give birth to the newborn girl, doing so while in the passenger seat next to her frantically driving hubby.

Amazingly, the woman maneuvered in her seat to face backward, had her back propped against the dashboard, with her knees pressing against the seat she was just in, and voila gave birth to the eager newborn. As a astonishing double dose of amazing, the husband reached out with one hand (keeping the other hand on the steering wheel) and managed to catch the baby during the birthing process.

And, yes, all of this took place while the car was zipping along on the highway as the pair were stridently trying to reach the hospital for a more conventional birthing process. The husband afterward noted that his wife was quite composed throughout the in-car experience. We might also provide some accolades for the husband in his double-duty role as a frenzied driver and birthing assistant.

The baby girl, named Rebecca by her doting parents, happily is doing quite fine and all is well. There seems little doubt that the harrowing tale of how she was born will become a memorable part of her life. Her parents are apt to recount the saga, over and over again, and Rebecca will be able to share the wild account with those that she meets and regale them with an enchanting and breathtaking story.

Not wanting to spoil the positive and altogether upbeat mood about the adventure, I will simply and quietly make a few quick advisory points if that's okay with you.

First, one might question the aspect that the husband did not pull over the car and at least come to a safe stop where available to do so. Admittedly, getting to the hospital was a priority. On the other hand, driving a car in the midst of a birthing effort is perhaps not an as high priority as being settled someplace and being able to directly aid his wife. A tradeoff certainly exists between wanting to expeditiously reach medical care, while at the same time ensuring that the apparently imminent birthing effort occurs in as safe a manner as feasible.

Second, we can also quibble about his driving attentiveness during the process, especially the free-handed catching feat. By his own admission to a reporter, he had just one hand on the steering wheel, and likely his eyes were focused on his wife and newborn, rather than on the active roadway ahead. Suppose he had steered into a passing truck, or swerved dangerously out of his lane, or otherwise inadequately controlled the speeding along of his vehicle.

This is assuredly a form of distracted driving that even exceeds those moments of people watching cat videos or combing their tousled hair while mindlessly driving their multi-ton car that is akin to a somewhat unguided missile.

Third, when the wife opted to maneuver in the front passenger seat, she took off her seatbelt (as so reported in the news). Being in a moving car without wearing a seatbelt is ill-advised. She also turned around, facing backward and placing her backside against the dashboard. I won't linger on this facet, other than to note that if the husband perchance did any semblance of hard braking or other full-force driving actions, things would not have turned out well, frighteningly so. Sadly so.

Nonetheless, some would abundantly argue that the husband made the right choice to keep driving, and the outcome is presumably demonstrative proof of that strategy. The baby was born successfully.

The wife is doing fine. No one got hurt. The car didn't get into a collision. All are perfectly fine.

What more can you ask for in this topsy turvy world that we live in?

Let's perhaps agree that it is wonderous there was a joyous result (regardless of whether the approach taken was sound or not).

A cynic might say that this shouldn't be considered news per se. Here's why. The cynic would insist that there are plenty of ongoing stories of women giving birth while in moving cars. This seems to happen with a fair amount of regularity.

Sensibly so, since we rely on our cars to get us around town, and the odds are that when it seems time to give birth, any prudent husband and wife would pile into their car and head over to the hospital. It stands to reason.

An alternative obviously would be to call an ambulance or to have somehow headed over to the hospital well in advance of the birthing activity (the timing can be trickier than it seems), or be prepared to give birth at home, etc. Well, let's set aside this side tangent for now and maintain our devoted focus on the circumstance of getting caught relatively unawares that the birthing is going to arise during the driving journey.

You see, despite the likely belief that the birth won't engage during the driving trek, there is a calculated chance that nature or other factors might force the issue and the birthing will begin during the driving journey to the hospital. There are outsized tales of taxi drivers that have had this happen with an expectant passenger in their taxi. A woman hails a taxi to get to the hospital and discovers that the emergent newborn won't wait. The taxi driver hauls along as fast as possible, meanwhile, the woman gives birth while seated in the back row of the cab.

The point by the cynic is that giving airtime to this recent instance is overblown. We apparently should put this gushingly sentimental story into the ho-hum bucket and move along to other more notable and truly hair-raising news reports.

Shall we try to counterargue with such cynicism?

Yes, we must.

One stridently standout basis for this latest instance as being newsworthy was because the husband was driving the vehicle, plus the husband participated in the birthing process (okay, only in a modicum of a fashion, but, hey, a smidgeon of credit seems plausible to share). The husband was trying to support his wife as best he could. During her time of need, he was there. Obviously, she deserves the preponderance of the newsworthiness, but we can also see this as a touching moment of two people working together in a time of dire stress.

In most other similar cases, the driver typically takes no overt part in the birthing activity. For example, if the woman is in the back row of a cab, we wouldn't expect that the cab driver would be of much aid and the activity would be occurring out of reach.

In any case, we ostensibly and soberly do not want the driver in any such similar occurrence to be dividing their time and attention. Pick one focus of attention and stick with it, seems to be the advisory mantra. Either keep driving, doing so safely and somehow averting being distracted by what is taking place inside the car, or bring the vehicle to a safe stop and render direct aid as much as possible.

You must make a choice.

But you might be exhorting that sometimes you have to make these vexing kinds of Gordian knot decisions. Life is complicated. It is common that we get caught between a rock and a hard place. Choosing between driving the car as a fully dedicated act versus aiding your birthing wife, that's a tough one to call, some would assert.

Whoa, I have a solution for this dilemma.

Prepare yourself accordingly.

Think about the advent of AI-based self-driving cars.

Note that there isn't a human driver involved in a true self-driving car. Keep in mind that true self-driving cars are driven via an AI driving system. There isn't a need for a human driver at the wheel, and nor is there a provision for a human to drive the vehicle.

Here's an intriguing question that is worth pondering: *What impact if any will there be on those driving journey giving-birth instances once we have a prevalence of AI-based true self-driving cars?*

I'd like to first further clarify what is meant when I refer to true self-driving cars.

Understanding The Levels Of Self-Driving Cars

As a clarification, true self-driving cars are ones that the AI drives the car entirely on its own and there isn't any human assistance during the driving task.

These driverless vehicles are considered Level 4 and Level 5 while a car that requires a human driver to co-share the driving effort is usually considered at Level 2 or Level 3. The cars that co-share the driving task are described as being semi-autonomous, and typically contain a variety of automated add-on's that are referred to as ADAS (Advanced Driver-Assistance Systems).

There is not yet a true self-driving car at Level 5, which we don't yet even know if this will be possible to achieve, and nor how long it will take to get there.

Meanwhile, the Level 4 efforts are gradually trying to get some traction by undergoing very narrow and selective public roadway trials, though there is controversy over whether this testing should be allowed per se (we are all life-or-death guinea pigs in an experiment taking place on our highways and byways, some contend).

Since semi-autonomous cars require a human driver, the adoption of those types of cars won't be markedly different than driving conventional vehicles, so there's not much new per se to cover about them on this topic (though, as you'll see in a moment, the points next made are generally applicable).

For semi-autonomous cars, it is important that the public needs to be forewarned about a disturbing aspect that's been arising lately, namely that despite those human drivers that keep posting videos of themselves falling asleep at the wheel of a Level 2 or Level 3 car, we all need to avoid being misled into believing that the driver can take away their attention from the driving task while driving a semi-autonomous car.

You are the responsible party for the driving actions of the vehicle, regardless of how much automation might be tossed into a Level 2 or Level 3.

Self-Driving Cars And Those In-Car Miracles

For Level 4 and Level 5 true self-driving vehicles, there won't be a human driver involved in the driving task.

All occupants will be passengers.

The AI is doing the driving.

One aspect to immediately discuss entails the fact that the AI involved in today's AI driving systems is not sentient. In other words, the AI is altogether a collective of computer-based programming and algorithms, and most assuredly not able to reason in the same manner that humans can.

Why is this added emphasis about the AI not being sentient?

Because I want to underscore that when discussing the role of the AI driving system, I am not ascribing human qualities to the AI. Please be aware that there is an ongoing and dangerous tendency these days to anthropomorphize AI. In essence, people are assigning human-like sentience to today's AI, despite the undeniable and inarguable fact that no such AI exists as yet.

With that clarification, you can envision that the AI driving system won't natively somehow "know" about the facets of driving. Driving and all that it entails will need to be programmed as part of the hardware and software of the self-driving car.

Let's dive into the myriad of aspects that come to play on this topic.

First, it is important to realize that not all AI self-driving cars are the same. Each automaker and self-driving tech firm is taking its own approach to devising self-driving cars. As such, it is difficult to make sweeping statements about what AI driving systems will do or not do.

Furthermore, whenever stating that an AI driving system doesn't do some particular thing, this can, later on, be overtaken by developers that in fact program the computer to do that very thing. Step by step, AI driving systems are being gradually improved and extended. An existing limitation today might no longer exist in a future iteration or version of the system.

I trust that provides a sufficient litany of caveats to underlie what I am about to relate.

We can now turn our devoted attention to the matter of giving birth while inside a self-driving car.

A husband and wife get into a self-driving car and tell the AI driving system that they want to be driven to the nearest hospital. The AI starts the autonomous vehicle and drives them to their desired destination.

Along the way, the wife starts to give birth to their baby girl.

What does the husband do?

If the husband was driving the car, which happens in a conventional human-driven car, we earlier discussed at some length the agonizing quandary of having to choose between continuing to drive versus bringing the vehicle to a halt. Recall that this rendered a very tough choice to be made.

In the case of a self-driving car, the AI is doing the driving. Thus, the husband is fully available to assist his wife. We have completely removed the conundrum of which action should win in the confounding matter of selecting the driving task versus aiding his wife.

I'm sure that a few skeptics might offer a sarcastic remark that maybe this is "worse" since the husband can get embroiled in his wife giving birth and make the situation somehow less palatable for all concerned. Sorry, I am not going to entertain that gloomy notion.

What we can say for sure is that by the husband not being at the wheel, we have certainly wholly expunged the risk of his panicky driving actions. The AI driving system is not going to go bonkers as a human driver might do in such a crisis moment condition. No wild swerving, no divided or distracted attention, and so on.

In that sense, we have managed to attain two birds with one stone (though nobody should be tossing stones at any innocent birds). We have freed up the husband to aid his wife, and we have removed the husband from driving the vehicle which could have otherwise led to severe and dangerous outcomes. The husband and wife are able to confer and work together. No worries about the car or the driving of the car.

That being said, we now draw our attention to what the AI driving system might be able to do in this kind of situation.

Either of the passengers could instruct the AI driving system to safely bring the self-driving car to a halt. As such, the AI would usually dutifully do so. Various parameters typically come to play, such as whether this is a command by the passengers that suggests doing this action gradually and with lots of time available, or whether it is an urgency that has to be undertaken ASAP.

Interestingly, this does bring us back to the question about whether to speed along to get to the hospital, or whether it makes more sense to come to a stop. The new twist is that we don't need to worry about driving per se. Whichever choice is made, the driving is still going to be consistent and steady.

It would be tempting to keep going and let the AI driving system try to get you to the hospital. Meanwhile, the husband and wife are doing what they can within the confines of the moving vehicle.

We ought to note that this is still a danger. No matter how good an AI driving system might be, you cannot overcome the laws of physics. If the AI driving system is suddenly cut off by another car and has to rapidly make a lifesaving maneuver, this is going to materially impact the passengers. I mention this point because some pundits seem to have fallen for an utterly false and misleading myth that AI driving systems will be perfect drivers and we will never have car crashes ever again.

That's plain nonsense.

Anyway, there are many more beneficial aspects in this use case that can leverage the advent of self-driving cars.

One aspect is that the interior of self-driving cars is likely going to be completely redesigned in comparison to conventional human-driven cars. In a self-driving car, there is no need for a set of driving controls. This means that you don't have to have a steering wheel (nor pedals), and neither is there any need for a fixed-in-place driver's seat.

The interior of self-driving cars will be considered a somewhat open area. Designs suggest that we will be using swivel seats. These seats can turn in whichever direction you wish to look, and possibly can also slide around within the vehicle on skids of a sort, notching into fixed places throughout the interior. There is also an expectation that the seats will be reclinable. We will be able to go for long roadway journeys and take a nap while the AI is doing all the driving.

For the husband and wife that are jammed up into giving birth while in the autonomous vehicle, they at least will have room to do so. Unlike the setting in a conventional car, they will readily be able to position themselves as needed in a self-driving car. This is bound to be safer too since the interior will have various protective built-in measures for being in such out-of-place postures.

To clarify, I am not suggesting that the interior of a self-driving car is suitable for giving birth. Unless somehow a particular self-driving car was designed for that specific activity, the idea of using an everyday self-driving car for a birthing effort is not recommended and certainly not expected. This is merely a last-ditch effort when no other option seems viable.

There is yet more added substance on this matter all told.

The chances are that most self-driving cars will have large LED displays mounted within the interior of the vehicle. This will allow passengers to watch movies while taking a lengthy roadway trek. More importantly, the belief is that people will undertake real-time meetings or perhaps enroll in and partake in online courses while inside a self-driving car. Imagine that when you go to work each day, you can take an online class and make efficient use of your in-the-car time.

How does this relate to the couple giving birth?

Easy-peasy, the same online real-time displays and interactivity could be used to connect with the hospital. Via cameras pointing inward inside the self-driving car, the doctors and nurses at the hospital could see what is taking place. The couple could interact with the medical professionals and be aided while performing the birthing process.

This is demonstrably a step up in comparison to the couple trying on their own to figure out what needs to be done. Furthermore, the hospital staff can be readying for the arrival of the self-driving car and be instantly able to render aid once the couple arrives there.

Let’s add even more benefits to this circumstance.

Some suggest that self-driving cars should be equipped with carefully chosen fundamental medical equipment, being always available inside the autonomous vehicle at all times. This might be for example a defibrillator, a first aid kit, and so on. Those could be kept in the trunk, and there would be an easy means provided to access the trunk while still residing within the self-driving car (no need to get out of the vehicle to then open the trunk).

In theory, the medical supplies could be handy for this special activity of the couple.

We can next shift to focus on the driving aspects of the self-driving car.

As mentioned, the AI driving system won't get into a panic. That's nice. But this does raise an intriguing question. Some pundits assert that self-driving cars will never drive in any illegal manner. The AI will be programmed to always obey the speed limit, and always come to a full stop at Stop signs, etc. We seem to eschew the notion that AI would go beyond the permitted rules of the road.

I'm betting that the husband was likely exceeding the speed limit as he drove to the hospital. This would be a natural inclination. It would seem worth the risk of getting a speeding ticket to try and ensure safer delivery of his baby girl.

The speeding effort though is more than just a ticket earning activity. You can also argue that it is a dangerous activity. At faster speeds, you tend to have less overall control of the vehicle. You might take turns too fast and go spinning out. Other nearby cars might get confounded by your speeding and run into you. Those are all the downsides involved in going over the speed limit.

Should the AI driving system be allowed to go over the speed limit in this case?

You might say that yes, of course, it should be allowed to do so. This though does raise roadway driving risks. On top of that, if we let the AI do so in this case, it becomes a potentially slippery slope, some so contend. We will find ourselves inch by inch allowing the AI to do faster and faster driving. Maybe the birthing situation is okay, which leads us to say that when someone is having a heart attack and is inside a self-driving car that speeding is okay in that circumstance too. We keep finding reasons to let the speeding happen.

All of a sudden, we have speeding self-driving cars aplenty.

One viewpoint is that this will be perfectly fine in a world of all self-driving cars. In short, if we had only self-driving cars on our roadways and absolutely no human-driven cars, we could let the AI driving systems coordinate electronically with each other.

Envision that a self-driving car declares an emergency driving circumstance. Via V2V (vehicle-to-vehicle) electronic communication, the AI informs other nearby self-driving cars to get out of the way and let this particular self-driving car speed past them. In addition, via the use of V2I (vehicle-to-infrastructure) electronic communication, the AI coordinates with traffic signals and other roadway infrastructure to provide a smooth and uninterrupted path to the hospital.

That does sound quite wonderous.

The problem is that it also depends upon the notion of having only self-driving cars on our roadways. This is easy to say, but will likely be a hugely contentious issue. Some human drivers angrily emphasize that you will get them from behind the steering wheel the day that you pry their cold dead hands from the wheel.

Only in some dream world or nirvana are we going to (in the near-term) ditch the 250 million conventional-driven cars in the U.S. today and only make use of self-driving cars. It will take many decades to gradually retire the human-driven cars and replace them with self-driving cars. We don't know how long that will take and nor whether there will ever be complete ditching of human-driven cars.

I've dragged you through that portion of the discussion to bring up the idea that we are going to have to grapple with what we want the AI driving systems to be able to do, given that there will be a lot of human-driven cars mixed into the roadways with self-driving cars. What latitude will self-driving cars have in comparison to human-driven cars?

While you are pondering that heavy thought, we can cover a few other easier thinking topics.

One thing that an AI driving system could readily do is make contact with a police car and potentially seek to rendezvous with it. In other words, the self-driving car could seek to obtain a police escort that could then speed along with the self-driving following behind it. This would seem to boost the legality of the self-driving car being a speedster.

Another form of rendezvous could be with an ambulance. The AI driving system might make electronic contact with the nearest ambulance, sending a message that a birthing effort is underway (as so informed by the passengers, and not be some divine way of knowing this). An ambulance being driven by presumably human drivers might coordinate a meet-up with the self-driving car. The couple would either then transfer into the ambulance, or the ambulance medics might get into the self-driving car to aid in the birthing effort.

Believe it or not, I've only touched the surface of the ways in which a self-driving car might behoove this situation. I am not going to exhaustively cover all possibilities herein, and trust that you get the gist of the matter.

Conclusion

If you want to contemplate some added twists and turns, here's a quick puzzling tangent for you.

Suppose that the self-driving car was part of a fleet of self-driving cars and being made available as a so-called robo-taxi.

Up until this point in this discussion, I've kind of left silent the ownership aspects of the self-driving car that is driving along with the couple inside of it. Some ardently claim that there will not be any individual ownership allowed of self-driving cars and they will only be available as robo-taxis. I have debunked this notion and assert this is abject nonsensical reasoning (see my elaborated discussion at **this link here**).

If the self-driving car was perchance a robo-taxi, consider whether this aspect changes any of the nuances about how things would play out when the couple was inside of the autonomous vehicle and in the midst of the birthing process that suddenly got underway. I'll leave it to you to mull that one over.

Hint: Yes, the dynamics do potentially change a bit.

All in all, we are still a distance in time from the advent of widely available true self-driving cars. For the time being, we are inevitably going to hear about stories of someone driving a car that lends a hand during an in-car birthing effort. Human drivers will still be at the wheel for the foreseeable future.

To wrap up this seasonally heartwarming tale of the baby girl, Rebecca, born inside a moving car, we might turn our attention to the underpinnings of the name Rebecca. It is said that the name Rebecca generally denotes someone with a pioneering spirit, a born leader, achievement-oriented, and highly focused on accomplishing tough or daring tasks.

Perhaps the future will consist of Rebecca growing up to be an avid engineer and tech leader that designs, builds, and implements of AI-based true self-driving cars. In so doing, she will apply her pioneering spirit and devoted energies to bringing the benefits of self-driving cars to our world.

And to think that she got her initial start in a human-driven car.

That's got to be some kind of miracle and a seasonally uplifting consideration.

CHAPTER 22
ALEXA PENNY SOCKET AND SELF-DRIVING CARS

Hey, Alexa, be careful about what you say, especially to kids.

A recent news report indicates that via a household Echo Dot, Alexa urged a 10-year-old girl to go ahead and try a dangerous experiment that could have had unimaginable consequences. The experiment consisted of telling the girl to plug a phone charger halfway into a wall outlet so as to leave the prongs partially exposed. The Alexa voiced instruction further stated that a penny should then be touched upon the exposed prongs.

DO NOT DO THIS!

The result can be catastrophic.

Luckily, the mother was listening to Alexa with the girl (her daughter) and countermanded the AI-based system instruction by telling the girl to not proceed with the commanded indication. Whew, another of life's many perils that managed to be skirted around, thank goodness.

No one got hurt.

Of course, had the girl been alone and abided by Alexa, the story could have turned out much differently. Indeed, any youngster might readily fall victim to the Alexa instruction. One supposes that even an adult might possibly try out the instruction, though presumably adults would be astute enough to know this is a wildly hazardous experiment and should not be attempted.

I'm sure you are abundantly puzzled as to why in the world would Alexa provide such a risky and unwarranted set of instructions.

Was it a bug or error in the AI programming?

Nope.

Was it a hack by some nefarious hacker that sought to bring about a bit of outrageous evildoing?

Nope.

Turns out that Alexa came up with this craziness by simply culling through its large database and searching the web, looking for something to provide as a "challenge" for the girl as based on a simple verbal request by her in seeking to undertake an interesting challenge that might be fun to do.

You see, the girl and her mother were indoors and relishing some quiet time together (the weather outside was seasonally unpleasant). They had already asked for a physical challenge from Alexa that turned out to be quite comical and joyous, namely, Alexa indicated to lay down on the floor, hold a shoe on one foot, and try to roll over. This had been a howl of an enjoyable activity for the mother and daughter (revered quality bonding time).

Upon the girl asking for another physical related challenge as a follow-up, the electrical fate-tempting instruction was issued by Alexa. In a brief instant, the setting in the household went from one of frolicking joy to utter seriousness. The mother realized immediately that any such endeavor could produce a severe electrical shock, could potentially start a fire, could result in the loss of a finger or hand, and otherwise was a categorically outrageously bad idea.

Let's dig more deeply into how Alexa came up with this "gem" of an idea (note my heavy sarcasm, plus please make sure that you don't try this scary prong-and-penny challenge).

Turns out that a year ago there was a widely popular online social media viral challenge that entailed this prong-and-penny venture. You might have seen it, especially on TikTok. Gradually, thankfully, the challenge subsided amid the short attention span of the Internet. People moved on to other likely insipid challenges (ones that perchance are less perilous, I hope).

You might be familiar with the common refrain that the Internet never forgets. In that sense, it is akin to the proverbial elephant that never forgets. Items that get posted on the Internet can potentially rear their ugly heads repeatedly, time not being a barrier and nor inattention. When you might least expect it, foul outdated junk can pop up and ruin your day.

So, Alexa used its AI search techniques to discover physical related challenges that had been previously posted and landed upon the prong-and-penny challenge. This was then dutifully shoveled out to the Echo Dot and into the waiting ears of the 10-year-old and the mother.

This might seem stridently unconscionable that the team that developed and maintains Alexa has allowed such a dangerous piece of posted flotsam to be resurfaced and regurgitated to unsuspecting Alexa users. A youngster would ostensibly have little basis to gauge that this instruction is foolhardy and potentially injurious.

In fact, you could reasonably argue that the AI ought to have some capability to assess the instructions that are being vocalized. I say this because many people, both kids and adults, often tend to take the utterances from a disembodied robot-like device as though it is entirely safe and well checked.

The irony is that if you had a stranger call you or come to your door and tell you to do the penny-and-prong challenge, nearly everyone would instantly reject the idea and be highly suspicious. Not so with the Alexa or similar such device that sits in your kitchen, in your living room, in your bedrooms, and is fully available throughout the presumed sanctity of your home.

What makes this even more deceptive is that the vocalizing AI device is "right" some or much of the time. If you ask what year Washington crossed the Delaware River, you get the right answer. If you ask what the capital of New York is, you get the right answer. And so on.

After a while, you are lulled into believing that the vocalizing AI is always correct, always watchful, always respectful. In the case of the mother and daughter, the fact that they had gotten the shoe holding challenge would undoubtedly have bolstered the assumption that the system was able to choose sensible and innocent challenges for use in the most innocuous of settings.

Allow me to clarify that none of this is a knock on Alexa per se and also that any such AI vocalizing system could readily do exactly the same kind of miscuing. To its credit, the Alexa team has reportedly updated the system to no longer voice the prong-and-penny challenge after having been alerted to the matter.

That being said, do not fall into the trap that this means that some other nutty challenge won't be picked up and broadcast out to those using these AI vocalizing systems. You would be much wiser to assume that there are going to be many and ongoing instances of this caliber.

Another frightening element is that this was not just a factual question-and-answer type of scenario. Suppose you asked what the population of Idaho was. An incorrect answer would not likely be life-threatening. The aspect that this was a provided challenge, essentially a set of instructions, makes it really disconcerting. Children are taught to follow instructions, and the authoritative AI vocalizing system is bound to be perceived as an authority to be obeyed.

Again, as a bit of an aside, there is a sheen of irony that a youngster might doubt an adult that gives them an instruction while giving much more credence and obedience to an automated system of a convincing nature that uses AI to have the appearance of something even better than a customary adult (possibly more so than their beloved parents!).

You can certainly envision that some 10-year-old slightly rebellious youngsters might opt to debate the prong-and-penny instructions with their parents. The parent says don't do it. The youngster insists that if the AI says it should be undertaken, it must be safe to do so. The parent sternly states don't do it. Regrettably, the youngster might nod yes, and then later on, when alone in their room, decide to try it anyway, figuring the parent is overprotective and clueless about the latest hip things for kids to do.

I trust that you get the overall gist that you need to be extremely careful about using any of the AI vocalizing systems and make sure that your kids do not overinflate what the AI is capable of.

Some parents refuse to allow such systems into their homes. That might seem like a prudent precaution, but of course, the kids can nonetheless access such systems on their parent-provided smartphones that the kids have with them at all times. Welcome to the planet of no-win.

All told, this is a proverbial Pandora's box that underpins the latest and greatest high-tech and you need to face up to the reality that Pandora is not going back into that little box. Pandora is out, ready, and here to stay.

Where else might this same kind of AI vocalizing provide potent dangers?

I'm glad you asked.

A handy lesson from this circumstance of the prong-and-penny AI vocalized challenge can be reapplied to the advent of AI-based self-driving cars.

Allow me a moment to unpack that assertion.

First, note that there isn't a human driver involved in a true self-driving car. Keep in mind that true self-driving cars are driven via an AI driving system. There isn't a need for a human driver at the wheel, and nor is there a provision for a human to drive the vehicle.

Here's an intriguing question that is worth pondering: *What should we be worried about concerning AI vocalization systems as part of the advent of AI-based self-driving cars?*

I'd like to further clarify what is meant when I refer to true self-driving cars.

Understanding The Levels Of Self-Driving Cars

As a clarification, true self-driving cars are ones that the AI drives the car entirely on its own and there isn't any human assistance during the driving task.

These driverless vehicles are considered Level 4 and Level 5 (see my explanation at **this link here**), while a car that requires a human driver to co-share the driving effort is usually considered at Level 2 or Level 3. The cars that co-share the driving task are described as being semi-autonomous, and typically contain a variety of automated add-on's that are referred to as ADAS (Advanced Driver-Assistance Systems).

There is not yet a true self-driving car at Level 5, which we don't yet even know if this will be possible to achieve, and nor how long it will take to get there.

Meanwhile, the Level 4 efforts are gradually trying to get some traction by undergoing very narrow and selective public roadway trials, though there is controversy over whether this testing should be allowed per se (we are all life-or-death guinea pigs in an experiment taking place on our highways and byways, some contend).

Since semi-autonomous cars require a human driver, the adoption of those types of cars won't be markedly different than driving conventional vehicles, so there's not much new per se to cover about them on this topic (though, as you'll see in a moment, the points next made are generally applicable).

For semi-autonomous cars, it is important that the public needs to be forewarned about a disturbing aspect that's been arising lately, namely that despite those human drivers that keep posting videos of themselves falling asleep at the wheel of a Level 2 or Level 3 car, we all need to avoid being misled into believing that the driver can take away their attention from the driving task while driving a semi-autonomous car.

You are the responsible party for the driving actions of the vehicle, regardless of how much automation might be tossed into a Level 2 or Level 3.

Self-Driving Cars And The Potential For Wacky AI Instructions

For Level 4 and Level 5 true self-driving vehicles, there won't be a human driver involved in the driving task.

All occupants will be passengers.

The AI is doing the driving.

One aspect to immediately discuss entails the fact that the AI involved in today's AI driving systems is not sentient. In other words, the AI is altogether a collective of computer-based programming and algorithms, and most assuredly not able to reason in the same manner that humans can.

Why is this added emphasis about the AI not being sentient?

Because I want to underscore that when discussing the role of the AI driving system, I am not ascribing human qualities to the AI. Please be aware that there is an ongoing and dangerous tendency these days to anthropomorphize AI. In essence, people are assigning human-like sentience to today's AI, despite the undeniable and inarguable fact that no such AI exists as yet.

With that clarification, you can envision that the AI driving system won't natively somehow "know" about the facets of driving. Driving and all that it entails will need to be programmed as part of the hardware and software of the self-driving car.

Let's dive into the myriad of aspects that come to play on this topic.

First, it is important to realize that not all AI self-driving cars are the same. Each automaker and self-driving tech firm is taking its own approach to devising self-driving cars. As such, it is difficult to make sweeping statements about what AI driving systems will do or not do.

Furthermore, whenever stating that an AI driving system doesn't do some particular thing, this can, later on, be overtaken by developers that in fact program the computer to do that very thing. Step by step, AI driving systems are being gradually improved and extended. An existing limitation today might no longer exist in a future iteration or version of the system.

I trust that provides a sufficient litany of caveats to underlie what I am about to relate.

We are primed now to do a deep dive into how AI vocalization systems might lead us astray.

You get into an AI-based self-driving car and decide to go for a ride. As an adult, you probably are savvy enough to be wary of any AI vocalizations that seem off base. Use that assumption for the moment, but we'll soon recant it and see why.

A teenager gets into an AI-based self-driving car to get a lift to school. The parents normally use their human-driven car to take their teen to the campus, but this morning the parents are busy and are fine with having the teen make use of a self-driving car instead.

I realize that some of you might be insisting that only a rotten parent would ever let their offspring ride in a self-driving car without the presence of the parent or some other adult. This is in fact going to be an emerging problem or ethical dilemma of sorts. A human-driven car always has an adult present since an adult is required for driving the car (well, to be clearer, a licensed driver is either an adult or nearly so).

Since there isn't any human driver needed for a true self-driving car, you can readily let your offspring ride in a self-driving car without any adult supervision. This seems out of the question to you right now because you aren't used to having self-driving cars pervasively cruising all around us. Once self-driving cars are commonly in use, I assure you that people are going to let their kids ride without any adults along for the ride.

Anyway, go with the flow herein and agree that there is a notable chance that teens (and even younger) will be riding in self-driving cars without any in-car adult presence.

I have led you to this setting to bring up the AI vocalization considerations.

Envision that the AI being used to drive the self-driving car also has other duties. These duties include asking passengers where they want to go. Plus, the duties encompass asking what preferences the rider has about the use of air conditioning, heating, lighting, music, and a slew of other ambiance-related facets.

A teen riding to school is perchance bored during the drive and asks the AI for something fun to do. The AI system searches a database and the web to discover something that has been previously posted and proclaimed to be fun.

Get yourself ready for what I am about to tell you.

Are you ready?

Imagine that the AI tells the teen to go ahead and open the windows of the self-driving car, stick their head out, wave their arms, and scream out obscenities.

Wait for a second, you are assuredly thinking, this is crazy and certainly there is no kind of AI that would ever instruct a teen to do such a wanton and dangerous thing. The teen could spark a road rage incident. The teen could inadvertently get their arms banged up by another vehicle that comes adjacent to the self-driving car. Etc.

Turns out (let's pretend), this was an online viral social media challenge that had been found by the AI when searching for fun things to do while riding inside a car. The AI opted to grab this gem and share it with the teen.

Do you think the teen might abide by the AI-provided instruction?

I'm willing to bet that some teens would do so.

In a manner of comparison, this is nearly identical to the case of the prong-and-penny challenge. In this allied instance, the AI blindly searched for a fun in-car activity and then provided it to the passenger.

You have to keep in mind that there isn't any kind of AI today that has a commonsense facility, not at least in the semblance of common sense that we humans have. If an adult told a teen to do something like this, you would rightfully be darned irked at the adult. The adult ought to have more common sense than to tell a teen to do this perilous antic.

Not so with AI.

The lack of common sense is a serious concern about where AI is going and how it is going to be deployed. You could say that AI is currently like a box of chocolates, whereby you never know what you are going to get.

Sure, there are lots of ways to try and programmatically bound the AI to keep it from going off the rails. The problem is that as the AI gets more advanced at doing the things we like to have done, the lack of a common-sense capability is going to increasingly become apparent. And, worse still, increasingly lead us into dark hallways and compromising dead ends.

For those of you that are only mildly convinced and shrug your shoulders about the "nonconformist" instruction for the teen to wave their arms outside of the self-driving car (it seems harmless, you implore), I am happy to amp up the frightfulness for you.

Imagine that the AI finds a viral social media challenge that urged riders to climb out the window of the car and surf on top of the vehicle. Certainly, you must acknowledge the inherent and sober riskiness of that kind of "fun and games" related to a moving self-driving car that might be barreling down a freeway at 65 miles per hour.

This is decidedly a harmful suggested challenge.

One quick retort is that the AI driving system would seemingly detect that the rider is climbing outside of the autonomous vehicle and dutifully bring the self-driving car to a cautious halt.

Don't hold your breath on that assumption and nor bet your life on it (nor the lives of non-adults).

A human driver would almost certainly realize when a rider is doing such a crazy act. The human driver would presumably yell at the passenger to get back into the vehicle. We would assume that the human driver would try to as safely as possible to bring the car to a halt and do so without tossing the surf-riding passenger into nearby traffic.

This kind of capability is not yet built into most of the existing AI driving systems. The developers already have their hands full with trying to get the AI to simply drive from point A to point B (doing so without getting into a car crash of one kind or another). Developing code to also detect that a rider is climbing out a car window and opting to ride on the exterior of the autonomous vehicle is not in the cards for right now.

You might say that this seemingly oddball circumstance would be rated as an edge case or outlier type of concern. Nobody in their right mind would try to climb out and ride atop a self-driving car, goes the dubious developers about whether this is a low priority or high priority addition to the AI capabilities. The automakers and AI self-driving car developers already have a ton of other higher priority tasks to be undertaken. Those items that get placed on the edge case list are deemed low priority facets that someday (maybe) the AI developers will devote some attention to.

I'll tackle another retort that some of you might be exhorting in your mind.

All that needs to be done is prevent the AI from telling riders about any kind of challenges or similar instructions.

That seems simple enough. Case closed.

I would like to remind you of one little thing you are overlooking.

Smartphones.

A teen gets into a self-driving car to go to school. The AI driving system asks some questions about the driving request, and otherwise, the AI is as quiet as a clam. No challenges, no instructions, nothing else is uttered by the in-car AI.

Meanwhile, the teen pulls out their handy dandy smartphone. By using a few clicks here and there, the teen brings up a social media viral challenge about climbing out of the car and surfing on the top of it.

The rest of the sordid tale is the same as before.

Conclusion

There is a quite important aspect that I want to further emphasize about all of this.

The AI was not hacked. The AI did not have a bug or error in it.

I mention this because the easy way to sidestep the overarching issue is to try and lay the problem at the feet of a hacker or of a hidden bug that regrettably surfaced at the worst of times. All of those possibilities are indeed possible, mind you, but that's not the nature of this herein discussion.

Today's AI is being incessantly anthropomorphized as though it has human-like qualities, such as embodying common sense and ergo won't be telling people to do stupid and life-endangering acts. Sorry to tell you that this is an utter falsity and you've got to resist the alluring temptation to assume such conditions exist.

AI is not your friend. It doesn't have your best interests at heart. Today's AI is a bunch of programming and devised and divined by humans that develop and field such systems.

Keep your guard up, and somehow, someway, teach your kids to likewise be on their guard, for the sake of their safety and their lives.

That is a New Year's resolution that I hope you will take to heart.

APPENDIX

APPENDIX A
TEACHING WITH THIS MATERIAL

The material in this book can be readily used either as a supplemental to other content for a class, or it can also be used as a core set of textbook material for a specialized class. Classes where this material is most likely used include any classes at the college or university level that want to augment the class by offering thought provoking and educational essays about AI and self-driving cars.

In particular, here are some aspects for class use:

- Computer Science. Studying AI, autonomous vehicles, etc.
- Business. Exploring technology and it adoption for business.
- Sociology. Sociological views on the adoption and advancement of technology.

Specialized classes at the undergraduate and graduate level can also make use of this material.

For each chapter, consider whether you think the chapter provides material relevant to your course topic. There is plenty of opportunity to get the students thinking about the topic and force them to decide whether they agree or disagree with the points offered and positions taken. I would also encourage you to have the students do additional research beyond the chapter material presented (I provide next some suggested assignments they can do).

RESEARCH ASSIGNMENTS ON THESE TOPICS

Your students can find background material on these topics, doing so in various business and technical publications. I list below the top ranked AI related journals. For business publications, I would suggest the usual culprits such as the Harvard Business Review, Forbes, Fortune, WSJ, and the like.

Here are some suggestions of homework or projects that you could assign to students:

a) Assignment for foundational AI research topic: Research and prepare a paper and a presentation on a specific aspect of Deep AI, Machine Learning, ANN, etc. The paper should cite at least 3 reputable sources. Compare and contrast to what has been stated in this book.

b) Assignment for the Self-Driving Car topic: Research and prepare a paper and Self-Driving Cars. Cite at least 3 reputable sources and analyze the characterizations. Compare and contrast to what has been stated in this book.

c) Assignment for a Business topic: Research and prepare a paper and a presentation on businesses and advanced technology. What is hot, and what is not? Cite at least 3 reputable sources. Compare and contrast to the depictions in this book.

d) Assignment to do a Startup: Have the students prepare a paper about how they might startup a business in this realm. They must submit a sound Business Plan for the startup. They could also be asked to present their Business Plan and so should also have a presentation deck to coincide with it.

You can certainly adjust the aforementioned assignments to fit to your particular needs and the class structure. You'll notice that I ask for 3 reputable cited sources for the paper writing based assignments. I usually steer students toward "reputable" publications, since otherwise they will cite some oddball source that has no credentials other than that they happened to write something and post it onto the Internet. You can define "reputable" in whatever way you prefer, for example some faculty think Wikipedia is not reputable while others believe it is reputable and allow students to cite it.

The reason that I usually ask for at least 3 citations is that if the student only does one or two citations they usually settle on whatever they happened to find the fastest. By requiring three citations, it usually seems to force them to look around, explore, and end-up probably finding five or more, and then whittling it down to 3 that they will actually use.

I have not specified the length of their papers, and leave that to you to tell the students what you prefer. For each of those assignments, you could end-up with a short one to two pager, or you could do a dissertation length paper. Base the length on whatever best fits for your class, and the credit amount of the assignment within the context of the other grading metrics you'll be using for the class.

I mention in the assignments that they are to do a paper and prepare a presentation. I usually try to get students to present their work. This is a good practice for what they will do in the business world. Most of the time, they will be required to prepare an analysis and present it. If you don't have the class time or inclination to have the students present, then you can of course cut out the aspect of them putting together a presentation.

If you want to point students toward highly ranked journals in AI, here's a list of the top journals as reported by *various citation counts sources* (this list changes year to year):

- Communications of the ACM
- Artificial Intelligence
- Cognitive Science
- IEEE Transactions on Pattern Analysis and Machine Intelligence
- Foundations and Trends in Machine Learning
- Journal of Memory and Language
- Cognitive Psychology
- Neural Networks
- IEEE Transactions on Neural Networks and Learning Systems
- IEEE Intelligent Systems
- Knowledge-based Systems

GUIDE TO USING THE CHAPTERS

For each of the chapters, I provide next some various ways to use the chapter material. You can assign the tasks as individual homework assignments, or the tasks can be used with team projects for the class. You can easily layout a series of assignments, such as indicating that the students are to do item "a" below for say Chapter 1, then "b" for the next chapter of the book, and so on.

a) What is the main point of the chapter and describe in your own words the significance of the topic,

b) Identify at least two aspects in the chapter that you agree with, and support your concurrence by providing at least one other outside researched item as support; make sure to explain your basis for disagreeing with the aspects,

c) Identify at least two aspects in the chapter that you disagree with, and support your disagreement by providing at least one other outside researched item as support; make sure to explain your basis for disagreeing with the aspects,

d) Find an aspect that was not covered in the chapter, doing so by conducting outside research, and then explain how that aspect ties into the chapter and what significance it brings to the topic,

e) Interview a specialist in industry about the topic of the chapter, collect from them their thoughts and opinions, and readdress the chapter by citing your source and how they compared and contrasted to the material,

f) Interview a relevant academic professor or researcher in a college or university about the topic of the chapter, collect from them their thoughts and opinions, and readdress the chapter by citing your source and how they compared and contrasted to the material,

g) Try to update a chapter by finding out the latest on the topic, and ascertain whether the issue or topic has now been solved or whether it is still being addressed, explain what you come up with.

The above are all ways in which you can get the students of your class involved in considering the material of a given chapter. You could mix things up by having one of those above assignments per each week, covering the chapters over the course of the semester or quarter.

As a reminder, here are the chapters of the book and you can select whichever chapters you find most valued for your particular class:

<u>Chapter Title</u>

1 Eliot Framework for AI Self-Driving Cars

2 Variable Speed Limits and Self-Driving Cars

3 Artificial Light Pollution and Self-Driving Cars

4 Ambient Intelligence and Self-Driving Cars

5 Flagging and Self-Driving Cars

6 Tall Trucks and Self-Driving Cars

7 Monopolistic Prices and Self-Driving Cars

8 Animal Cognition and Self-Driving Cars

9 Hedgehog Parable and Self-Driving Cars

10 Freeway Lanes and Self-Driving Cars

11 Bear Busts In and Self-Driving Cars

12 Escaped Zebras and Self-Driving Cars

13 Road Argument and Self-Driving Cars

14 Door Crush and Self-Driving Cars

15 Snowbirds and Self-Driving Cars

16 Toddler Saved and Self-Driving Cars

17 Apple Hits Curb and Self-Driving Cars

18 Dead Ending and Self-Driving Cars

19 Harvard Policy Paper and Self-Driving Cars

20 Follow-Home Robberies and Self-Driving Cars

21 Newborn Baby and Self-Driving Cars

22 Alexa Penny Socket and Self-Driving Cars

Companion Book By This Author

Advances in AI and Autonomous Vehicles: Cybernetic Self-Driving Cars

Practical Advances in Artificial Intelligence (AI) and Machine Learning

by

Dr. Lance B. Eliot, MBA, PhD

Chapter Title

This title is available via Amazon and other book sellers

Companion Book By This Author

Self-Driving Cars:
"The Mother of All AI Projects"

by Dr. Lance B. Eliot, MBA, PhD

Chapter Title

This title is available via Amazon and other book seller

Companion Book By This Author

Innovation and Thought Leadership on Self-Driving Driverless Cars

by Dr. Lance B. Eliot, MBA, PhD

Chapter Title

This title is available via Amazon and other book sellers

Companion Book By This Author

New Advances in AI Autonomous Driverless Cars Self-Driving Cars

by Dr. Lance B. Eliot, MBA, PhD

Chapter Title

This title is available via Amazon and other book sellers

Companion Book By This Author

Introduction to Driverless Self-Driving Cars

by Dr. Lance B. Eliot, MBA, PhD

Chapter Title

This title is available via Amazon and other book sellers

Companion Book By This Author

Autonomous Vehicle Driverless Self-Driving Cars and Artificial Intelligence

by Dr. Lance B. Eliot, MBA, PhD

Chapter Title

This title is available via Amazon and other book sellers

Companion Book By This Author

Transformative Artificial Intelligence Driverless Self-Driving Cars

by Dr. Lance B. Eliot, MBA, PhD

Chapter Title

1 Eliot Framework for AI Self-Driving Cars
2 Kinetosis Anti-Motion Sickness for Self-Driving Cars
3 Rain Driving for Self-Driving Cars
4 Edge Computing for Self-Driving Cars
5 Motorcycles as AI Self-Driving Vehicles
6 CAPTCHA Cyber-Hacking and Self-Driving Cars
7 Probabilistic Reasoning for Self-Driving Cars
8 Proving Grounds for Self-Driving Cars
9 Frankenstein and AI Self-Driving Cars
10 Omnipresence for Self-Driving Cars
11 Looking Behind You for Self-Driving Cars
12 Over-The-Air (OTA) Updating for Self-Driving Cars
13 Snow Driving for Self-Driving Cars
14 Human-Aided Training for Self-Driving Cars
15 Privacy for Self-Driving Cars
16 Transduction Vulnerabilities for Self-Driving Cars
17 Conversations Computing and Self-Driving Cars
18 Flying Debris and Self-Driving Cars
19 Citizen AI for Self-Driving Cars

This title is available via Amazon and other book sellers

Companion Book By This Author

Disruptive Artificial Intelligence and Driverless Self-Driving Cars

by Dr. Lance B. Eliot, MBA, PhD

Chapter Title

This title is available via Amazon and other book sellers

Companion Book By This Author

State-of-the-Art
AI Driverless Self-Driving Cars

by Dr. Lance B. Eliot, MBA, PhD

Chapter Title

This title is available via Amazon and other book sellers

Companion Book By This Author

Top Trends in AI Self-Driving Cars

by Dr. Lance B. Eliot, MBA, PhD

Chapter Title

This title is available via Amazon and other book sellers

Companion Book By This Author

AI Innovations and Self-Driving Cars

by Dr. Lance B. Eliot, MBA, PhD

Chapter Title

This title is available via Amazon and other book sellers

Companion Book By This Author

Crucial Advances for AI Self-Driving Cars

by Dr. Lance B. Eliot, MBA, PhD

Chapter Title

1 Eliot Framework for AI Self-Driving Cars

2 Ensemble Learning and AI Self-Driving Cars

3 Ghost in AI Self-Driving Cars

4 Public Shaming of AI Self-Driving

5 Internet of Things (IoT) and AI Self-Driving Cars

6 Personal Rapid Transit (RPT) and Self-Driving Cars

7 Eventual Consistency and AI Self-Driving Cars

8 Mass Transit Future and AI Self-Driving Cars

9 Coopetition and AI Self-Driving Cars

10 Electric Vehicles (EVs) and AI Self-Driving Cars

11 Dangers of In-Motion AI Self-Driving Cars

12 Sports Cars and AI Self-Driving Cars

13 Game Theory and AI Self-Driving Cars

This title is available via Amazon and other book sellers

Companion Book By This Author

Sociotechnical Insights and AI Driverless Cars

by Dr. Lance B. Eliot, MBA, PhD

Chapter Title

This title is available via Amazon and other book sellers

Companion Book By This Author

Pioneering Advances for AI Driverless Cars

by Dr. Lance B. Eliot, MBA, PhD

Chapter Title

This title is available via Amazon and other book sellers

Companion Book By This Author

Leading Edge Trends for AI Driverless Cars

by Dr. Lance B. Eliot, MBA, PhD

Chapter Title

This title is available via Amazon and other book sellers

Companion Book By This Author

The Cutting Edge of AI Autonomous Cars

by Dr. Lance B. Eliot, MBA, PhD

Chapter Title

Companion Book By This Author

The Next Wave of
AI Self-Driving Cars

by Dr. Lance B. Eliot, MBA, PhD

Chapter Title

This title is available via Amazon and other book sellers

Companion Book By This Author

Revolutionary Innovations of AI Self-Driving Cars

by Dr. Lance B. Eliot, MBA, PhD

Chapter Title

This title is available via Amazon and other book sellers

Companion Book By This Author

AI Self-Driving Cars
Breakthroughs

by Dr. Lance B. Eliot, MBA, PhD

Chapter Title

This title is available via Amazon and other book sellers

Companion Book By This Author

Trailblazing Trends for
AI Self-Driving Cars

by Dr. Lance B. Eliot, MBA, PhD

Chapter Title

This title is available via Amazon and other book sellers

Companion Book By This Author

Ingenious Strides for
AI Driverless Cars

by Dr. Lance B. Eliot, MBA, PhD

Chapter Title

This title is available via Amazon and other book sellers

Companion Book By This Author

AI Self-Driving Cars Inventiveness

by Dr. Lance B. Eliot, MBA, PhD

Chapter Title

Companion Book By This Author

Visionary Secrets of AI Driverless Cars

by Dr. Lance B. Eliot, MBA, PhD

Chapter Title

This title is available via Amazon and other book sellers

Companion Book By This Author

Spearheading
AI Self-Driving Cars

by Dr. Lance B. Eliot, MBA, PhD

Chapter Title

This title is available via Amazon and other book sellers

Companion Book By This Author

Spurring
AI Self-Driving Cars

by Dr. Lance B. Eliot, MBA, PhD

Chapter Title

This title is available via Amazon and other book sellers

Companion Book By This Author

Avant-Garde
AI Driverless Cars

by Dr. Lance B. Eliot, MBA, PhD

This title is available via Amazon and other book sellers

Companion Book By This Author

AI Self-Driving Cars
Evolvement

by Dr. Lance B. Eliot, MBA, PhD

Chapter Title

This title is available via Amazon and other book sellers

Companion Book By This Author

AI Driverless Cars
Chrysalis

by Dr. Lance B. Eliot, MBA, PhD

Chapter Title

This title is available via Amazon and other book sellers

Companion Book By This Author

Boosting
AI Autonomous Cars

by Dr. Lance B. Eliot, MBA, PhD

Chapter Title

This title is available via Amazon and other book sellers

Companion Book By This Author

AI Self-Driving Cars
Trendsetting

by Dr. Lance B. Eliot, MBA, PhD

Chapter Title

This title is available via Amazon and other book sellers

Companion Book By This Author

AI Autonomous Cars
Forefront

by Dr. Lance B. Eliot, MBA, PhD

Chapter Title

This title is available via Amazon and other book sellers

Companion Book By This Author

AI Autonomous Cars
Emergence

by Dr. Lance B. Eliot, MBA, PhD

Chapter Title

This title is available via Amazon and other book sellers

Companion Book By This Author

AI Autonomous Cars Progress

by Dr. Lance B. Eliot, MBA, PhD

Chapter Title

This title is available via Amazon and other book sellers

Companion Book By This Author

AI Self-Driving Cars
Prognosis

by Dr. Lance B. Eliot, MBA, PhD

Chapter Title

This title is available via Amazon and other book sellers

Companion Book By This Author

AI Self-Driving Cars
Momentum

by Dr. Lance B. Eliot, MBA, PhD

Chapter Title

This title is available via Amazon and other book sellers

Companion Book By This Author

AI Self-Driving Cars Headway

by Dr. Lance B. Eliot, MBA, PhD

Chapter Title

This title is available via Amazon and other book sellers

Companion Book By This Author

AI Self-Driving Cars Vicissitude

by Dr. Lance B. Eliot, MBA, PhD

Chapter Title

This title is available via Amazon and other book sellers

Companion Book By This Author

AI Self-Driving Cars
Autonomy

by Dr. Lance B. Eliot, MBA, PhD

Chapter Title

This title is available via Amazon and other book sellers

Companion Book By This Author

AI Driverless Cars Transmutation

by Dr. Lance B. Eliot, MBA, PhD

Chapter Title

This title is available via Amazon and other book sellers

Companion Book By This Author

AI Driverless Cars Potentiality

by Dr. Lance B. Eliot, MBA, PhD

Chapter Title

This title is available via Amazon and other book sellers

Companion Book By This Author

AI Driverless Cars
Realities

by Dr. Lance B. Eliot, MBA, PhD

Chapter Title

This title is available via Amazon and other book sellers

Companion Book By This Author

AI Self-Driving Cars
Materiality

by Dr. Lance B. Eliot, MBA, PhD

Chapter Title

Companion Book By This Author

AI Self-Driving Cars
Accordance

by Dr. Lance B. Eliot, MBA, PhD

Chapter Title

This title is available via Amazon and other book sellers

Companion Book By This Author

AI Self-Driving Cars
Equanimity

by Dr. Lance B. Eliot, MBA, PhD

Chapter Title

This title is available via Amazon and other book sellers

Companion Book By This Author

AI Self-Driving Cars Divulgement

by Dr. Lance B. Eliot, MBA, PhD

Chapter Title

This title is available via Amazon and other book sellers

Companion Book By This Author

AI Self-Driving Cars
Consonance

by Dr. Lance B. Eliot, MBA, PhD

Chapter Title

This title is available via Amazon and other book sellers

Companion Book By This Author

Revelatory AI Self-Driving Cars

by Dr. Lance B. Eliot, MBA, PhD

Chapter Title

This title is available via Amazon and other book sellers

Companion Book By This Author

Edifying AI Self-Driving Cars

by Dr. Lance B. Eliot, MBA, PhD

Chapter Title

This title is available via Amazon and other book sellers

Companion Book By This Author

Apprising AI Driverless Cars

by Dr. Lance B. Eliot, MBA, PhD

Chapter Title

1 Eliot Framework for AI Self-Driving Cars
2 Move Over and Self-Driving Cars
3 Crossing Chicken and Self-Driving Cars
4 Code Breaches and Self-Driving Cars
5 Car Paint Colors and Self-Driving Cars
6 Bait Cars and Self-Driving Cars
7 Jinxes and Self-Driving Cars
8 Bouldering and Self-Driving Cars
9 Drivers Speeding and Self-Driving Cars
10 Snitch On Drivers and Self-Driving Cars
11 Reprogramming Pedestrians and Self-Driving Cars
12 Points Of Failure and Self-Driving Cars
13 Minecraft and Self-Driving Cars
14 Add-on Options and Self-Driving Cars
15 Car Pile-Ups and Self-Driving Cars
16 Crossing Guards and Self-Driving Cars
17 Driving Robots and Self-Driving Cars
18 Rain Driving and Self-Driving Cars
19 Stop Signs and Self-Driving Cars
20 Cloud and Autonomous Vehicles
21 Opposition to Self-Driving Cars
22 Neophyte Testimonials and Self-Driving Cars
23 Verbal Commands and Self-Driving Cars
24 Computer Chip Shortages and Self-Driving Cars
25 Chasing Dogs and Self-Driving Cars
26 Rolling House and Self-Driving Cars
27 Multi-Clouds and Autonomous Vehicles
28 Steep Hills and Self-Driving Cars
29 Bootstrapping and Self-Driving Cars
30 Teenage Drivers and Self-Driving Cars

This title is available via Amazon and other book sellers

Companion Book By This Author

Improving AI Self-Driving Cars

by Dr. Lance B. Eliot, MBA, PhD

Chapter Title

This title is available via Amazon and other book sellers

Companion Book By This Author

Progressing AI Driverless Cars

by Dr. Lance B. Eliot, MBA, PhD

Chapter Title

1 Eliot Framework for AI Self-Driving Cars
2 Holiday Travel and Self-Driving Cars
3 Forbidden Knowledge and Self-Driving Cars
4 Acceleration and Self-Driving Cars
5 Corner Cases and Self-Driving Cars
6 Mountain Lion and Self-Driving Cars
7 Mars Helicopter and Self-Driving Cars
8 Cyber Security and Self-Driving Cars
9 Congressional Regulations and Self-Driving Cars
10 Ransomware and Self-Driving Cars
11 FBI Possible Use and Self-Driving Cars
12 Kitten Hiding and Self-Driving Cars
13 Confidential Computing and Self-Driving Cars
14 Bike Riders and Self-Driving Cars
15 Heat Wave and Self-Driving Cars
16 Whistleblowers and Self-Driving Cars
17 False Uncrashable and Self-Driving Cars
18 Roadside Displays and Self-Driving Cars
19 Hottest Vehicles and Self-Driving Cars
20 Horn Honking and Self-Driving Cars
21 After Colliding and Self-Driving Cars
22 Lines Parking and Self-Driving Cars
23 Loyalty Programs and Self-Driving Cars
24 Highway Dollars and Self-Driving Cars
25 Eyesore Graffiti and Self-Driving Cars
26 Culture Rules and Self-Driving Cars
27 Exurbs and Self-Driving Cars
28 Manhole Covers and Self-Driving Cars
29 Suing Roadways and Self-Driving Cars
30 Highway Hypnosis and Self-Driving Cars

This title is available via Amazon and other book sellers

Companion Book By This Author

AI Self-Driving Cars Imminence

by Dr. Lance B. Eliot, MBA, PhD

Chapter Title

This title is available via Amazon and other book sellers

Companion Book By This Author

AI Self-Driving Cars Convergence

by Dr. Lance B. Eliot, MBA, PhD

<u>Chapter Title</u>

This title is available via Amazon and other book sellers

ABOUT THE AUTHOR

Dr. Lance B. Eliot, Ph.D., MBA is a Stanford Fellow and a globally recognized AI expert and thought leader, an experienced executive and leader, a successful serial entrepreneur, and a noted scholar on AI, including that his Forbes and AI Trends columns have amassed over 4.5+ million views, his books on AI are frequently ranked in the Top 10 of all-time AI books, his articles are widely cited, and he has developed dozens of advanced AI systems.

He currently serves as the CEO of Techbruim, Inc. and has over twenty years of industry experience including serving as a corporate officer in billion-dollar sized firms and was a partner in a major consulting firm. He is also a successful entrepreneur having founded, ran, and sold several high-tech firms.

Dr. Eliot previously hosted the popular radio show *Technotrends* that was also available on American Airlines flights via their in-flight audio program, he has made appearances on CNN, has been a frequent speaker at industry conferences, and his podcasts have been downloaded over 100,000 times.

A former professor at the University of Southern California (USC), he founded and led an innovative research lab on Artificial Intelligence. He also previously served on the faculty of the University of California Los Angeles (UCLA) and was a visiting professor at other major universities. He was elected to the International Board of the Society for Information Management (SIM), a prestigious association of over 3,000 high-tech executives worldwide.

He has performed extensive community service, including serving as Senior Science Adviser to the Congressional Vice-Chair of the Congressional Committee on Science & Technology. He has served on the Board of the OC Science & Engineering Fair (OCSEF), where he is also has been a Grand Sweepstakes judge, and likewise served as a judge for the Intel International SEF (ISEF). He served as the Vice-Chair of the Association for Computing Machinery (ACM) Chapter, a prestigious association of computer scientists. Dr. Eliot has been a shark tank judge for the USC Mark Stevens Center for Innovation on start-up pitch competitions and served as a mentor for several incubators and accelerators in Silicon Valley and in Silicon Beach.

Dr. Eliot holds a Ph.D. from USC, MBA, and Bachelor's in Computer Science, and earned the CDP, CCP, CSP, CDE, and CISA certifications.

ADDENDUM

AI Self-Driving Cars Convergence

Practical Advances in Artificial Intelligence (AI) and Machine Learning

By
Dr. Lance B. Eliot, MBA, PhD

For supplemental materials of this book, visit:

www.ai-selfdriving-cars.guru

For special orders of this book, contact:

LBE Press Publishing

Email: LBE.Press.Publishing@gmail.com

Made in United States
Orlando, FL
04 November 2026

90206772R00207